Praise, Praise, Praise for Perennials For Dummies!

"A wonderful introduction to the world of perennials! With warmth, wit, and the wisdom that comes only from her years hunkered down in the dirt, Marcia Tatroe has written the ideal introductory book for all budding perennial lovers."

— Lauren Springer, garden designer, columnist, and author of *The Undaunted Garden*

"Humorous, down-to-earth information anyone can understand. Covers every detail of creating a flower garden from beginning to end. I'm impressed — a book filled with valuable lessons covering each phase of building a garden, keeping one from making timely mistakes. It could help any beginner have a successful, flourishing flower garden."

— Judy Wigand, owner of Judy's Perennials, San Marcos, CA

"Whether you live in the sun-bleached subtropics or the misty snow belt, you will be able to determine just what perennials grow best for you, how to combine them for the optimal effect through the season, and, perhaps most importantly, you will have some real design concepts instilled in you. . . . I know no other book that presents these ideas more intelligently."

— Panayoti Kelaidis, Plant Evaluation Coordinator, Denver Botanic Gardens

". . . this is an outstanding reference for beginners and first time homeowners . . . clearly explains how to retrieve garden information online."

— Carol Stocker, *Boston Globe*, Boston, Massachusetts

". . . a thorough, readable beginners' guide. . . . Readers will enjoy the straightforward, yet light-hearted tone."

— Cheryl Dorschner, *Burlington Free Press*, Burlington, Vermont

"This book has much to recommend it . . . a simple, well-laid-out introduction to basic gardening . . ."

— *Library Journal*

". . . easy to read and fun to thumb through . . . a wealth of information on all aspects of gardening. . . . A good choice for beginning gardeners, *Gardening For Dummies* would also be a good gift for longtime growers."

— Beth Dolan, *The Tampa Tribune,* Tampa, Florida

". . . you'll find you're in the company of the real geniuses — the folks who can help you dig through the mounds of gardening information available and get growing soon."

— Amy Green, *The Journal Constitution,* Atlanta, Georgia

"The beauty of *Gardening For Dummies* . . . is its clear, jargon-free text. This should be a great relief for you if you're truly interested in learning about the subject, but afraid to spend big bucks on a serious gardening book that will only amaze and confuse you."

— *Country Decorator* magazine

™

BUSINESS AND GENERAL REFERENCE BOOK SERIES FROM IDG

References for the Rest of Us!™

Do you find that traditional reference books are overloaded with technical details and advice you'll never use? Do you postpone important life decisions because you just don't want to deal with them? Then our *...For Dummies*™ business and general reference book series is for you.

...For Dummies business and general reference books are written for those frustrated and hard-working souls who know they aren't dumb, but find that the myriad of personal and business issues and the accompanying horror stories make them feel helpless. *...For Dummies* books use a lighthearted approach, a down-to-earth style, and even cartoons and humorous icons to diffuse fears and build confidence. Lighthearted but not lightweight, these books are perfect survival guides to solve your everyday personal and business problems.

"More than a publishing phenomenon, 'Dummies' is a sign of the times."
— The New York Times

"... you won't go wrong buying them."
— Walter Mossberg, Wall Street Journal, on IDG's ...For Dummies™ books

"A world of detailed and authoritative information is packed into them..."
— U.S. News and World Report

Already, hundreds of thousands of satisfied readers agree. They have made *...For Dummies* the #1 introductory level computer book series and a best-selling business book series. They have written asking for more. So, if you're looking for the best and easiest way to learn about business and other general reference topics, look to *...For Dummies* to give you a helping hand.

™

IDG BOOKS WORLDWIDE

7/96r

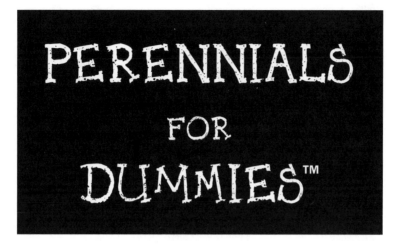

PERENNIALS FOR DUMMIES™

by Marcia Tatroe
and the Editors of the
National Gardening Association

IDG BOOKS WORLDWIDE

IDG Books Worldwide, Inc.
An International Data Group Company

Foster City, CA ♦ Chicago, IL ♦ Indianapolis, IN ♦ Southlake, TX

Perennials For Dummies™

Published by
IDG Books Worldwide, Inc.
An International Data Group Company
919 E. Hillsdale Blvd.
Suite 400
Foster City, CA 94404
http://www.idgbooks.com (IDG Books Worldwide Web site)
http://www.dummies.com (Dummies Press Web site)

Copyright © 1997 IDG Books Worldwide, Inc. All rights reserved. No part of this book, including interior design, cover design, and icons, may be reproduced or transmitted in any form, by any means (electronic, photocopying, recording, or otherwise) without the prior written permission of the publisher.

Library of Congress Catalog Card No.: 96-80236

ISBN: 0-7645-5030-6

Printed in the United States of America

10 9 8 7 6 5 4 3 2 1

1B/RS/QS/ZX/IN

Distributed in the United States by IDG Books Worldwide, Inc.

Distributed by Macmillan Canada for Canada; by Transworld Publishers Limited in the United Kingdom and Europe; by WoodsLane Pty. Ltd. for Australia; by WoodsLane Enterprises Ltd. for New Zealand; by Longman Singapore Publishers Ltd. for Singapore, Malaysia, Thailand, and Indonesia; by Simron Pty. Ltd. for South Africa; by Toppan Company Ltd. for Japan; by Distribuidora Cuspide for Argentina; by Livraria Cultura for Brazil; by Ediciencia S.A. for Ecuador; by Addison-Wesley Publishing Company for Korea; by Ediciones ZETA S.C.R. Ltda. for Peru; by WS Computer Publishing Company, Inc., for the Philippines; by Unalis Corporation for Taiwan; by Contemporanea de Ediciones for Venezuela. Authorized Sales Agent: Anthony Rudkin Associates for the Middle East and North Africa.

For general information on IDG Books Worldwide's books in the U.S., please call our Consumer Customer Service department at 800-762-2974. For reseller information, including discounts and premium sales, please call our Reseller Customer Service department at 800-434-3422.

For information on where to purchase IDG Books Worldwide's books outside the U.S., please contact our International Sales department at 415-655-3023 or fax 415-655-3299.

For information on foreign language translations, please contact our Foreign & Subsidiary Rights department at 415-655-3021 or fax 415-655-3281.

For sales inquiries and special prices for bulk quantities, please contact our Sales department at 415-655-3200 or write to the address above.

For information on using IDG Books Worldwide's books in the classroom or for ordering examination copies, please contact our Educational Sales department at 800-434-2086 or fax 817-251-8174.

For press review copies, author interviews, or other publicity information, please contact our Public Relations department at 415-655-3000 or fax 415-655-3299.

For authorization to photocopy items for corporate, personal, or educational use, please contact Copyright Clearance Center, 222 Rosewood Drive, Danvers, MA 01923, or fax 508-750-4470.

LIMIT OF LIABILITY/DISCLAIMER OF WARRANTY: AUTHOR AND PUBLISHER HAVE USED THEIR BEST EFFORTS IN PREPARING THIS BOOK. IDG BOOKS WORLDWIDE, INC., AND AUTHOR MAKE NO REPRESENTATIONS OR WARRANTIES WITH RESPECT TO THE ACCURACY OR COMPLETENESS OF THE CONTENTS OF THIS BOOK AND SPECIFICALLY DISCLAIM ANY IMPLIED WARRANTIES OF MERCHANTABILITY OR FITNESS FOR A PARTICULAR PURPOSE. THERE ARE NO WARRANTIES WHICH EXTEND BEYOND THE DESCRIPTIONS CONTAINED IN THIS PARAGRAPH. NO WARRANTY MAY BE CREATED OR EXTENDED BY SALES REPRESENTATIVES OR WRITTEN SALES MATERIALS. THE ACCURACY AND COMPLETENESS OF THE INFORMATION PROVIDED HEREIN AND THE OPINIONS STATED HEREIN ARE NOT GUARANTEED OR WARRANTED TO PRODUCE ANY PARTICULAR RESULTS, AND THE ADVICE AND STRATEGIES CONTAINED HEREIN MAY NOT BE SUITABLE FOR EVERY INDIVIDUAL. NEITHER IDG BOOKS WORLDWIDE, INC., NOR AUTHOR SHALL BE LIABLE FOR ANY LOSS OF PROFIT OR ANY OTHER COMMERCIAL DAMAGES, INCLUDING BUT NOT LIMITED TO SPECIAL, INCIDENTAL, CONSEQUENTIAL, OR OTHER DAMAGES. FULFILLMENT OF EACH COUPON OFFER IS THE RESPONSIBILITY OF THE OFFEROR.

Trademarks: All brand names and product names used in this book are trade names, service marks, trademarks, or registered trademarks of their respective owners. IDG Books Worldwide is not associated with any product or vendor mentioned in this book.

 is a trademark under exclusive license to IDG Books Worldwide, Inc., from International Data Group, Inc.

About the Author

Marcia Tatroe is a garden designer, lecturer, and writer who lives on the southeastern edge of Denver, Colorado. She settled on a career in gardening after studying art and interior design in Southern California, raising kids, and actively wondering what she would be when she grew up. In the meantime, she was fortunate to have the opportunity to live and garden in areas as diverse as Highland, California; Tacoma, Washington; Lompoc, California; the Netherlands; and south-central England. When she discovered folks would actually pay to hear her gush on about gardening, there was no looking back.

A former Master Gardener of several years for Colorado State University's Cooperative Extension Program, Marcia is currently on the board of directors of Xeriscape Colorado! and a teacher for Denver Botanic Gardens. An inveterate plant addict, she squeezes an ever-changing collection of over 2,000 perennials into a small suburban lot. Time spent tending the garden is one of her greatest passions, and she hopes it's contagious.

The National Gardening Association is the largest member-based, nonprofit organization of home gardeners in the U.S. Founded in 1972 (as Gardens for All) to spearhead the community-garden movement, today's National Gardening Association is best known for its bimonthly magazine, *National Gardening* ($18 per year). Some half-million gardeners worldwide read each issue of this publication, which reports on all aspects of home gardening. The National Gardening Association supplements these publishing activities with online efforts, such as on CompuServe (type GO GARDEN) and the World Wide Web (http://www.garden.org).

Other National Gardening Association activities include

- ✔ **Growing Science Inquiry and GrowLab:** Funded in part by the National Science Foundation, these projects provide science-based curricula for students in kindergarten through grade 8.

- ✔ **The *National Gardening Survey:*** Conducted by the Gallup Company since 1972, the *National Gardening Survey* is the most detailed research about gardeners and gardening in North America.

- ✔ **Youth Garden Grants:** Every year, the National Gardening Association awards grants (worth more than $500 each) of gardening tools and seeds to schools, youth groups, and community organizations.

Mission statement: "The mission of the National Gardening Association is to sustain the essential values of life and community, renewing the fundamental links between people, plants, and the earth. Through gardening, we promote environmental responsibility, advance multi-disciplinary learning and scientific literacy, and create partnerships that restore and enhance communities."

For more information about the National Gardening Association, write to 180 Flynn Ave., Burlington, VT 05401, U.S.A. or call 800-LETSGRO (538-7476).

ABOUT IDG BOOKS WORLDWIDE

Welcome to the world of IDG Books Worldwide.

IDG Books Worldwide, Inc., is a subsidiary of International Data Group, the world's largest publisher of computer-related information and the leading global provider of information services on information technology. IDG was founded more than 25 years ago and now employs more than 8,500 people worldwide. IDG publishes more than 275 computer publications in over 75 countries (see listing below). More than 60 million people read one or more IDG publications each month.

Launched in 1990, IDG Books Worldwide is today the #1 publisher of best-selling computer books in the United States. We are proud to have received eight awards from the Computer Press Association in recognition of editorial excellence and three from *Computer Currents'* First Annual Readers' Choice Awards. Our best-selling *...For Dummies*® series has more than 30 million copies in print with translations in 30 languages. IDG Books Worldwide, through a joint venture with IDG's Hi-Tech Beijing, became the first U.S. publisher to publish a computer book in the People's Republic of China. In record time, IDG Books Worldwide has become the first choice for millions of readers around the world who want to learn how to better manage their businesses.

Our mission is simple: Every one of our books is designed to bring extra value and skill-building instructions to the reader. Our books are written by experts who understand and care about our readers. The knowledge base of our editorial staff comes from years of experience in publishing, education, and journalism — experience we use to produce books for the '90s. In short, we care about books, so we attract the best people. We devote special attention to details such as audience, interior design, use of icons, and illustrations. And because we use an efficient process of authoring, editing, and desktop publishing our books electronically, we can spend more time ensuring superior content and spend less time on the technicalities of making books.

You can count on our commitment to deliver high-quality books at competitive prices on topics you want to read about. At IDG Books Worldwide, we continue in the IDG tradition of delivering quality for more than 25 years. You'll find no better book on a subject than one from IDG Books Worldwide.

John J. Kilcullen

John Kilcullen
CEO
IDG Books Worldwide, Inc.

Eighth Annual Computer Press Awards ≥1992

Ninth Annual Computer Press Awards ≥1993

Tenth Annual Computer Press Awards ≥1994

Eleventh Annual Computer Press Awards ≥1995

IDG Books Worldwide, Inc., is a subsidiary of International Data Group, the world's largest publisher of computer-related information and the leading global provider of information services on information technology. International Data Group publishes over 275 computer publications in over 75 countries. Sixty million people read one or more International Data Group publications each month. International Data Group's publications include: **ARGENTINA:** Buyer's Guide, Computerworld Argentina, PC World Argentina; **AUSTRALIA:** Australian Macworld, Australian PC World, Australian Reseller News, Computerworld, IT Casebook, Network World, Publish, Webmaster; **AUSTRIA:** Computerwelt Osterreich, Networks Austria, PC Tip Austria; **BANGLADESH:** PC World Bangladesh; **BELARUS:** PC World Belarus; **BELGIUM:** Data News; **BRAZIL:** Annuário de Informática, Computerworld, Connections, Macworld, PC Player, PC World, Publish, Reseller News, Supergamepower; **BULGARIA:** Computerworld Bulgaria, Network World Bulgaria, PC & MacWorld Bulgaria; **CANADA:** CIO Canada, Client/Server World, ComputerWorld Canada, InfoWorld Canada, NetworkWorld Canada, WebWorld; **CHILE:** Computerworld Chile, PC World Chile; **COLOMBIA:** Computerworld Colombia, PC World Colombia; **COSTA RICA:** PC World Centro America; **THE CZECH AND SLOVAK REPUBLICS:** Computerworld Czechoslovakia, Macworld Czech Republic, PC World Czechoslovakia; **DENMARK:** Communications World Danmark, Computerworld Danmark, Macworld Danmark, PC World Danmark, Techworld Denmark; **DOMINICAN REPUBLIC:** PC World Republica Dominicana; **ECUADOR:** PC World Ecuador; **EGYPT:** Computerworld Middle East, PC World Middle East; **EL SALVADOR:** PC World Centro America; **FINLAND:** MikroPC, Tietoverkko, Tietoviikko; **FRANCE:** Distributique, Hebdo, Info PC, Le Monde Informatique, Macworld, Reseaux & Telecoms, WebMaster France; **GERMANY:** Computer Partner, Computerwoche, Computerwoche Extra, Computerwoche FOCUS, Global Online, Macwelt, PC Welt; **GREECE:** Amiga Computing, GamePro Greece, Multimedia World; **GUATEMALA:** PC World Centro America; **HONDURAS:** PC World Centro America; **HONG KONG:** Computerworld Hong Kong, PC World Hong Kong, Publish in Asia; **HUNGARY:** ABCD CD-ROM, Computerworld Szamitastechnika, Internetto online Magazine, PC World Hungary, PC-X Magazin Hungary; **ICELAND:** Tolvuheimur PC World Island; **INDIA:** Information Communications World, Information Systems Computerworld, PC World India, Publish in Asia; **INDONESIA:** InfoKomputer PC World, Komputek Computerworld, Publish in Asia; **IRELAND:** ComputerScope, PC Live!; **ISRAEL:** Macworld Israel, People & Computers/Computerworld; **ITALY:** Computerworld Italia, Macworld Italia, Networking Italia, PC World Italia; **JAPAN:** DTP World, Macworld Japan, Nikkei Personal Computing, OS/2 World Japan, SunWorld Japan, Windows NT World, Windows World Japan; **KENYA:** PC World East African; **KOREA:** Hi-Tech Information, Macworld Korea, PC World Korea; **MACEDONIA:** PC World Macedonia; **MALAYSIA:** Computerworld Malaysia, PC World Malaysia, Publish in Asia; **MALTA:** PC World Malta; **MEXICO:** Computerworld Mexico, PC World Mexico; **MYANMAR:** PC World Myanmar; **NETHERLANDS:** Computer! Totaal, LAN Internetworking Magazine, LAN World Buyers Guide, Macworld Netherlands, Net, WebWereld; **NEW ZEALAND:** Absolute Beginners Guide and Plain & Simple Series, Computer Buyer, Computer Industry Directory, Computerworld New Zealand, MTB, Network World, PC World New Zealand; **NICARAGUA:** PC World Centro America; **NORWAY:** Computerworld Norge, CW Rapport, Datamagasinet, Financial Rapport, Kursguide Norge, Macworld Norge, Multimediaworld Norge, PC World Ekspress Norge, PC World Nettverk, PC World Norge, PC World ProduktGuide Norge; **PAKISTAN:** Computerworld Pakistan; **PANAMA:** PC World Panama; **PEOPLE'S REPUBLIC OF CHINA:** China Computer Users, China Computerworld, China InfoWorld, China Telecom World Weekly, Computer & Communication, Electronic Design China, Electronics Today, Electronics Weekly, Game Software, PC World China, Popular Computer Week, Software Weekly, Software World, Telecom World; **PERU:** Computerworld Peru, PC World Profesional Peru, PC World SoHo Peru; **PHILIPPINES:** Click!, Computerworld Philippines, PC World Philippines, Publish in Asia; **POLAND:** Computerworld Poland, Computerworld Special Report Poland, Cyber, Macworld Poland, Networld Poland, PC World Komputer; **PORTUGAL:** Cerebro/PC World, Computerworld/Correio Informático, Dealer World Portugal, Mac*In/PC*In Portugal, Multimedia World; **PUERTO RICO:** PC World Puerto Rico; **ROMANIA:** Computerworld Romania, PC World Romania, Telecom Romania; **RUSSIA:** Computerworld Russia, Mir PK, Publish, Seti; **SINGAPORE:** Computerworld Singapore, PC World Singapore, Publish in Asia; **SLOVENIA:** Monitor; **SOUTH AFRICA:** Computing SA, Network World SA, Software World SA; **SPAIN:** Communicaciones World España, Computerworld España, Dealer World España, Macworld España, PC World España; **SRI LANKA:** Infolink PC World; **SWEDEN:** CAP&Design, Computer Sweden, Corporate Computing Sweden, Internetworld Sweden, it.branschen, Macworld Sweden, MaxiData Sweden, MikroDatorn, Nätverk & Kommunikation, PC World Sweden, PCaktiv, Windows World Sweden; **SWITZERLAND:** Computerworld Schweiz, Macworld Schweiz, PCtip; **TAIWAN:** Computerworld Taiwan, Macworld Taiwan, NEW ViSiON/Publish, PC World Taiwan, Windows World Taiwan; **THAILAND:** Publish in Asia, Thai Computerworld; **TURKEY:** Computerworld Turkiye, Macworld Turkiye, Network World Turkiye, PC World Turkiye; **UKRAINE:** Computerworld Kiev, Multimedia World Ukraine, PC World Ukraine; **UNITED KINGDOM:** Acorn User UK, Amiga Action UK, Amiga Computing UK, Apple Talk UK, Computing, Macworld, Parents and Computers UK, PC Advisor, PC Home, PSX Pro, The WEB; **UNITED STATES:** Cable in the Classroom, CIO Magazine, Computerworld, DOS World, Federal Computer Week, GamePro Magazine, InfoWorld, I-Way, Macworld, Network World, PC Games, PC World, Publish, Video Event, THE WEB Magazine, and WebMaster; online webzines: JavaWorld, NetscapeWorld, and SunWorld Online; **URUGUAY:** InfoWorld Uruguay; **VENEZUELA:** Computerworld Venezuela, PC World Venezuela; and **VIETNAM:** PC World Vietnam.   1/24/97

Dedication

To my patient husband, Randy Tatroe, who typed this whole darn book from my unintelligible scribblings (and with only a reasonable amount of grumbling).

Author's Acknowledgments

Putting this book together has taken the combined efforts of a huge number of behind-the-scenes hands and talent. All the folks listed in the credits page deserve a big thank-you. Each and every one of them was critical to this book's creation and deserves a hearty round of applause.

Michael MacCaskey and his stalwart staff at *National Gardening* magazine deserve a special thanks for their support and advice. Among them, Regan Eberhart was a real help. Sometimes, writing a book feels exactly like stepping in to fly an airplane after the pilot has fainted at the controls — Regan was always there to "talk me down."

This book owes a mammoth debt to the Helen Fowler Library at Denver Botanic Gardens and especially to the head librarian, Susan Eubank. She cheerfully dropped whatever she was doing whenever I needed her help with research. To her credit, she never once raised her voice when she called to beg the return of overdue books.

Thanks also to Lauren Springer, Angela Overy, and Rob Proctor — veteran writers all — who offered advice, encouragement, and superb photographs.

My apologies to my poor neglected garden, which I vow to take *really* good care of in the coming year. It deserves better treatment.

The National Gardening Association (NGA) thanks editors Emily Stetson and Regan Eberhart for keeping the book on track, and Charlie Nardozzi, NGA senior horticulturist, for gamely jumping onboard here and there as needed. Likewise, thanks are extended to NGA and *National Gardening* magazine staff: David Els, president and publisher; Michael MacCaskey, editor; Linda Provost, art director; and Larry Sommers, marketing. Special thanks to David Cavagnaro and Todd Davis for providing the majority of the excellent photographs.

Certainly and effusively, we thank the team at IDG Books Worldwide, Inc. In Chicago, thanks go to Kathy Welton, vice president and publisher; Sarah Kennedy, executive editor; Stacy Collins, brand manager; and Jamie Klobuchar, assistant brand manager — all of whom were essential to first launching and then landing this project. In Indianapolis, Shannon Ross, project editor, and Christine Meloy Beck, copy editor, worked with us in the trenches and contributed enormously to this book — many thank-yous to you both.

Publisher's Acknowledgments

We're proud of this book; please send us your comments about it by using the Reader Response Card at the back of the book or by e-mailing us at feedback/dummies@idgbooks.com. Some of the people who helped bring this book to market include the following:

Acquisitions, Development, and Editorial

Project Editor: Shannon Ross

Acquisitions Editor: Sarah Kennedy, Executive Editor

Associate Permissions Editor: Heather H. Dismore

Copy Editor: Christine Meloy Beck

Technical Editor: The National Gardening Association

Editorial Manager: Kristin A. Cocks

Editorial Assistants: Ann Miller, Constance Carlisle, Chris H. Collins

Production

Project Coordinator: Cindy L. Phipps

Layout and Graphics: Linda M. Boyer, Elizabeth Cárdenas-Nelson, J. Tyler Connor, Dominique DeFelice, Maridee V. Ennis, Angela F. Hunckler, Todd Klemme, Jane E. Martin, Drew R. Moore, Anna Rohrer, Brent Savage

Proofreaders: Nancy L. Reinhardt, Rachel Garvey, Robert Springer, Carrie Voorhis, Ethel M. Winslow, Karen York

Indexer: Richard Evans

Special Help

Illustrations by Ron Hildebrand; Photography by David Cavagnaro, R. Todd Davis, Angela Overy, Rob Proctor, Lauren Springer, Randy Tatroe

General and Administrative

IDG Books Worldwide, Inc.: John Kilcullen, CEO; Steven Berkowitz, President and Publisher

IDG Books Technology Publishing: Brenda McLaughlin, Senior Vice President and Group Publisher

Dummies Technology Press and Dummies Editorial: Diane Graves Steele, Vice President and Associate Publisher; Judith A. Taylor, Brand Manager; Kristin A. Cocks, Editorial Director

Dummies Trade Press: Kathleen A. Welton, Vice President and Publisher; Stacy S. Collins, Brand Manager

IDG Books Production for Dummies Press: Beth Jenkins, Production Director; Cindy L. Phipps, Supervisor of Project Coordination, Production Proofreading and Indexing; Kathie S. Schutte, Supervisor of Page Layout; Shelley Lea, Supervisor of Graphics and Design; Debbie J. Gates, Production Systems Specialist; Tony Augsburger, Supervisor of Reprints and Bluelines; Leslie Popplewell, Media Archive Coordinator

Dummies Packaging and Book Design: Patti Sandez, Packaging Specialist; Kavish+Kavish, Cover Design

◆

The publisher would like to give special thanks to Patrick J. McGovern, without whom this book would not have been possible.

◆

Contents at a Glance

Cartoons at a Glance

By Rich Tennant • Fax: 508-546-7747 • E-mail: the5wave@tiac.net

page 279

page 7

page 95

page 153

page 219

page 41

Table of Contents

Introduction

• •

*I*f your only experience with gardening until now has been tending houseplants, you're in for a real treat when you turn your hand to perennial gardening. Anyone can grow perennials; houseplants are the ones that give gardening a bad name. I'll let you in on a secret — I couldn't keep a houseplant healthy if my life depended on it. (When I entertain guests, I run out and buy robust replacements so that I'm not embarrassed by the dead and dying plants hanging around from the last party.) But I can grow hundreds of perennials. Most perennials are much less demanding and tolerate much more abuse than you may have been led to believe.

The only trick to creating a little bit of heaven in your own yard is choosing perennials suited to the conditions where you live. Every corner of the world has flowers that grow better there than anywhere else on earth. Every location also has flowers that don't survive there no matter what you do. Concentrate on the flowers in the first group, instead of pining for the flowers in the second group, and you absolutely can't fail.

Like all nonessential activities in life, gardening, first and foremost, ought to be fun. Don't get bogged down in *shoulds* and *should nots* — just go with your own instincts. If you aren't having a good time, you're either trying too hard or attempting to live up to someone else's expectations.

About This Book

This book is just to get you started; the best lessons come by trial and error in your own garden. Every gardener's experience is unique, so treat all gardening advice — including mine — with a healthy dose of skepticism. Be especially skeptical whenever what you read contradicts your own garden. Your garden tells you what it likes and doesn't like.

How to Use This Book

You don't need to read this book from cover to cover — it's not a romance novel or a who-done-it thriller, for heaven's sake. Instead, let it serve as a reference you can turn to whenever a particular need arises. Use the Table of Contents or the Index to guide you to the section you need, or simply skim through chapters or parts of the book that look relevant to you.

Before you actually put your shovel to the ground, be sure to give some attention to the fundamentals of selection, care, and feeding. These basics, covered in the following chapters, are all interrelated — overlooking any one of them can be fatal (for your perennials, that is):

- **Chapter 4:** Choosing perennials compatible with your climate
- **Chapter 11:** Soil preparation
- **Chapter 14:** How to plant
- **Chapter 15:** Watering
- **Chapter 16:** Fertilizing
- **Chapter 17:** Taking care of the garden

The color section of this book includes photographs of several complete gardens and over 100 common perennials. Because the name you may call a particular perennial depends on where you live, these flowers are arranged alphabetically by botanical name (see Chapter 1 for a discussion of common versus botanical names). The text refers you to this color section for photographs of the topic at hand.

What You Can Skip

After you read the basics (outlined in the preceding section), everything else is optional. If you have no interest in garden design or growing your own perennials, skip right past those chapters. If you don't have a single pest in your garden, you can leave Chapter 18 unthumbed until you run into trouble (sooner or later, insects turn *every* garden into an all-you-can-eat buffet). Part VI is filled exclusively with fun and extraneous information, so you can save it for the next time you visit your dentist's office and need some light reading material.

How This Book Is Organized

I've arranged this book into six parts, each one covering a different aspect of gardening. For easy reference, each part is divided into chapters, which are divided into sections, which are divided into paragraphs, which are divided into sentences, which are . . . well, you get the idea.

Part I: Perennial Joy

Perennial is a fairly broad term. The first chapter of this book explains what a perennial is (for flower-gardening intents and purposes) and includes reasons why you would even want to contemplate digging up part of your yard to make room for perennials (reasons you can use to convince your spouse that doing so is a sensible idea). Chapters 2 and 3 are purely optional design advice.

Part II: The Part of Plans

Planting your flowers without rhyme or reason is perfectly okay — don't let anyone tell you otherwise. But, in case you do care about such things as color, texture, and form, this part contains 15 designs for a variety of situations and climates. (I'm a garden designer — I can't help myself.)

Part III: Cast of Characters

Of the thousands of perennials currently available from mail-order catalogs and garden centers, this encyclopedic section describes in detail a few of the easiest and most widely available plants to pique your interest. But don't limit yourself to only these selections; many more perennials are out there waiting to come home with you.

Part IV: Making Your Bed

You may not believe it now, but constructing the flower bed can be among the most rewarding and enjoyable aspects of growing perennials. Part IV contains all the information you need to build your flower bed from the ground up (or to supervise hired labor intelligently).

Part V: Care, Feeding, and Propagation

After you give perennials a place in your landscape, most of them require regular attention to look and perform their very best. In this part, I cover watering, fertilizing, various maintenance considerations, dealing with pests, and growing your own perennials.

Part VI: The Part of Tens

The last part contains all the *et cetera* information — the nonessentials of perennial gardening. You can find lists of flowers that combine beauty with diverse practical uses, such as providing fodder for your table. You can also find a few ideas for embellishing your garden with natural or man-made objets d'art (and some not so d'art).

Icons Used in This Book

Gardening is a visual art, so using icons to depict certain kinds of information is only natural in a gardening book. When you see the following icons beside a paragraph, here's what you can expect to find:

Gardening is, by nature, environmental. Any activity that brings you up close and personal with the earth and nature's bounty is sure to make you more sensitive to ecological issues. I use the Eco-Smart icon to highlight tips or information that can make your gardening practices even better for the environment.

A big part of gardening involves keeping the grim reaper out of the flower bed. Flower Killer icons can help by calling your attention to any practices or products that can suck the life out of your prized perennials.

Sometimes, it seems as though gardeners speak a language all their own. In this book, I try to avoid all that botanical mumbo-jumbo. But some gardening terms are worth learning, if for nothing else than to get the sales clerk at the local nursery to understand what you want. Whenever you see the Garden Jargon icon, limber up your tongue and prepare for a lesson in Gardenese.

Which plants grow well for you and which ones die the moment their roots hit the soil depends on your climate, soil type, and many other factors unique to your garden. However, some perennials seem to have the fortitude of a Saturday morning cartoon hero, no matter where they're planted. I indicate these rough-and-tumble plants with the Perennial Superhero icon.

What's a flower book without a splash of color? This book contains color photographs of over 100 perennials and several complete gardens. Whenever I refer to a plant or garden that's pictured in the color insert, you see the Photo Op icon beside that paragraph.

In the midst of digging, weeding, watering, pinching, pruning, and planting, you can easily lose sight of the big picture. Remember icons adorn paragraphs that help you put everything in perspective. (For added effect, you may want to read these pearls of wisdom in your mother's voice.)

The truth is, most flowers love sun — lots and lots of sun. But don't despair if you live in the shade of a giant oak tree or a ten-story apartment building — some perennials thrive in shady conditions. If you're looking to liven up a shady patch of bare earth, look for the Shady Character icon to help you pick the best perennials for the job.

Gardeners get the tools of their trade from a variety of sources, from mail-order catalogs to local nurseries to the Internet. Look for the Source icon to find out where you can stock up on garden supplies.

Gardening should be fun, so don't let yourself get caught up in a sticky situation. Thorny Issue icons serve as beacons to steer you clear of common gardening blunders that can cause you to lose time, money, and patience.

A favorite pastime of gardeners is sharing trade secrets with other gardeners. Look for the Tip icon to find helpful hints that can make you the most popular gardener on the block.

Although gardening is a relatively safe hobby, you do need to be aware of some potential health and safety hazards. Some plants and plant-care products are deadly poisonous. Treat paragraphs with the Warning icon the same way you treat warning labels on household chemicals: Read them carefully and heed their advice.

Where to Go from Here

Be honest. You've probably already read the chapters that first caught your fancy. Few folks ever tackle the Introduction first. If you are the rare exception, stop reading this introduction right now. Instead, thumb through the pages and read the bits that interest you most. That will be enough of an orientation to what this book covers.

Part I
Perennial Joy

"That should do it."

In this part . . .

*B*efore you're willing to get dirty, sweaty, and sore from planting a garden of perennials, you may want to find out just what a perennial is and what it can do for you. You may also want to investigate the various styles of flower beds to find the one that appeals to your unique sense of taste (and to the unique features of your yard). Part I can help on all these counts. Armed with this information, you can become your own "exterior decorator" — putting together a flower bed in which the interplay of color, texture, shape, and size enhances each individual flower.

Chapter 1

Perennials: the Plant That Keeps On Going

● ●

In This Chapter

▶ An introduction to perennials

▶ The function of roots, stems, leaves, and flowers

▶ A crash course in plant names and descriptions

▶ A case of Perennial Fever

● ●

*P*erennial flowers are in the midst of a popularity surge. Actually, perennials never lost their appeal in gardening circles, but when perennial gardens start popping up in the landscapes of every new gas station or shopping mall, you can't help but notice that a mainstream insurgence is afoot.

Nurseries can hardly keep up with the demand as the public clamors for more varieties. (After they've gotten a taste of the mundane, gardeners start craving the new and the rare.) Fund-raising garden tours sell out. Plant clubs and societies find their membership rolls swelling. Subscription rates of gardening magazines soar.

With this book, you can discover for yourself what all the fuss is about. You don't need to hire a professional gardener to surround your home with perennials — you can grow them yourself. Perennials are as easy to grow as they are fulfilling.

What Makes a Perennial a Perennial?

Rather than bury you here in Chapter 1 under dozens of terms concerning every facet of perennial gardening, I've decided to define most terms as they come up in the appropriate chapters. This chapter includes only a few of the most basic definitions to help you make sense of the topic at large. (Relax, there isn't a quiz at the end of this chapter.)

The many meanings of "perennial"

A *perennial* is any plant that lives for three or more years *when it's grown in conditions to its liking.* Notice that just because a plant dies in less than three years doesn't mean that it isn't a perennial (otherwise, I know several people who would claim that there's no such thing as a perennial — at least not in their yards). The fact that you can't get Mexican sage to last a week in-your Alaskan flower bed doesn't mean that Mexican sage isn't a perennial. Like all perennials, Mexican sage has the *potential* to live a long and full life, if you grow it in the proper conditions.

This book is really just about one type of perennial plant — the *herbaceous flowering perennial.* Technically, the term "perennial" includes such giants as the majestic, centuries-old redwood and the oak tree in the city park. Unlike trees and shrubs (which have woody stems forming their twigs, branches, and trunks) *herbaceous* perennials have soft, fleshy stems.

Perennials that hail from cold climates usually indulge in a winter nap, called a period of *dormancy.* (A few herbaceous perennials go dormant in summer, instead, playing a convincing game of opossum for their uninitiated gardeners.) During the period of dormancy, the perennial *dies back to the ground* — that is, allows its stems and foliage to die. The above-ground parts of a dormant plant are truly dead, but the roots are alive and well. In fact, the roots may be actively growing even when the top is resting.

In more moderate climates, most herbaceous perennials are *evergreen* (meaning that their above-ground parts are alive and kicking all year long) because they don't need a coping mechanism such as dormancy to escape extreme temperatures.

Anatomy of a perennial

Growing perennials is much easier if you have at least a fundamental understanding of how the flowers are put together. Significant variations exist within this large group of plants, but they all share a few characteristics, as shown in Figure 1-1.

Roots

In addition to serving as the anchor that holds the perennial in place, roots also pull water and nutrients from the soil and carry these essentials to the stems. The roots even store extra water and nutrients in case times get tough.

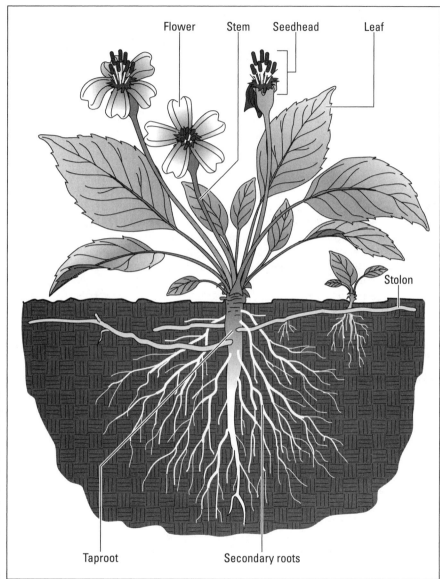

Flower   Stem   Seedhead   Leaf

Stolon

Figure 1-1:
The basic
parts of a
perennial
plant are
the roots,
stem,
leaves,
flowers,
and
seedheads.

Taproot   Secondary roots

The two main types of roots are *fibrous roots* and *taproots*. Fibrous-rooted perennials have a network of branching roots. Taprooted perennials have a fleshy central root (like a carrot), with smaller secondary roots growing off the main root (refer to Figure 1-1). Whereas taproots can reach quite deeply into the ground, fibrous roots generally occur primarily in the top 12 inches (30 cm) of soil.

Stems

Stems are the framework of the perennial, supporting the leaves and flowers. They also transport water and nutrients from the roots to the leaves and flowers, and vice versa. Stems take many forms. Some are squared, and some are rounded. They may be upright or low and spreading; single or branched.

Stem tissue is sometimes specialized to create thickened underground repositories, where the plant can stash extra food and water. These lumps of tissue take many forms, such as *rhizomes, corms,* or *tubers* (all of which I convert into plain English for you in Chapter 10).

Perennials may also spread by modified stems called *stolons* (or *runners*) that travel just beneath the surface of the ground (refer to Figure 1-1). The stolons often send up new shoots along their length, either close by or quite some distance from the original clump, varying by the type of perennial. Some perennials make pests of themselves — spreading far too quickly by runners. But these plants can also provide you with lots of new plants, as Chapter 19 explains.

Leaves

Although stems *can* manufacture food for the plant, this function is primarily the role of the leaves. Leaves also help the plant regulate its moisture content and internal temperature by allowing water to evaporate from their surfaces or by wilting, when necessary, to reduce their exposure to sun and air. Leaves come in a huge variety of shapes, sizes, and textures and can occur singly or as one of several leaves attached in a group on a single stalk.

A cluster of leaves at the base of the plant is called a *basal rosette.* Stems and flower stalks rise from this clump of leaves and often die back to the basal rosette at the end of the growing season.

Flowers

You may think that plants form flowers solely for your viewing pleasure (and so you have something to present to your sweetheart on Valentine's Day). But flowers are the reproductive structure of a perennial. The bright, sweet-smelling flower blossom is meant to attract pollinators such as bees, flies, butterflies, birds, moths, and bats. These creatures get a meal of nectar or pollen in exchange for carrying bits of pollen to other flowers in the garden. When a bee brushes pollen from one Shasta daisy onto another — bingo! — pollination occurs.

Very small flowers are often wind-pollinated, producing prodigious amounts of pollen in a hit-or-miss system that greatly affects hay fever sufferers. However, most garden flowers are chosen for their very showy blossoms, which don't cause hay fever.

Flowers have evolved into a vast multitude of different shapes, sizes, and colors to lure and accommodate their various pollinators. Flowers can be held on a single stem or in multiples on spikes; in flattened clusters or loosely branched.

What appears to be a single flower may actually be a cluster of many tiny flowers, forming a *flowerhead*. One example is the daisy, which is called a *composite* because it's composed of two kinds of flowers: the tiny tubular flowers forming the center button and the frill of petals around the outside edge.

Seedheads

After a flower is pollinated, it forms seed. The flower deteriorates — first fading and wilting, and then turning brown and dropping petals. If you don't cut off the dead bloom at this point, most flowers *go to seed* — that is, form seedpods or capsules. Some seedheads are as attractive as the flowers themselves. If you leave these seedheads on the plant, you can enjoy their beauty long after all the flowers are gone.

Flowers that develop seeds and germinate in your garden are said to *self-sow* or *volunteer.* The baby plants that come up are called *seedlings.*

Some perennials are sterile and don't make viable seed. You can't grow more of these plants from seed, but you can chop the plants up and grow each part into a new plant that's identical to the parent. See Chapter 19 to find out how to do this.

Playing the Perennial Name Game

True gardenholics tend to go on and on about plant names. You may catch them at the nursery asking, "Which Latin name is *most* correct, the old one or the new one?" Real garden snobs even get into heated debates about how to pronounce a particular plant name. Such disputes are commonplace because the gardening community has no final authority for plant names. Botanical spellings and pronunciations go in and out of favor like hairstyles.

This book relies on the *Naamlijst Van Vaste Planten (List of Names of Plants)* by H.J. van de Laar (Research Station for Nursery Stock, Boskoop, the Netherlands, 1995) as its primary authority. Secondary sources include the *Western Garden Book,* by the editors of Sunset Books and *Sunset* magazine (1995); *The New Royal Horticultural Society Dictionary of Gardening,* edited by Anthony Huxley (1992); and *The Plant Finder,* devised and compiled by Chris Philip (1993).

Common names

Of course, ordinary people don't go around using long, Latin botanical names in everyday conversation. Instead, they use a sort of botanical nickname, called a *common name*. Common names are less formal and easier to pronounce than botanical names. They're also less precise. Just as your Aunt Norma calls you "pumpkin" and Uncle Bob calls you "Big Guy," many perennials have several nicknames.

Often, the common name describes some distinguishing characteristic of the plant. For example, the plant called blue star has starry blue flowers. Sometimes, however, the origin of the name is lost in the mythology of a former time. Does anyone have a clue just who was the Susan of black-eyed Susan fame?

Finding that several unrelated flowers share the same common name isn't unusual at all. Unfortunately, regular English flower names are often just as silly as their highfalutin Latin cousins, if for different reasons. For example, I can think of two distinct plants that share the name "mock orange," and five different plants that go by "dusty miller." At least three unrelated perennials are called coneflowers: *Echinacea, Rudbeckia,* and *Ratibida.* On the other hand, many plants have no common name! Go figure.

The long and short of it is that you're going to have to pay some attention to plant names — if only to avoid buying and planting the wrong flower.

TIP

A flower called "Bob"

You can call your Shasta daisy "Bob" if you want, and no one can challenge you. But imagine what kind of chaos would exist if no standardized method for naming plants existed. Fortunately, we do have such a system, called *botanical nomenclature.*

Unfortunately, botanical nomenclature is composed of pseudo-Latin, Greek, and the names of botanists and explorers. You find some really intimidating and unpronounceable combinations, such as *Paeonia mlokosewitschii* (which is a yellow peony, not a serious new disease).

Obviously, folks who name plants have a really fun sense of humor. (Or is it just the opposite?) But don't be put off by the names. You already know quite a few of these proper botanical names. *Aster, Chrysanthemum, Dahlia, Geranium, Hibiscus, Iris* — these are all botanical names that you're probably already familiar with and are comfortable using. Others, such as *Lilium, Rosa,* and *Tulipa,* are altered very little from their common names.

Learning new botanical names is a good way to impress your friends with your gardening savvy. It's also a sort of secret gardener's handshake, one that makes you appear to be a very serious gardener, indeed.

Plant name nonsense

The proper botanical name of a plant consists of two parts, much in the same way that people have a first and a last name. However, in plant language, the last name comes first.

The "family name" — the "Smith" of Joe Smith, if you will — is the *genus.* (This name is always capitalized and italicized.) A genus is a family of closely related plants. Just as in your own family, some of the cousins look a lot alike, and others don't bear much resemblance at all. Also like your family, some closely related individuals have very different comfort levels. One uncle lives in Phoenix, Arizona, and loves the heat. His sister thinks that Oxford, England, is quite warm enough, thank you very much.

The second name, the "Joe" part of Joe Smith, is the *species* name. The species name usually describes some feature of the plant, alludes to its preferred habitat, or serves as a tribute to whoever first discovered the plant. But botanists disguise these references in pseudo-Latin, of course, just to keep things interesting. Consider, for example, *Hosta undulata. Hosta* is the genus name. The species name, *undulata,* describes the undulating shape of the leaf.

Occasionally, a third name follows the species name — the variety. *Varieties* are members of the same species that are different enough to deserve their own name. Just as you may have one redhead in a family of brunettes, some plants are quite dissimilar to their siblings. So you have *Phlox divaricata alba,* which is the name of the white form of a flower that is normally blue.

The word *cultivar* is made up of the two words "cultivated variety." Whoever discovered or created the plant decided that it was special enough to have its own name. The cultivar name comes after the species or variety and is bracketed by single quotation marks. For example, a very nice form of *Lychnis coronaria* with a pink blush is called *Lychnis coronaria* 'Angel Blush'.

Some unexpected benefits of big names

The botanical naming system has some real advantages, even if those advantages aren't readily apparent at first:

- ✔ **Standardization:** Each plant has the same name anywhere on earth. Even if you don't speak a lick of Russian, you can still talk perennials to a Muscovite — the botanical name of a plant is the same in Russian as it is in English. This standardization is particularly valuable when you buy plants. You don't ever need to *say* the botanical name but, for accuracy, check the nursery card to make sure that the coneflower you're buying is really the one you want.

✔ **Pronunciation:** Botanical Latin doesn't have a right or wrong pronunciation, despite what you may have been told. Latin is a *written* language, for heaven's sake. No one can say with any certainty how it was spoken. I've heard many a gardening expert pronounce the same name two different ways in a single lecture. Don't let anyone suck you into an argument over whether *Clematis* should be CLEM-a-tis or clem-AH-tis. Neither is more correct than the other.

✔ **Plant characteristics:** Botanical names can tell you a great deal about a plant. The species name is often very descriptive. For example, if you live near the ocean and are choosing plants that must tolerate salt spray and ocean breezes, look for those with the species name *maritima,* which means *from the seaside.* Marsh-loving plants are often called *palustrus,* so look for that name if you want to plant on a wet, poorly drained site. If you consider a snow shovel a gardening tool, you should know that plants that do well in very cold regions are often named *frigida.*

Botanical names also give you some idea of what the plant looks like. *Alba* means white, *purpurea* is purple, *atropurpurea* is dark purple, and *purpuraceous* is purplish. If you make your own potpourri, you may be especially interested in flowers with the species name *fragrantissima,* which indicates very fragrant plants.

Going Perennial

Why grow perennials and not annuals? For two very good reasons: Perennials offer more visual interest than annuals, and (despite what you may think) perennials are actually easier to manage than annuals in the long run.

A tribute to the changing seasons

Unlike static landscapes, perennial flower beds celebrate and, to some extent, choreograph the passing seasons. The institutional annual-flower displays, ever popular in municipal plantings, look exactly the same from the day they're planted until the first blackening frost. In sharp contrast, perennials reflect the passing seasons and are constantly changing and evolving. Tulips and daffodils give way to summer's bounty, and asters and chrysanthemums announce Indian summer.

The ephemeral quality of most perennials is part of their charm. I've heard gardeners say that they refuse to grow the tall bearded iris because it only blooms for a couple of weeks in spring. To me, that reasoning makes about as much sense as forgoing sweet corn because it's only available for a short season in late summer. Tall bearded iris and other transient pleasures restore nature's rhythm to modern lives that are too often confined to a virtual reality of temperature-controlled interiors and silk plants.

Easy to grow — within reason

Most perennials are endlessly forgiving as long as you plant their roots downward and point their leaves toward the light. In fact, perennials are such versatile plants that a few misconceptions about them have inevitably taken root.

The novice gardener who chooses perennials to avoid having to replant annually is going to be disappointed to discover that many perennials don't survive the three years that, by definition, classify them as perennials. Many perennials are short-lived under any circumstances, and even the long-lived ones only endure when conditions are to their liking.

At a nursery this past spring, a gentleman asked me for advice about a particularly difficult site he had — a dry spot under a shallow-rooted tree where no direct sunlight got through. He wanted me to recommend a perennial so he wouldn't have to spend the money to replant annuals there every year. He also wanted the plant to have evergreen foliage and flowers all summer long. When I finally found a plant that met all these exacting requirements, the man said that he wasn't too crazy about that particular choice and asked me to please show him some other options. He wasn't happy to learn that there were no other options, and I'm sure that, to this day, he thinks I was just being thick-headed.

Some perennials are, indeed, tough and resilient enough to grow in a crack in concrete, even during the hottest and driest summers. A few perennials outlive the gardener who planted them. Old, abandoned homesteads in the American West are often distinguished by non-native flowers still thriving — without a care, mind you — decades after the structures have collapsed.

Most traditional flowers are easy to grow, especially if you keep your expectations realistic. Perennials promise to bring even the most casual gardener endless hours of delight (peppered with occasional moments of frustration as a reality check). Wherever you live and whatever the conditions you have to offer, you can find perennial flowers that can oblige.

A Flower for Every Personality

With all the fervor of a new religious cult, the interest in perennial flowers has taken the gardening world by storm. The craze isn't so surprising when you consider the great variety and diversity these flowers offer the gardener. Perennial gardening has a facet to suit every character type or need:

- **The Type-A gardener:** People with a competitive disposition can find an outlet for their energies at plant shows and other such contests. They can line their walls with awards and blue ribbons to their heart's content. Every community hosts a plethora of opportunities — from garden-club flower shows to county fairs. Growing winning flowers takes much less time, money, and space than many similar endeavors — say, raising show horses or collecting antique cars.

- **The pack-rat gardener:** The collector who has run out of shelf space inside the house can turn to the garden for new ground. You can find two general types of perennial collectors: the specialist and the generalist.

  - The *specialist* falls in love with a particular plant and ends up with 150 daylilies (or iris or hostas or — well, you get the point). These folks often have to move to a larger property to accommodate their ever-expanding collections. Most single-flower nurseries have their origins in a collection run amok.

  - The *generalist* wants one of every flower ever grown. I'm in this category, so I know it well. The if-it's-new-I-want-it crowd attends lectures on botanical explorations to remote parts of the planet, eagerly awaiting each new introduction from the high mountains of Tadzhikistan or the rain forests of Brazil. Serious garden designers disapprove of the collector's garden, because it deteriorates into an unrelated hodgepodge of diverse habitats. Art is not the goal here. Meeting the cultural needs of these many treasures takes precedence.

- **The therapeutic gardener:** A neighbor of mine is a busy professional whose hectic schedule leaves her few opportunities to relax and indulge in complete calm and quiet. Her perennial garden is her therapy, providing an escape from the demands of clients and family. Puttering around in the garden guarantees fresh air and exercise with compensation that a spa or a gym can't offer. Gardening pays back hard work with a sense of pride and accomplishment — not to mention dazzling displays of color and beauty.

✓ **The nature lover:** This person is stuck in the city or suburbia but longs for the countryside. The nature lover wants critters to liven up the landscape. Every passing bird, bee, and butterfly is invited to drop in for a visit, and some inevitably stay and set up housekeeping. Gardens bring nature "up close and personal" by supplying food and shelter to all manner of wildlife.

✓ **The nonconformist:** Most yards are pretty much the same up and down both sides of the street — lawn, one shade tree, and a few shrubs. A tour of the interiors of these same houses would reveal an entirely different scenario; you would find the varied interests and personalities of the homeowners proudly displayed. Perennial gardening provides the perfect opportunity for public display of the same kind of self-expression. Adding a flower bed is an effective antidote to all the sameness of a suburban street (see Figure 1-2).

Figure 1-2:
Adding just a few perennial flowers to an entryway transforms a dull landscape into one that says WELCOME.

Perennial gardening is so popular and timely that it's even spilled onto the Internet. If you have access to the Internet, check out the Perennial Plant Association (http://garden.cas.psu.edu/ppa.html), an organization for landscapers, nurseries, designers, educators, and the general public. If you get really caught up in growing perennials, you may want to join this association yourself. Members have access to an annual symposium, a membership directory for networking, and guides to regional meetings and gardens. A bounty of gardening information is also available at the National Gardening Association's Web site (http://www.garden.org). You can find a guide to Web sites of other gardening associations at GardenNet (http://trine.com/GardenNet/GardenAssn/assnguil.htm).

Chapter 2
Finding Your Style

· ·

In This Chapter

▶ Planning before you dig

▶ Getting in touch with your own taste

▶ Going formal or *au naturel*

▶ Building beds and borders

▶ Considering color, texture, and form

· ·

Unless you're an old hand at creating gardens, you probably find the very suggestion of flower-bed design intimidating. The word *design* brings to mind obscure concepts involving focal points, sight lines, color charts, and so-called experts shaking their heads in disbelief at your attempts at creativity. Dump all those misconceptions and just remember that flower-bed design is simply a process that encourages you to take the time to thoroughly think through what you plan to do before you actually start. Good design happens automatically when you arrange all the various building blocks discussed in this chapter into a satisfying layout. Most important, each garden should also reflect the builder's personal taste and needs.

There's no one right way to design your garden. Don't let anyone (not even me!) impose his or her own views and prejudices on you. Your garden should be uniquely your own. My goal in this chapter is to help you define and develop your own taste. All the following design advice is meant to serve only as a guide, not as a set of rules for you to blindly follow.

Blue Jeans or Evening Gown?

For starters, forget everything you've ever read about design theory. Burn the color wheel and toss out all those suggestions for genteel combinations. You have a built-in sense of what feels right *to you* — which is all that really matters.

Mistakes are inevitable, but flower-garden foul-ups are among the easiest and least costly landscape disasters to remedy. Misplaced flowers don't come crashing down and destroy your roof during a bad storm. They don't overhang the fence and annoy the neighbors. The taste police won't issue you a ticket for using clashing colors. The worst errors in judgment are easily dug up and moved (or killed with herbicide, if all else fails).

So how do you get an idea of what you want your flower garden to look like? You have to do some soul-searching and investigating:

1. **Make a file or a notebook to keep track of your observations.**

2. **Visit public gardens or just take a critical look around your neighborhood.**

   You can even sign up for a couple of garden tours or watch garden shows on television.

3. **Ask yourself _what_ about each garden appeals or doesn't appeal to you.**

4. **Write down any particular flowers that catch your fancy.**

   Be sure to note what you like about the flower and what you don't.

   If you don't know what a particular flower is, knock on the gardener's door and ask. Gardeners are generally flattered and pleased to discuss their gardens.

5. **Keep visual records.**

   You may want to take some snapshots of the best ideas you find so that you can study them at your leisure. Look through magazines and cut out inspiring illustrations or make color copies from books. Remember: plagiarism doesn't apply to garden design. You can copy whatever you like.

After you compile all this information, you are likely to find some trends emerging. Are you more taken with a tidy formal style that has clearly defined edges and geometric shapes? Or do you prefer a carefree mix with the casual air of a wild meadow? Are you attracted to subtle pastel colors or a bright, carnival-like atmosphere?

Formality for the neat and orderly

If you like topiary and Grecian urns, or if you get uncomfortable when your plants touch, consider using some aspects of the formal design. The formal flower garden is neat and orderly, relying on strong visual lines. A formal garden may be based on geometric patterns and often is divided into parts, with each part a mirror image of the opposite part. Color and form are usually repeated regularly within the formal design.

In defense of serendipity

The most carefully considered plans don't always turn out the way you intended. Sometimes, forces of nature mess up your best ideas. Other times, the flowers themselves become contrary. For example, you observe two flowers in bloom that would be perfect together, and you cleverly decide to plant them next to each other. Then your plans are foiled. As if by mutual consent, the bloom times of these two flowers never again coincide.

But just as often, one flower takes seed next to another and creates magic. Honest garden designers have to admit that some of their best efforts are entirely accidental. These brilliant combinations can't occur if you're too quick to pull out every wandering seedling. Besides, if you're too tidy in the garden, you can get an overly planned look — much like model homes. They seldom have a lived-in, comfortable feel about them.

A rigidly formal design can be quite labor-intensive — every dead or stunted plant leaves an obvious gap, interrupting the line or grid pattern.

To get a feel for what a formal arrangement looks like, turn to Chapter 5 and look for the section called "A Jewel-Tone Garden."

Informality — but with a guiding hand

The informal design feels refreshingly free from rules and order, but it works best when you thoughtfully arrange it to create a subtle balance between the various colors and forms of the flowers. The informal gardening style is much like natural make-up. The goal is to appear less studied and fussy, but not to let nature have its way unrestricted. You can get a taste for what happens when nature is allowed to go its own way by visiting an overgrown vacant lot — not a pretty sight!

The popular cottage garden style embodies the rustic, unaffected, informal garden. If you like to color outside the lines, you're probably more comfortable with an informal garden design. (You can find an example of a cottage garden in the color photo section of this book.)

Beds and Borders

Whether arranged formally or informally, flower beds come in two basic configurations — the *border* or the *island bed*.

Whether planning beds or borders, keep the shapes fairly simple for ease of maintenance and to prevent the viewer from feeling the motion sickness that squiggly lines can cause. Curves should undulate softly, not sharply zig and zag — especially when bordering the lawn. Flowers along sharp edges inevitably lose their heads to the errant lawnmower — no matter how careful you are.

Walking the border

The grand perennial border, as big as a city block, was the height of fashion for the 19th century manor house, when skilled labor was cheap and plentiful. The tradition is still preserved in botanical gardens and historic houses, but grand borders are impractical for most gardens today.

The term *border* now refers to any flower bed located alongside a wall, fence, hedge, or pavement — as shown in Figure 2-1. A border garden is usually long and narrow as it follows the contours of the backdrop. The edges can be straight or curved. Two borders are sometimes divided by a central walk between them and often fit well into the narrow side yard of the average suburban lot.

Figure 2-1:
A flower bed along a wall, hedge, or fence is called a border.

A gardening term you may hear tossed about is *mixed border.* The *traditional* or *herbaceous border* excludes any type of plant except herbaceous perennial flowers. The mixed border, on the other hand, contains a medley of flowering plants, including small trees, well-behaved shrubs, bulbs, annual flowers, herbs, vines, and perhaps even vegetables. Much of the mixed border's popularity today is due to the limited size of the modern lot. These days, garden space must do double or even triple duty. Another part of the mixed-border appeal is due to current fashion. Gardeners presently like the look of a variety of different plants grown together.

Stranded on a deserted island bed

The *island bed* is a free-standing flower bed surrounded on all sides by lawn, gravel, or pavement. Island beds can be any shape or size. Like border gardens, island beds can be mixed, but for some unknown reason, you never see the term "mixed island beds."

The main advantage of the island style is that you can place the bed wherever conditions are ideal for the flowers that you want to grow. The middle of the lawn, for example, may be the only sunny spot you have. Island beds also counter the tendency to confine all the landscaping to the perimeter of the property — which can create an awkward appearance, sort of like pushing all your furniture up against the walls. Unlike flower beds grown against a barrier, island beds encourage you to walk around them and view their splendor from a variety of angles, as shown in Figure 2-2.

Figure 2-2:
You can walk around an island bed and view it from all sides.

Usually, island beds work best when you place them off to one side, rather than smack dab in the middle of the space that they occupy.

The Interaction of Various Design Elements

An interesting and attractive flower bed involves a complex interplay of many separate parts. Putting together such a garden can be a delicate balancing act. Too much sameness can easily become dull and boring; too much variety can slip into chaos.

On the other hand, continually remind yourself that no garden design is *wrong*. Most gardeners are constantly playing around with their compositions, moving flowers to try new and better combinations (part of the appeal of gardening with perennials is their cheerful acceptance of such treatment).

As you tinker with your flower beds (on paper or in the dirt), pay special attention to the three most important design elements: color, texture, and form.

Color

Folks have some pretty weird notions about color. One view says that certain colors reflect a more sophisticated palette than others. According to this theory, if you let orange into your garden, you must be a country bumpkin with several vehicles rusting on the front lawn, whereas pastel lovers naturally favor Mozart and Dom Pérignon. Don't let this kind of ridiculous dogma interfere with your gardening decisions.

Color fashion is always arbitrary. After a few decades of having the pastel garden represent good taste in garden design, stronger colors have recently begun to enjoy a surge in popularity. Thank goodness. How the color of the monarch butterfly and flamboyant sunsets ever came to be so badly maligned is still a great mystery to me. (Hopefully, pink won't be tapped next as gauche and tacky!)

Another trap you want to avoid is the myth of clashing colors. No natural law governs color compatibility. In nature, anything goes. You need to determine what colors *you* like together, regardless of convention. This decision shouldn't be difficult, because most folks have very definite color preferences. You can plan a garden around your favorite color, repeat the colors you use inside your home, or find some other creative approach. Ideas are all around you.

You can seek inspiration from many non-garden sources. While living in Holland, I fell in love with the vivid door colors commonplace in parts of Europe. After I painted my front door cobalt blue in a fit of nostalgia for those days, planning an entrance flower garden to match seemed only natural. In this case, the door was the sole motivation for a blue, yellow, and white flower bed. In another example, I came across a wonderful photograph in a magazine. It showed a basket of red onions, eggplants, and purple corn, accented with purple herbs and magenta and blue flowers. I was so moved that I planned an entire border around these dusky, brooding tones.

You also need to decide whether to stick with a single color, to use two or three colors, or to go wild and embrace the whole spectrum of the rainbow. Coordinating flower colors is much like putting together an outfit. You start by choosing one color and then go from there. Wearing all one color is perfectly acceptable; for example, a blue sweater with blue slacks and blue socks. You can do exactly the same thing in the garden. But to keep monotony at bay, you may decide to vary the tones of blue. Of course, you can't really have a completely monochromatic color scheme in the garden, because the foliage color always contrasts with the flowers.

Try various color combinations by cutting out pictures from garden catalogs and putting them together until the arrangement pleases you. Or go to a nursery, pick up your favorite perennial in bloom, and carry it around, placing it next to other flowers until you discover attractive associations (matching the water, sunlight, and soil needs of the plants to each other and to your garden site is equally important). In fact, an easy way to choose perennials for your garden is to buy one-third of the flowers that you need to fill your garden while they're in bloom in the spring, buy another one-third in bloom in the summer, and one-third while in bloom in the fall. This way, you can be absolutely certain that they go together.

Look closely at a variety of flowers, and you notice that very few of them are solid colors. Most have shadings, and nearly all have contrasting centers. An effective design trick is to pick up these shades or center colors in neighboring flowers. For example, placing a white daisy with a yellow center next to a yellow lily visually ties the two together. You can also use intermediate colors to soften hard companions. If you have crayon reds and yellows fighting for your attention, adding either orange or pale yellow calms both of them down.

Texture

Texture in the garden may be actual or perceived. You can touch the soft fuzz of lamb's ear or the waxy smoothness of 'Autumn Joy' sedum. Perceived texture is created by the varying shapes and sizes of flowers and foliage, the interplay of light and shadow, and background materials, whether hard surfaces or mulch. A brick wall has an entirely different tactile quality than a wooden fence. A smooth, painted fence has a different nature than one constructed of rough, unpainted cedar.

Looking beyond the blooms

When selecting flower colors, give some thought to the background. White flowers against a white wall don't make much of a statement and may even blend in so well that they become invisible at 20 paces. Light colors stand out better against dark surfaces, and the reverse is also true. Pale pastel colors such as pink, lavender, and soft yellow look best in soft light — either early or late in the day, in shade, or in overcast climates. Strong reds, purples, oranges, and yellows are more dynamic and stand up better to intense sunlight. White becomes luminescent at dusk or by moonlight.

In addition to background, don't overlook foliage when considering flower color. Leaves of silver, gray, blue, purple, or red, as well countless shades of green, add another dimension to the flower bed. For more on colored foliage, see Chapter 9. For additional information on using flower color and for three garden plans based on a pastel, a hot-color, and a jewel-toned scheme, see Chapter 5.

Fine texture generally feels more elegant and formal; coarse is more casual or rustic. Complete uniformity of either texture is almost always too dull. Generally, you want to aim for some contrast — varying the proportion of coarse to fine to suit your taste. Using one-third large foliage and flowers, one-third medium-sized, and one-third small is always safe.

Traditional hedge plants have fine foliage; they don't call attention to themselves, so they form a somewhat neutral backdrop. Bold, large-leafed perennials have the opposite effect. They are attention-grabbing and bring drama and excitement to the mix.

Shape, size, and form

Other variables that merit your attention are size, shape, and form. Stimulating and intriguing gardens always depend on some diversity among all three of these elements, as shown in Figure 2-3. Perennials occur in countless different forms. They may be rounded, either loosely or in tight domes. They may be upright or prostrate and spreading. Interesting arrangements play these characteristics against one another. For example, place low 'Wargrave Pink' geranium in front of tall bearded iris. The contrast and tension between the two forms highlights each one against the other.

Figure 2-3:
Add dimension to your flower beds by choosing flowers with varying heights.

As important as contrasting form is varying flower and foliage size and shape. Flowers can be borne singly or in multiples. They can be spikes or spires, flattened or rounded, clusters, balls, daisies, stars, bell-, cup-, or saucer-shaped, clouds of tiny blossoms, or asymmetrical. Size varies just as widely — from $^1/_4$ inch (0.5 cm) to dinner plate proportions. Foliage is equally diverse in size, shape, and arrangement, as you can see in Figure 2-4.

Repeating size, shape, and form has a calming effect. Using a variety livens things up. In cooking, you adjust the various seasonings and flavors until their blend suits you, and you do the same with flower-garden design. You try out many combinations until you discover the ones that you like. As with color experiments, the simplest way to try out combinations is with photos cut out of garden catalogs or by going to a nursery and actually placing pots of perennials next to one another until you get the right mix for your taste.

Accent

To further spice things up, consider using an accent or two in the flower bed. An accent can be anything that stands out or calls attention to itself — such as a strategically placed piece of sculpture; a bird bath; a large, bold plant; or a bright spot of contrasting color. For accents to be effective, they must be used sparingly. A single specimen of blue oat grass is conspicuous, but a grouping of the same grass blends together and doesn't have the same emphasis.

Figure 2-4:
Think about the form of flowers and foliage as well as their colors. To create a pleasing blend, use an assortment of different sizes and shapes.

Succession of bloom

During the Victorian era, the goal of a garden was to have the whole border burst into a blaze of color at once. When money (and space) was no object, a large estate may have maintained three separate perennial borders — each planned to peak at a different season. Today, most of us find this style a bit overwhelming. I recently saw a slide presentation of a restored design from this period and was reminded of a tourist returning from Hawaii, sporting flowers on every article of clothing. It was just too much.

A flower garden can be planned so that instead of one brief moment of splendor, its beauty can span the whole year, with something happening at every season. Or you can focus on whichever parts of the year you prefer. If you are away from home from the end of June until the middle of August every year, you may want to concentrate on having flowers in spring, fall, and winter. For a summer home, you may choose to plant only those flowers that bloom while you're there to enjoy them.

Planning for a succession of bloom gives you the opportunity to pack a great deal into a small space. Generally, the aim is to have a third of the garden in bloom in the spring, a third in the summer, and a third in the fall. You can accomplish this plan quite simply by figuring out approximately how many plants fit into your allotted space, divide this number by three, and then purchase that number of flowers for each season. You can extend the color by choosing a few long-blooming flowers or flowers that have attractive seedheads. To further maximize your space, plant scads of bulbs. You can mix them right into the root zones of the other perennials without causing competition problems for either. (See Chapter 10 for more information on using bulbs in your perennial garden.)

You can also choose to completely switch your color scheme from one season to the next. You may have pastels for spring, passionate jewel tones for summer, and hot colors to complement the pumpkins in autumn. Because most perennials only bloom for a few weeks at a time, making such changes within the flower bed isn't difficult. If any flower blooms at the wrong season and causes a color catastrophe with its unintended neighbors, simply cut the offending blossoms and enjoy them in a vase inside the house.

Winter interest

For gardeners who live in cold climates, winter brings a well-needed respite from gardening. But that doesn't mean that the garden must be absolutely bare during this quiet season. Seedheads and the stark silhouettes of grasses stand in dramatic contrast to a blanket of snow. Many perennials are at least partly evergreen. Winter may never have the same exuberance as the rest of the year, but the trade-off is the possibility of a peaceful stroll that is uninterrupted by the nagging of myriad unfinished garden tasks. Time moves more slowly in winter — which can be a good thing.

Planning a garden in cyberspace

From magazines in a waiting room to your neighbor's backyard, many sources of inspiration are available to you during the planning phase of perennial gardening. A recent addition to the slew of garden-planning resources is the World Wide Web.

For example, the University of South Carolina runs a really cool site at `http://www.usc.edu/dept/garden/`. Here, you visit the USC Telegarden: a patch of virtual land entirely managed by members via the Internet. As a guest, you can move a mechanical arm around the garden to look at its various parts; as a member, you can plant seeds and tend to the garden! Telegardening is a fascinating way to experiment with different gardening designs and plans — and without pulling a single muscle!

You can also go online to visit the National Wildflower Research Center in Austin, Texas.

This organization grows a variety of interesting display gardens — formal gardens, theme gardens, and even sensory gardens for people with visual impairments. Viewing these display gardens can give you ideas for your own patch of dirt. To look at some of National Wildflower Research Center gardens via their Web site, visit `http://www.wildflower.org/` (the site also provides directions for visiting these gardens in person).

If you really want to get serious about landscaping, The Australian Correspondence Schools offer a course in Landscaping Home Gardens. They also offer a variety of other courses for home gardeners: propagation, cottage garden design, organic gardening, herbs, and many more. Check out their Web site at `http://www.qldnet.com.au/acs/home.htm`.

Chapter 3

Planning Your Attack

. . . .

In This Chapter

▶ Diagramming your property

▶ Choosing the best site for your garden

▶ Understanding microclimates

▶ Mapping the flower bed

▶ Keeping records of it all

. . . .

*T*his chapter discusses two of the most important tools a gardener can have — a pencil and paper. Although your first impulse may be to just get out there and dig, the effort you put into planning and sketching your perennial flower bed will pay off in spades . . . literally!

Yards rarely have one perfect site for a flower bed. Instead, you must weigh the pros and cons of each potential site in order to make your decision. Next, you determine the dimensions of the bed and work out how many perennials you need to plant to fill up the site. Drawing your plan on graph paper makes this process easier and gives you the chance to try out various schemes. Remember, corrections on paper are quick erasures — corrections in the garden require digging up and moving actual flowers.

Throughout the process of planning, planting, and tending your flower bed, you should keep some sort of record of your work — that is, unless your memory is much better than mine!

Figuring Out Where to Put the Flower Bed

The first step in deciding where to plant your flower bed is to do an overall inventory of your property. When you bought your house, you probably received a plat plan showing the boundaries of the lot and the position of the main structures on it. If you recall seeing such a document, dig through your paperwork to retrieve it. Make a copy of this plan so that you can doodle away on it without wrecking the original.

If you don't have a plat plan, you can draw up a basic diagram of your property showing the general outline of the boundaries (rectangle, square, wedge, and so on) and the approximate position of any structures. Don't bother to get out a measuring tape or hire a surveyor; pinpoint accuracy is not necessary.

Now walk around your property, noting every relevant detail on your diagram. If you're already certain that you want the flower bed at the front or the back of the house, inventory only the area that you're considering. Even if you don't want to go to the trouble of drawing or diagramming, at least write these features down or make a mental note of what is where:

- ✓ **The house and any other structures, such as a detached garage or shed:** Note the location of windows, doors, porch swings, overhangs, driveways, sidewalks, patios, terraces, decks, walks, fences, retaining walls, built-in barbecues, mailboxes, clotheslines, play equipment, drain spouts, sprinkler heads, and valve boxes.

- ✓ **Utilities:** Note the location of meters, boxes, underground lines, utility poles, fire hydrants, street lights and other exterior lighting, exterior electrical outlets, water faucets, and air conditioners.

Call your local utility company to locate power lines before you dig. Digging into underground electrical wires can be extremely dangerous, and you also need to watch out for cable lines, gas lines, water mains, and even sewer lines — how would you like to crack your shovel into one of those? Yuck!

- ✓ **Existing plants:** Note the position of shrubs, trees, and lawn. Also note any of your neighbor's hedges, trees, and shrubs that you can see or that shade your property.

- ✓ **Topographical details:** Indicate slopes, low places, ditches, ponds, and streams. Mark outcrops of rock or boulders. Note erosion or wet areas.

- ✓ **Environmental details:** Mark the location of sun and shade patterns (keeping in mind that these patterns change seasonally) and the direction of prevailing winds.

Exploiting microclimates

Generally, within the boundaries of any property are many smaller areas where conditions differ — sometimes quite radically — from the prevailing environment. These mini-climates (called *microclimates*) can be colder, warmer, drier, wetter, sunnier, or shadier than the areas surrounding them.

Microclimates are sometimes formed by geographic features, such as low-lying depressions where water or frost collects. Very often, however, microclimates are the result of buildings or fences deflecting wind and retaining warmth. A courtyard, for example, is the ultimate microclimate, protected from the elements on all sides. But even small structural variations can have a big impact. The overhanging eaves in Figure 3-1, for example, completely block rainfall to the soil underneath, forming a radically different microclimate. The soil shaded by the eaves is much drier than the soil only inches away, out from under the eaves.

Figure 3-1:
For a garden under the eaves, choose flowers that can tolerate dry conditions or be prepared to supply the garden with extra water.

You can take advantage of microclimates to grow a broader selection of plants than your overall climate conditions normally support. And you aren't limited to choosing perennials compatible to the various microclimates on your property — you can also *create new microclimates* to suit the plants you want to grow. Fences and walls, shelter belts of trees and shrubs, or trellising can block drying winds or provide shade. If necessary, you can remove trees to let in more light. If you want to have a shade garden on a sunny property, construct a wall or a trellis-covered structure to make a shady microclimate.

Remember, too, that conditions in your garden are constantly changing as your landscape evolves and matures. Trees have the biggest effect. Most developments start out bare and sunny, but they gradually evolve into woodlands. Then a single storm or disease may suddenly fell a large percentage of the trees, altering the local environment quite drastically again.

Making the ground-breaking decision

After you develop an intimate sense of your property, sit down with your diagram and draw an oval on every spot where you think that you have room for a flower bed. Pick one of these spots to be your first project.

Allowing your enthusiasm to race ahead of your common sense is all too easy. Start small — even if you plan to convert an entire five acres to flower beds, eventually. You can plan and plant the other sites on your property in future years. Put in one bed at a time so that you can easily stop whenever you reach the limit of your time and endurance.

Studying your finished map gives you a fair idea of where flower gardens can fit into your landscape. Here are some tips to keep in mind when making your choice:

- ✔ Give priority to any site with at least five to six hours of direct sunlight a day, if you have such a site. A sunny location, rather than a shady one, offers the most flexibility and many more varieties of flowers to choose from.

- ✔ Consider your climate. In very hot regions, the best orientation for flowers is usually where they catch morning sun and afternoon shade.

- ✔ Choose an area roomy enough for a 100- to 200-square-foot (9- to 19-square meter) flower bed with space left over to stroll or sit and enjoy the view. Very small or narrow sites are the most difficult to work with because they're too cramped for many combinations or seasonal variety.

- ✔ Flower beds by entrances always create a warm welcome. (See Chapter 6 for an entrance garden plan.)

- ✔ Consider a location where you spend a great deal of time or where you like to entertain, such as next to a deck or patio.

- ✔ Place a flower garden where you can view it from a window inside the house. Looking at flowers makes doing dishes feel less like a chore.

- ✔ Flower gardens are often the best solution for any place too wet, dry, or shady for lawn to grow. Although the selection of flowers that can grow in these sites is limited, you still have dozens to choose from. By choosing shade-adapted perennials, you can replace these bare spots with color and texture (see Figure 3-2).

Figure 3-2:
If you have a spot that's too shady for grass to grow, plant a flower bed of shade-tolerant perennials.

Sketching Out Size and Shape

After you decide where to put your first flower bed, you're ready to experiment with many possible shapes and sizes, both at the site and on paper. Although planning ahead is important, do try to use some restraint. If you're too picky, the planning stage can go on indefinitely. At some point, you must get on with digging!

Use a garden hose to outline curved shapes on the ground. Stretch a string between stakes to make straight lines and sharp angles. Combine the two methods to try out both straight edges and curves. After you come up with a pleasing shape, go inside the house and view your artwork from windows overlooking the area. Check out your design from as many perspectives as possible to make sure that it looks good from all angles. When I'm satisfied with a shape, I like to leave it overnight to see how it looks to me the next day.

Measure your flower bed and transfer the dimensions to your paper (see Figure 3-3). One inch on ¹/₄-inch graph paper translates to 4 feet on the tape measure (1 cm translates to just under 0.5 m). Measure the widest points and guess a bit at the curves. Approximate measures are close enough.

I use graph paper divided into ¹/₄-inch squares, because it's readily available and the only tools you need to work with are a ruler and a pencil. These graphs are also large enough scale to represent each perennial with a decent-sized circle. (No flower needs a smaller space than one square.) If your flower bed can't fit on one sheet of standard notebook paper, it's too large. Divide the bed in halves or thirds and plan to build it in stages.

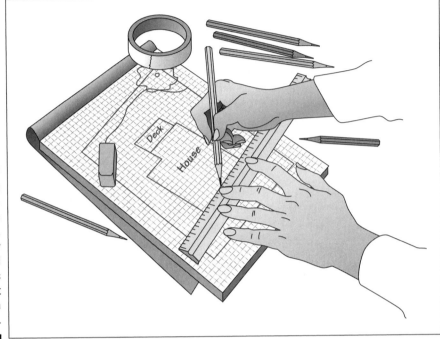

Figure 3-3:
By drawing
sample
plans first,
you can try
several
options
without
breaking a
sweat.

Filling Your Plan with Actual Perennials (Wow!)

After you have your outline down on paper, you can play around with the placement of the flowers within the bed. (You may want to make several copies of your plan before starting so that you can try several combinations.) In general, you can choose from two main styles for arranging flowers:

- ✔ **Group them together in sloppy-shaped ovals.** Perennials are tradition-ally clustered in odd-numbered groups of three, five, or seven. Massing each type of flower within the border creates blocks of conspicuous color.

- ✔ **Mix them all up, more or less randomly or in geometric patterns.** The random method scatters flowers throughout the space, giving you an informal look, sort of like a field of wildflowers or a meadow.

If you opt for the random look, don't try to map out the position of every individual plant on graph paper. Just buy the plants you want and arrange them on the ground in their containers. Keep moving them around until you find an composition you like.

No matter what style of flower bed you're creating, pick out about a dozen different types of perennials. The next step is estimating how many of each perennial to buy to fill up your flower bed. Spacing is arbitrary, depending on whether you like the subway-at-rush-hour look or prefer room for your flowers to spread out.

The easiest way to determine the number of flowers you need is to look up the mature size of each perennial and count how many you can realistically smash into the space allotted in your plan. I try to allow one foot (30 cm) for each small perennial, two feet (60 cm) for medium, and three feet (90 cm) for large.

Guess low. During the construction phase, you always end up making several trips to the nursery, anyway. You can pick up more plants if you need them, but most nurseries don't take plants back when you've bought too many.

Keeping Records As You Go

One of the best gardening tips I can give you is to create some sort of system to keep track of what you're doing in your garden. Labels inevitably get lost or misplaced. Plants die, and you can't remember just what that brown mass of leaves once was. Many times, nurseries guarantee plants to live for a certain length of time, so you need to keep a record of these plants and a file of the receipts for them.

I use a four-tiered approach. You can use any or all of these ideas, or come up with your own system:

- Use a manila folder to hold receipts and miscellaneous stuff (such as "how to plant" brochures) that often arrives with catalog orders.

- Fill a recipe file box with index cards. Whenever you buy a new plant, create a card with the plant's name in one corner and the date and place of purchase in the other. You can add any other information, such as description and care requirements, in the space below. If you can find a catalog photo of the plant, cut it out and paste it onto the back of the card (if the plant dies, at least you'll have something to remember it by).

  Alphabetize your cards and keep a collection of your failures at the back of the file — I'm not going to tell you how many of my plants have ended up in the "dead file" section! If you're really organized, you can keep the plants in separate files alphabetically by flower bed or location. Some people even name their flower beds after something, such as constellations or family members.

✔ Stick a label into the ground next to each plant, as shown in Figure 3-4. If the plant comes with a nursery label, use that. Otherwise, write the name on the back of an extra plastic label in pencil (ink wears off). You can also buy more attractive and permanent plant labels at your garden center.

✔ Keep a journal. You can find beautiful gardening diaries, but I simply buy a datebook in January, when they're on sale, and use that. My plan is to jot down every detail of my gardening year — such as the weather, bug plagues, when I put the plants in the ground, disasters, and successes.

My heart is in the right place, but my garden journals always seem to suffer the same fate as my kids' baby books. I make oodles of entries in late winter and early spring, when I'm enthusiastic but not so busy. But every year, around April, the entries stop. Having a record of when the first and last frosts occurred and when the flea beetles made their annual assault would be so helpful — if only I'd stick with it! If you're more disciplined than I am, your journal will reward you with detailed information that you can use in later years. To put it in gardening terms, you reap what you sow.

Figure 3-4:
Labels are the gardener's cheat sheet.

Part II
The Part of Plans

In this part . . .

When you're faced with a seemingly endless expanse of bare dirt and no immediate inspiration, knowing where to start can be difficult. If you find yourself stumped, Part II offers 12 garden plans to get you going. These plans suit a variety of locations, circumstances, and climates — and all are just as appropriate for the small yard as for the large one.

I've drawn the plans in this part to $\frac{1}{4}$-inch scale, so you can use an ordinary ruler and carpenter's tape to translate the measurements to the actual flower bed. One inch on the plan equals four feet on the ground; 2.5 centimeters equal 1.2 meters. Don't spend too much time trying to re-create a perfect rendering of the design on your site; distances can be approximate. Mark the outside dimensions of the bed and prepare the soil according to the instructions in Chapter 16.

Chapter 4

Gardening by Climate

. . . .

In This Chapter

▶ Making peace with your climate

▶ Planning a cold-hardy garden

▶ Gardening in a subtropical and coastal climate

▶ Coping with water shortages, salty gales, and drying winds

▶ Dealing with extreme heat and humidity in the land of exotic
bulbs and flowering shrubs

▶ Creating a colorful raised bed with bullet-proof flowers

. . . .

*E*very gardener sincerely believes that his or her own climate is the
worst on the face of the planet. Although some people offer up southwestern England and Portland, Oregon, as examples of the perfect gardening
climate, I strongly suspect that gardeners in these halcyon regions have
their own, equally valid complaints.

The cold-climate gardener who has to shovel snow from early fall until late
spring isn't likely to feel compassion for the tropical gardener who experiences a few flakes once in five years. Yet that rare snowfall is just the type of
record-breaking event that causes the worst damage to gardens.

Find the climate in this chapter that most closely approximates your own
and take a look at the sample garden plan I suggest for that climate. All six of
the plans in this chapter are drawn to $^1/_4$-inch scale so that you can use an
ordinary ruler and carpenter's tape to translate the measurements to the
actual flower bed. One inch (2.5 cm) on the plan equals 4 feet (1.2 m) on the
ground. Don't spend a great deal of time trying to draw an exact replica of
the design; distances can be approximate.

Follow these basic steps to construct your garden:

1. **Mark the outlines of the flower bed, according to the instructions in Chapter 3.**

2. **Prepare the soil, using the directions in Chapter 11.**

3. **Buy your perennials.**

   The tables that accompany each garden plan tell you how many of each perennial you need.

Substitutions and modifications are easy. If you can't find a certain plant, or if the perennial in the plan is not appropriate to your climate, simply switch to a different perennial. Choose a plant that's the same height and color as the original suggestion to preserve the character of the design, or break out and pick something entirely different. But make sure that the substitutions you make share the same light, water, and soil requirements as the rest of the flower bed.

4. **Plant your garden.**

   Chapter 14 explains how to plant your garden. Part V tells you how to care for your garden after it's in the ground.

Choosing What to Grow Based on Where You Live

From time to time, gardeners in every region have to contend with challenges caused by various natural disasters — floods, hurricanes, tornadoes, hail, drought, brush fires, and plagues of locusts, to name a few. But you aren't likely to base your plant choices on these extreme incidents — unless, of course, hail or drought are normal annual occurrences in your region (in which case you'd better give serious thought to defensive gardening, covered in Chapter 17 — or, better yet, consider moving). Instead, gardeners base plant choices on *average* conditions.

Unfortunately, averages are almost always deceiving. After all, a plant whose roots are frozen solid and whose petals are on fire is, on average, experiencing mild temperatures. When trying to interpret weather data, you need to know whether a local average temperature of 70° F (21° C) is the result of a never-ending chain of balmy 70° F days or a series of alternating 100° F (38° C) highs and 40° F (4.5° C) lows. Where I live, sorry to say, the latter condition is definitely the case.

GARDEN JARGON

Zoning out

In an attempt to make some sense of the climate chaos, and to help you predict which plants are likely to do well in your region, gardening gurus have created standardized charts, called *zone maps,* mostly based on low temperature averages.

When you pick up a perennial at your local nursery, you're likely to see a zone rating on the label — for example, "Hardy to Zone 5." This zone rating corresponds to an average wintertime low temperature on a particular zone map. For example, according to the

United States Department of Agriculture (USDA) Zone Map, a zone 5 perennial can, in general, withstand low temperatures to –20° F. But according to the Western European Plant Hardiness Zone Map, a zone 5 perennial can generally withstand an average winter low of –23° C (which is –10° F!).

Because zone maps vary from place to place, I use average low temperatures (in Celsius and Fahrenheit) throughout this book instead of zone ratings.

Wintertime: looking beyond the lows

Average low temperatures create a useful guideline, but many factors other than a plant's tolerance to cold determine hardiness. Whether a particular freeze actually damages a plant depends on several factors:

- ✔ **What stage of growth the plant is in when the freeze occurs:** Is the plant big enough to take a few hits, or is it still a helpless baby?

- ✔ **The length of the cold spell:** They all seem endless, but some cold spells really are longer than others.

- ✔ **The windchill factor:** What's the perceived temperature, taking into account the bluster effect?

- ✔ **What the weather was like before and after the freeze:** Are you going from hot to cold or from cold to colder?

- ✔ **The presence or absence of snow cover:** Believe it or not, plants actually *prefer* a blanket of snow in winter.

Even a hint of frost may be fatal to a tropical or subtropical perennial. Most plants from temperate regions avoid winter by going into a dormant state and indulging in a version of horticultural hibernation, but early and late freezes can catch plants off-guard and kill an otherwise hardy and healthy plant. Winter wetness can also be fatal to plants that demand well-drained soil, which explains why lavender is completely hardy in my garden in relatively dry Denver, Colorado, but not in wetter regions where the temperature doesn't drop as low.

Although most perennials disdain frost, some actually insist on a period of chilling in order to rest and recuperate, regardless of the weather. If deprived of winter cold, such perennials sulk, becoming short-lived or refusing to bloom. For this reason, if you live in a warm-winter climate, you must refrigerate tulips and daffodils for a few weeks before planting them outside.

The many factors that make up your climate

Winter is only one of many elements of climate that affect a plant's success or failure. When a plant is labeled hardy to 30°, for example, you need to know *which* 30°. Consider the vast differences between San Diego, California, and Miami, Florida — both of which have average winter lows around 30° to 35° F (–1° to –2° C).

- ✔ San Diego nearly qualifies as a desert, with only 9 inches (23 cm) of rainfall annually, whereas Miami receives a soggy 57 inches (1.45 m) of rain per year.

- ✔ San Diego is a considerably cooler climate, experiencing only a few days each year when the temperature rises over 90° F (32° C). Miami averages 55 days per year with temperatures over 90° F.

- ✔ Night temperatures in San Diego and Miami are also quite dissimilar. The record overnight low for Miami in the summer is a warm 70° F (21° C), but you won't catch residents of San Diego out after dark without a sweater.

Extreme gardening

Some people go to real extremes to grow their favorite flower outside of its natural environment. Reports of desperate Gulf Coast gardeners dumping buckets of ice on peonies throughout the winter or of gardeners in cold climates tenting their gardens in burlap illustrate just how far some people are willing to go to thwart nature.

A gardener in frigid Colorado is even rumored to have wrapped an Australian tree fern with an electric heating cable to fend off the arctic cold. The gardener awoke one night to a flaming fern after the cable shorted out and set fire to his prized specimen.

You make less work for yourself — and for your local fire department — if you stick to perennials that are adapted to your own particular region.

All the preceding factors profoundly affect the best plant choices for these localities, even though they share the same average low wintertime temperature.

To plan for a garden in your region — a garden that will actually grow, that is — you have to take into account many more factors than low-temperature averages and the length and severity of winters. In addition, consider all the following factors as you plan your perennial garden:

- **Different soil types:** Differing soil types influence which perennials are likely to succeed in your garden. Most perennials are surprisingly flexible and adapt contentedly to whatever soil you plant them in, as long as you meet their basic requirements for fertility, water, and drainage. Others are finicky about soil acidity or alkalinity. The more extreme your soil, the more restricted your plant choices become.

  You can modify any soil to suit a wider range of flowers — but only within limitations. Changing a highly alkaline desert soil into an acid loam isn't impossible, but it *is* a pain in the azalea. And the solution is usually only temporary, anyway. For more details on soil types, check out Chapter 11.

- **Average rainfall and drainage:** Perennials vary greatly in their water requirements. Those originating in swamps, ponds, and wet meadows clearly enjoy wet feet (although many such perennials are surprisingly drought tolerant for short periods). However, not all water-lovers can grow in standing water. Many stream-bank natives, for example, need the abundant dissolved oxygen that running water carries. Dry-land perennials can rot from a single heavy rainfall if drainage is poor. To find out more about water requirements, turn to Chapter 15.

- **Average hours and intensity of sunlight:** A plant's sunlight prerequisites can change markedly from one climate to the next. How many hours of sunlight are sufficient depends on the quality and intensity of the light.

  You can get a fair idea of the sun's strength in your area by considering how long it takes to get a sunburn. In Denver, where 15 minutes of midday sun fries the average person to a crisp, even sun-worshipping plants are content with only a couple of hours of sunlight each day. Many perennials that need full sun exposure in cooler climates end up begging for protection from the afternoon sun in hot, sunny regions. The reverse is also true. Some shade-lovers can accept full sun when grown in cool, overcast climates, such as in Seattle or London.

- **Overnight temperatures:** The high overnight temperatures in some regions can affect the longevity of certain plants more than winter cold. Many traditional perennials don't get the rest they need when hot and humid days are followed by high nighttime temperatures. Some perennials can adapt to extreme summer heat and humidity if the winter is cold enough to stimulate a dormant rest period. However, a few perennials from cool climates can't tolerate heat with high humidity under any circumstance.

✔ **Relative humidity:** The average humidity in your region greatly influences your garden's water needs. Your perennials can dehydrate at astonishing speeds in arid climates but don't dry out so quickly in humid areas. On the other hand, moist air encourages fungal and bacterial diseases. You may not want to use perennials prone to these maladies if the relative humidity in your area routinely keeps pace with the air temperature.

✔ **Air and soil temperature:** Perennials dislike very high air and soil temperatures. They sulk and stop growing when things get toasty, and soil that's too hot is lethal to plant roots.

All the factors that make up your gardening climate are interrelated. For example, relative humidity, sun exposure, and air and soil temperature all help determine an individual plant's water requirements. A plant that never needs a single drop of irrigation in a cool and rainy climate may be perpetually thirsty in an arid region and may insist on supplemental water three times a week.

Keeping the faith

Don't be put off by all the variables that make up your climate. Every climate supports a vast number of plant choices, so you can find perennials to indulge even your most eclectic tastes, no matter where you live.

To get an idea of what flowers grow well near your home, visit public gardens. Also check out flower beds in parks, commercial developments, and street plantings. Use the average wintertime low temperature (or zone designations) that you find in plant catalogs as a guide when trying unfamiliar offerings. Many catalogs and books now include a range of hardiness ratings. The lower number indicates the plant's winter cold tolerance; the higher number shows how warm a summer the plant can tolerate.

Trying new plants is always a bit of a gamble, but one well worth the risk. Climate recommendations are always approximate, and they are constantly being updated as new information becomes available. Plant successes and failures often defy logic, anyway. My neighbor can't grow garden phlox, yet phlox do beautifully for me in what appear to be nearly identical conditions.

My policy is to give each new plant three chances to live. If the plant fails the first time, I try planting it again in a different location in the garden. If a plant strikes out three times, I abandon the feat as impossible — unless, of course, it's one of those plants that I really *must* have to make my life complete. In that case, I may grant a stay of execution. So far, I haven't resorted to ice baths, heating cables, or a retractable roof over the garden — but you never know.

Cultivating Cold-Climate Perennials

On some winter mornings, would you be less surprised to find polar bears romping through your garden than rabbits or squirrels? Is your garden more likely to sprout Popsicles than perennials?

Extreme cold is the greatest limitation for some gardeners. In regions where winter temperature minimums *average* between −30° to −40° F (−35° to −40° C) (and occasionally dip even lower than that), where the windchill adds to the arctic effect, and where erratic shifts in heat and cold can occur during any season, you need perennials with the constitution of a junkyard dog.

Only the strong survive

A record-breaking cold spell can damage even the hardiest plants — I've witnessed more than one especially severe winter badly burn or kill seemingly bullet-proof junipers. In addition, rainfall is often unpredictable in cold climates, and summers may be either prone to drought or wet and humid, depending on where you live. The frost-free growing season is often unreasonably short in these climates — lasting only three to four months. Some areas are lucky to get 60 consecutive days without frost.

Gardens in cold-winter climates tend to be *high summer* gardens. Because the gardening season is short, plants rush to bloom, with most peaking at about the same time. Instead of bemoaning the short season, plan a garden party for mid to late summer and amaze your friends from more temperate climes.

Winter hardiness depends on a number of elements beyond low temperatures. The perfect winter would gradually become colder as the days grew shorter in the fall, stay consistently cold throughout the winter months, and slowly warm up again the following spring. The reality falls far short of this ideal. Summer ends abruptly when a late summer blizzard assaults the garden and knocks down a few tree limbs and power lines. Temperatures jump all over the thermometer, and bitter cold alternates with a few balmy days.

Here are just a few of the ways in which winter's capriciousness can wreak havoc with your perennials:

- ✔ Early hard freezes, arriving in fall before your perennials have had time to adjust to cold weather, can cause winter injury.
- ✔ A late spring frost can sometimes damage even the most cautious plant.
- ✔ Snowstorms right smack in the middle of the growing season are most distressing. When such storms occur, many gardeners seriously contemplate a move to warmer climes. Fortunately, midsummer freezes are rare events.

Winter sun and thaw also pose a significant threat to plants. Many plants that don't survive winter die not because they got too cold, but because they warmed slightly on a sunny day and then were unable to readjust quickly enough when frigid temperatures returned. From a plant's point of view, once frozen, it's better to stay frozen.

Snow serves as the down comforter of mulches. A thick layer of snow keeps the ground solidly frozen and unaffected by constantly fluctuating air temperatures. Flowers tucked cozily under this insulating blanket aren't tempted to break dormancy prematurely — they much prefer to hit the snooze button a few times. If an unusually warm spell breaks the winter freeze, you may gratefully throw off your coat, hat, and mittens to revel in the temporary warmth. But the garden that indulges in the horticulture equivalent of throwing off winter garb can't bundle itself back up again when winter inevitably comes back in force.

If a winter warm spell lasts long enough to melt the snow cover, vulnerable new growth gets zapped by the next passing storm. In regions where snow cover is reliable and durable, such fluctuations of weather don't harm perennials as much.

Perennials that are only marginally hardy in your region may survive winter if you plant them on the north side of a building. In this normally shady location, plants are least likely to thaw on sunny winter days.

Planning a winter-proof flower bed

Imagine a flower bed made up of a group of perennials as tough and sturdy as any dandelion, but with some of the most beautiful and graceful blooms available. The garden in Figure 4-1 represents a good plan if your climate has very cold, snowy winters and humid summers, with an annual precipitation greater than 25 inches (63.5 cm). (These weather-proof bruisers are hardy to −40° F [−40° C], but they also do well in climates with warmer low-temperature averages.)

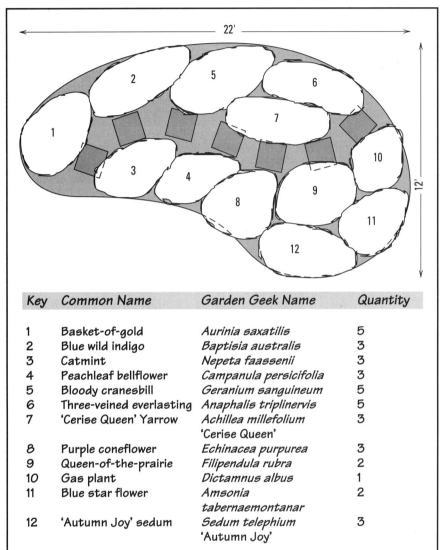

Key	Common Name	Garden Geek Name	Quantity
1	Basket-of-gold	*Aurinia saxatilis*	5
2	Blue wild indigo	*Baptisia australis*	3
3	Catmint	*Nepeta faassenii*	3
4	Peachleaf bellflower	*Campanula persicifolia*	3
5	Bloody cranesbill	*Geranium sanguineum*	5
6	Three-veined everlasting	*Anaphalis triplinervis*	5
7	'Cerise Queen' Yarrow	*Achillea millefolium 'Cerise Queen'*	3
8	Purple coneflower	*Echinacea purpurea*	3
9	Queen-of-the-prairie	*Filipendula rubra*	2
10	Gas plant	*Dictamnus albus*	1
11	Blue star flower	*Amsonia tabernaemontanar*	2
12	'Autumn Joy' sedum	*Sedum telephium 'Autumn Joy'*	3

Figure 4-1: This island bed of perennials thrives in a cold-region garden.

Plant this garden in full sun and give it a thorough soaking once a week during the growing season, if rainfall isn't sufficient. This garden rewards you year-round with the following procession of blooms (many of which appear in this book's color insert):

❀ This garden awakens in spring with bright yellow basket-of-gold, covered with masses of tiny flowers on spreading mounds of grayish foliage. Basket-of-gold blooms contentedly right through late spring snowfalls. Soft blue clouds of catmint soon follow the basket-of-gold. Tuck a few crocuses or small species tulips in and around both basket-of-gold and catmint for extra spring color.

❀ Spikes of deep blue wild indigo rise above bluish foliage. Following a month of bloom, dark, pea-like pods form at the ends of the stems — leave them on for winter drama or cut to add to dried flower bouquets.

❀ Bloody cranesbill is unabashedly magenta, with handsome foliage that does double duty by turning brilliant red in autumn. 'Cerise Queen' yarrow has finely cut leaves and large, flat-topped flower clusters on long stems — perfect for cutting. Both bloody cranesbill and yarrow are available in more subdued color forms, if you prefer a softer pink.

❀ Gas plant produces loose spikes of showy pink flowers over crisp, thick, green leaflets. White peachleaf bellflower features wide-open blossoms and tall, upright stalks. Long, arching stems of blue star appropriately carry constellations of smoky blue star-shaped flowers. In autumn, the foliage becomes a clear yellow, if an early freeze doesn't burn it.

❀ Summer brings sparkling purple coneflowers with bristly, bright orange centers and queen-of-the-prairie — a large, impressive plant with pink cotton-candy plumes towering above dramatic foliage.

❀ In midsummer, small white star flowers appear amid the linear, silver leaves of pearly everlasting. In late summer, the rounded flowerheads of 'Autumn Joy' sedum open pink and then age to a rust color over waxy, succulent leaves. If an early snow doesn't smash the seedheads, leave them uncut to grace the garden all winter long.

Dressing Up the Drylands

The cold-winter/dry-summer climate encompasses a large area of western North America, including the high plains of the United States and Canada. This climate also occurs in central Asia and parts of the former Soviet Union. Summers are devilishly hot, except at higher elevations. Low winter temperatures average –20° F (–29° C) and erratic temperature fluctuations can wreak havoc on the garden and affect plant hardiness.

Within these areas lie a few so-called *banana belts* where fruit orchards flourish. A commercial peach and cherry production near your home is an indication of relatively steady and even winter temperatures. In these locations, you can safely flaunt many hardiness recommendations and grow less hardy perennials than gardeners in other areas within your region can.

Some common challenges of this climate include the following:

✔ **Generally poor soils:** The dirt in this climate is usually stony, sandy, or highly alkaline clay. Humus content is very low. (See Chapter 11 for more information about soils.)

✔ **Notoriously low humidity:** The entire region is exceedingly dry. Locals tease that you don't even need a towel to dry off after you shower.

✔ **Unreliable snow cover:** Because of the low humidity, snow usually evaporates before it has a chance to soak in.

✔ **Not enough rain:** The average annual rainfall of 8 to 15 inches (20 to 38 cm) isn't adequate for traditional perennials without generous supplemental irrigation.

Conserving water with xeriscaping

Water is a scarce and precious resource in these arid regions. Coping with inevitable shortages has given rise to the *xeriscape movement* — combining good horticulture with water conservation to create flower gardens every bit as lush, full, and vibrant as those in more temperate climates.

Xeriscape may sound like one of those phony words that desperate Scrabble players make up in an attempt to bluff a high score. But the term actually combines *xeric* (a dry habitat or a plant from such a place) with *landscape* to create *xeriscape* — literally, a dry landscape. Unfortunately, xeriscape is easily mispronounced as "zero-scape," resulting in a complete misunderstanding. Many folks equate xeriscaping with covering the ground from house front to curb with rock and gravel — and they know they don't want that. These gravelscapes unquestionably save water, but xeriscaping advocates much more.

Xeriscape is a system, not a style. A xeriscape can be as formal as Versailles or as casual as a cottage garden. You can't drive up and down the street and pick out the xeriscapes; only the water bill tells the story. Xeriscaping relies on fixing poor soils, grouping together plants with similar needs, mulch, and efficient irrigation. But the most important factor is choosing perennials with low water needs. Many flowers that hail from regions of the world with similar climates do fine on naturally occurring precipitation. In fact, seasonal blazes of flowers are the distinguishing feature of semi-arid regions. Recreating this effect in your garden is only natural.

A few characteristics help you estimate a flower's water needs. Although not 100 percent accurate, these characteristics are good indicators. Most drought-tolerant plants employ one or more of the following adaptations:

✔ **Succulent leaves:** Fat, fleshy leaves and stems act as water storage tanks. You probably recognize cacti as an example, but 'Autumn Joy' sedum also exhibits this feature.

✔ **Large roots:** Roots are an underground water storage system. Many prairie and desert natives have massive roots — some reported to weigh as much as a grown man.

✔ **Silver or gray hairy leaves:** Light colored, fuzzy leaves reflect intense sunlight and shade the leaf surface.

✔ **Small leaves:** Cacti take this feature to the extreme. The smaller the leaf, the less surface area exposed to drying winds and sunlight.

Planting your own xeriscape

With an abundance of shimmering silvery foliage and lively crayon colors, the garden shown in Figure 4-2 stands up to the harshest summer sunlight and drought.

Put this garden where it will receive at least six hours of direct sunshine each day. The soil doesn't need to be particularly fertile, but it must be well drained. After planting, cover the exposed soil with several inches of mulch. Water deeply whenever the soil dries out until the plants are actively growing, and once or twice a month thereafter or as needed. Chapter 15 helps you determine how often to water your garden.

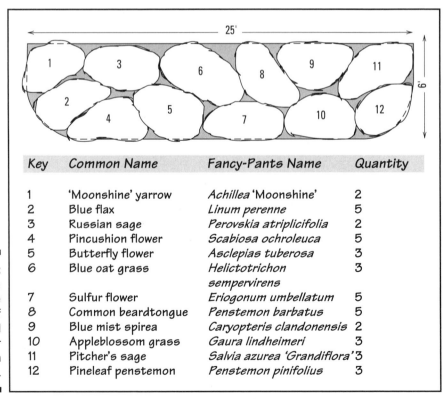

Key	Common Name	Fancy-Pants Name	Quantity
1	'Moonshine' yarrow	*Achillea* 'Moonshine'	2
2	Blue flax	*Linum perenne*	5
3	Russian sage	*Perovskia atriplicifolia*	2
4	Pincushion flower	*Scabiosa ochroleuca*	5
5	Butterfly flower	*Asclepias tuberosa*	3
6	Blue oat grass	*Helictotrichon sempervirens*	3
7	Sulfur flower	*Eriogonum umbellatum*	5
8	Common beardtongue	*Penstemon barbatus*	5
9	Blue mist spirea	*Caryopteris clandonensis*	2
10	Appleblossom grass	*Gaura lindheimeri*	3
11	Pitcher's sage	*Salvia azurea* 'Grandiflora'	3
12	Pineleaf penstemon	*Penstemon pinifolius*	3

Figure 4-2: Here is a sample border of perennial flowers for dry-region gardens.

These rugged plants bring attractive foliage and a long blooming season to the dry flower garden. Leave all the seedheads uncut until spring for a full year of texture and interest. With proper care, this garden rewards you with the following brilliant blooms (many of which are pictured in this book's color insert):

❀ Blue flax is a short-lived perennial that pops up in every nook and cranny to become a filler for the whole garden if you allow it to spread. The silver gray flowers of blue flax complement the lemon yellow tones of 'Moonshine' yarrow nearby.

❀ Acid yellow sulfur flowers age to rust red. Creamy pincushion flowers provide a soft bridge next to intense orange butterfly flower. Silvery blue oat grass catches every passing breeze. Russian sage stands at the rear of the bed and sends up steel blue spikes in late summer.

❀ Scarlet common beardtongue and soft orange pineleaf penstemon attract hummingbirds into areas that they don't usually frequent. Appleblossom grass's delicate white blossoms resemble butterflies on slender, arching stems.

❀ Brilliant blue pitcher's sage (also called azure sage), one of the latest flowers to bloom in fall, joins blue mist spirea, a small shrub featuring sky blue whorls that dry to the color of straw. Blue mist spirea's dried flowerheads poke up through winter snows to grace the off-season garden.

Gardening Where It's Mild and Moist All Year Long

Newcomers to Seattle, Washington, are warned against standing too long in one place lest they start to collect moss on their north side. The same can be said of most of the northwest U.S., British Columbia, and Great Britain. All share a gentle climate where the weather is mild year-round, even though the changing seasons are also clearly defined.

Some characteristics of this type of climate include the following:

✔ **Cool summers:** Summers are cool and overcast, punctuated by an occasional spell of bright, sunlit days. When I lived in England, I heard folks comment that there were two days of summer, but those two days were not necessarily in a row.

✔ **Mild winters:** Snow falls most winters, but not often enough to make a nuisance of itself. Killing frosts can (and do) sneak down from the arctic, but not with any great regularity. And even then, the temperatures rarely plummet below 0° F (–18° C).

> ✔ **Moderate, steady rainfall:** Rainfall is moderate and conveniently spaced throughout the seasons. Even so, periods of extended drought are not at all uncommon. Resulting water shortages seem like irony in a region with a reputation for being constantly damp and rainy.

Perennial paradise

This moderate, marine climate is a genuine Shangri-La for perennial gardening. Winters are sufficiently cold to satisfy bulbs and other flowers that require a period of chilling. But winters aren't frigid enough to exclude tender choices that can't tolerate an annual arctic freeze. (See Chapter 10 for more information on bulbs.)

Mild summers spare flowers the "crispy midsummer stage" that gardens in hot summer regions have to endure. A few flowers don't get adequate sunlight to bloom in these moderate regions, however. Others refuse to open except on sunny days. You may as well leave these sun worshippers to more appropriate climates. For consolation, remind yourself of all the woodland wildflowers, ferns, roses, and rhododendrons that you can grow to perfection.

Pastels for a sparkling island bed

One advantage of living in an overcast climate is that you can safely use even the quietest pastel tones without fearing that the harsh sunlight will wash out the colors. The garden in Figure 4-3 is composed of muted pinks, buttery yellows, lavender, and blue. All these colors glow softly in overcast light.

Locate this island bed in the sunniest section of your property, where it gets at least six hours of unobstructed sunlight each day. Don't fret if clouds get in the way — filtered sunlight is sufficient. Choose a site relatively free of tree roots for ease of preparation and to limit competition between the trees and flowers for water and nutrients. You can place this garden off to one side in an expanse of lawn or surround it on all sides with a mulched path. Build the path wide, so that you can walk freely around the bed to admire the following flowers from every angle.

 ❀ Delphiniums are the signature flower of the cool-summer perennial garden. They tower to impressive heights — each stately spike crowded with flat, open-faced blossoms. You may want to stake these plants so they don't fall face down in the mud (a much less elegant repose). Bold but elegant 'Casablanca' lilies stand up to the imposing delphinium with large, gleaming white flowers that send their spicy fragrance throughout the garden.

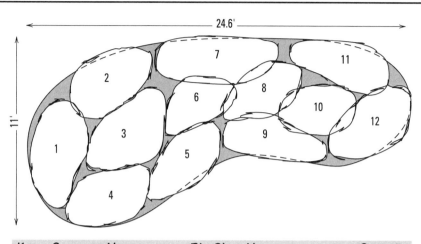

Key	Common Name	Big Shot Name	Quantity
1	Strawberry cinquefoil	*Potentilla nepalensis* 'Miss Willmott'	3
2	Frikart's aster	*Aster frikartii*	3
3	Maiden grass	*Miscanthus sinensis* 'Morning Light'	3
4	Lupine	*Lupinus* 'Gallery Yellow'	3
5	Geranium	*Geranium oxonianum* 'Claridge Druce'	2
6	Pincushion flower	*Scabiosa columbaria* 'Pink Mist'	3
7	Lady's mantle	*Alchemilla mollis*	3
8	Delphinium	*Delphinium* Pacific Giant Strain	5
9	Calamint	*Calamintha grandiflora*	5
10	Lily	*Lilium* 'Casa Blanca'	5
11	Great masterwort	*Astrantia major*	3
12	'Purple Rain' sage	*Salvia verticillata* 'Purple Rain'	3

Figure 4-3:
This island bed features perennials that thrive in places like Seattle, Washington, and London, England.

❀ Another star performer in the cool-summer climate is the graceful lupine. The individual flowers are quite distinctive, looking like little Dutch wooden shoes attached by their heels to each flower spike.

❀ Whorls of tiny lavender blossoms grace candelabra-like stems of 'Purple Rain' sage, contrasting sweetly with neighboring masterwort's delicate pink blossoms. (Look for a photo of *Salvia verticillata* 'Purple Rain' in this book's color insert.)

❀ The white and green variegated foliage of calamint has a strong, minty aroma and small, bright pink, tubular flowers that play off 'Claridge Druce' geranium, with its grayish green foliage and lilac pink blossoms.

❀ Pincushion flower is aptly named, as each individual flower looks like a pincushion sitting on a lacy doily. Nearby lady's mantle, often grown solely for its heavily folded foliage, has an equally attractive froth of chartreuse flowers (look under *Alchemilla mollis* in the color photo section of this book).

❀ 'Miss Willmott' cinquefoil has strawberry-like leaves and cherry pink flowers. The subtle variegation of 'Morning Light' maiden grass adds a touch of grace and can provide an accent to the winter landscape if left in the garden.

Growing Perennials in Warm, Dry Maritime Climates

If a flower-gardening paradise exists, the mild maritime climates of parts of California, Australia, New Zealand, South America, and South Africa and Mediterranean Greece, Turkey, and Italy approach it. Moderated by the ocean's influence, these regions suffer no extremes of heat or cold to test a plant's endurance. Much as in a greenhouse environment, cool and misty conditions prevail at all seasons. All these maritime regions have their own diverse and rich native floral palette, which gardeners have eagerly exchanged over the years. New Zealand flax is probably more common in California now than in its native home.

Frosts are infrequent in most maritime regions and almost unheard of in some (such as the southern parts of the California coast). The farther you travel inland from the sea or toward the Poles, or the higher you climb in elevation, the more likely you are to experience regular winter frosts. But even these frosts aren't of the killer arctic nature. The temperature rarely dips much below 30° F (–1° C). Summers are equally mild, dominated by foggy mornings and humid sea breezes. A few heat lovers don't get adequate sunshine, but most perennials thrive in this benevolent climate — as long as they get enough water.

Water, water everywhere, but . . .

Ah, water — the one shortcoming in regions that would otherwise approach true gardener's paradise. Scarce rainfall is a reality for many coastline communities. Their green lushness is an illusion created by liberal irrigation with imported water. Today, this scarce resource is running out. Water shortages and periodic rationing are increasingly common in all arid and semi-arid regions around the world.

The wise maritime gardener plans for water shortages by choosing from the large number of perennials that need little or no irrigation to prosper.

Planning for mild but thirsty climates

Figure 4-4 shows a garden plan for a climate that's mild year-round, with an annual rainfall below 25 inches (64 cm). Consider a garden like this one if you live in a region that's similar to Santa Barbara, California; Johannesburg, South Africa; or Sydney, Australia.

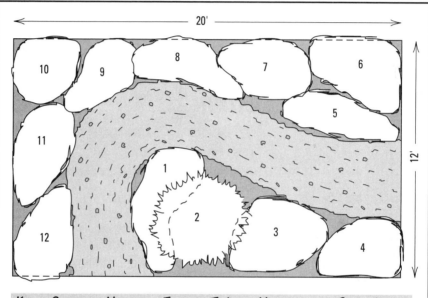

Key	Common Name	Tongue-Twister Name	Quantity
1	African daisy	*Osteospermum barberae*	5
2	New Zealand flax	*Phormium tenax*	1
3	Sea lavender	*Limonium perezii*	3
4	Fortnight lily	*Dietes vegeta*	5
5	African lily	*Agapanthus 'Peter Pan'*	3
6	Matilija poppy	*Romneya coulteri*	1
7	Crocosmia	*Crocosmia 'Lucifer'*	5
8	Lavender cotton	*Santolina chamaecyparissus*	3
9	Gazania	*Gazania hybrids*	7
10	Orchid rockrose	*Cistus purpureus*	1
11	French lavender	*Lavandula dentata*	3
12	Common thrift	*Armeria maritima*	5

Figure 4-4: This bed of perennials is perfect for gardeners who live in coastal or inland-coastal regions of the world.

The walk in Figure 4-4 permits ever-changing perspectives and views as it meanders through the flower bed. Use brick or stone for permanence, or choose gravel (with its satisfying crunch underfoot) for a more casual setting. For more about garden walks, see Chapter 12.

The plan in Figure 4-4 comprises *drought tolerant* perennials that can survive with only occasional supplemental water. For this garden, I chose a tough group of plants that can withstand salt-laden gales as well as seasonal, drying desert winds. All these flowers bloom for a long season, and most have evergreen foliage.

Photographs of most of the following flowers appear in this book's color insert — look for them alphabetically according to their botanical names.

❀ Not for the timid, New Zealand flax dominates the garden with red, sword-shaped leaves that can reach 9 feet (nearly 3 meters). Substitute *Phormium tenax* 'Bronze Baby', 'Dark Delight', or another dwarf hybrid where a shorter form seems more appropriate. Smoky lavender African daisies take on a sultry air when planted next to the purplish red fans of the flax.

❀ Sea lavender features large, loose clusters of purple flowers standing high above shiny green foliage. White iris-like blossoms of fortnight lily echo the color of sea lavender, with purple spots on their upper petals and yellow spots on the lower.

❀ Stately Matilija poppy matches the scale of the flax at 8 feet (2.4 m) tall, with salad-plate-sized white crimped poppies with golden centers rising above deeply cut sage green leaves.

❀ 'Peter Pan' is a dwarf African lily only 18 inches (45 cm) tall and long blooming, with dark blue flower clusters and evergreen straplike foliage. You don't have to clap your hands to bring this fairy-tale perennial to life!

❀ Fiery 'Lucifer' really sparks things up with bolts of bright scarlet, tubular flowers dancing like flames among stiffly upright, narrow leaves. Silvery and aromatic lavender cotton and sea lavender cool the flames, their blossoms serving as an added bonus.

❀ Any gazania is compatible in this arrangement, but my favorite (if you can find it) has soft, pink daisies and silver leaves.

❀ Orchid rockrose is a compact shrub that has single, purplish, roselike flowers. Each delicately wrinkled petal is accented at the base with a red spot.

❀ Compact common thrift has cheerful pompoms for flowerheads, which it carries on tall stems over grasslike tufts of foliage. Common thrift blooms almost all year and is available in white, rose pink, or wine red. Plant either a mix of colors or all one variety, whichever you prefer.

Creating Steamy Subtropical Gardens

Subtropical regions experience mild, wet winters and hot, humid summers. The deep south of the U.S., southeastern China, southern India, the east cape of South Africa, coastal Argentina, and parts of Australia share these conditions.

When the winter-weary head to the balmy subtropics, some folks are disappointed to find that many of their old garden favorites can't make the journey with them. Most traditional perennials originate in cooler climates and require a period of winter rest to bounce back hearty and vigorous the following spring. The lack of reliable chilling, coupled with relentless year-round humidity and consistently high nighttime low temperature averages, takes its toll on plants that aren't adapted to those conditions.

Still, gardeners new to the subtropics need not despair. Although many dependable cooler-clime standbys (such as peonies, bleeding hearts, delphiniums, bearded iris, lupines, and lady's mantle) do wimp out from the endless heat and humidity, the trade-off is an abundance of tender treasures that you can set free from the conservatory or the windowsill to take up permanent residence in the garden. Extravagantly exotic bulbs — stately amaryllis, sultry Lily of the Nile *(Agapanthus), Crocosmia,* elegant fortnight lily *(Dietes),* gladiolas, and fragrant crinum — spread like weeds in the subtropics . . . to the genuine envy of gardeners in frostier climates.

The subtropical garden's riotous spring display also has few rivals. Camellias, dogwoods, magnolias, azaleas, and flowering vines all bloom together with reckless and colorful abandon.

It's not the heat; it's the humidity

Most hot and humid regions experience just enough cold to make growing truly tropical plants a risky proposition. Even gardens in the warmest parts of these areas routinely experience a hard freeze once every 15 or 20 years, sometimes with an occasional snowfall.

Periods of very heavy rainfall alternate with prolonged dry spells in these regions, so plants must be able to contend with both extremes. Soil types range from nearly perfect, fertile, well-drained loam to sticky, heavy clay and pockets of pure sand, and from overly acidic to highly alkaline. (See Chapter 11 for the dirt on soil types.)

Where rainfall is heavy and drainage is poor, amending the soil thoroughly and building raised beds are critical to successful perennial gardening. Most perennials can't tolerate wet feet for long and may rot if left standing in water puddles.

In general, the same perennials bloom earlier in the year and are shorter-lived when they are grown in warmer climates. Perennials also tend to be taller and less sturdy in the subtropical garden than their counterparts grown in cold-weather climates. Whenever one is available, choose a dwarf variety, because it's less likely to flop over without staking. Frequent division — as often as once a year — helps many types maintain their vigor. See Chapter 19 to find out how to divide your perennials.

Planning a subtropical garden

For the garden in Figure 4-5, I've chosen a tough group of perennials that laugh off summer's muggiest heat. This mix of wildflowers and traditional perennials include several that, if you regularly *deadhead* (pluck off the dying blooms, as described in Chapter 17), bloom for most of the year. Give this garden plan a try if your winters are mild and wet and your summers are hot and humid.

Some tips for growing and maintaining the flower bed in Figure 4-5 follow:

- ✔ **Unless your site is very fast draining, raise the bed at least 1 foot (30 cm) higher than ground level and fill the box with a sandy soil mix.** (See Chapter 12 to find out how to create a raised bed.) Plan to irrigate this garden deeply once a week during long dry spells. (For tips on how and when to water, see Chapter 15.)

- ✔ **Plant this subtropical garden in the fall or, at the very latest, in early winter.** You want to give these newly transplanted perennials several months to become settled and establish strong roots before they have to deal with excessive summer heat.

- ✔ **Over the winter, lay down a thick, loose blanket of mulch (see Chapter 13) to protect frost-tender perennials like velvet sage and Transvaal daisies.** If you don't want to bother with trying to babysit these plants during the winter, you can treat them as annuals, replacing them each year that they don't come back.

- ✔ **In late winter, give the bed a thorough cleaning and cut back old, tired foliage to get everything off to a new start.** If any of the perennials become mildewed during the growing season, cut them down to the tuft of leaves at the base of the plant (see Chapter 17), and the new foliage generally comes up free of mildew.

The pastel tones in this garden balance and soften the bright accents of scarlet hibiscus, golden yarrow, and coreopsis.

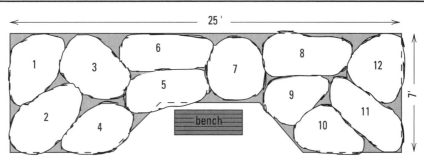

Key	Common Name	Impress-Your-Neighbor Name	Quantity
1	Transvaal daisy	*Gerbera jamesonii* 'Coral Gables'	3
2	Tickseed	*Coreopsis grandiflora* 'Sunray'	5
3	Lemon daylily	*Hemerocallis lilioasphodelus*	2
4	Showy evening primrose	*Oenothera speciosa*	3
5	Shasta daisy	*Leucanthemum maximum* 'Little Miss Muffet'	2
6	'Coronation Gold' yarrow	*Achillea* 'Coronation Gold'	3
7	Velvet sage	*Salvia leucantha*	1
8	Purple coneflower	*Echinacea purpurea*	2
9	Red-hot poker	*Kniphofia uvaria*	2
10	Rigid verbena	*Verbena rigida*	3
11	Rose mallow	*Hibiscus moscheutos* Southern Belle Series	2
12	Obedient plant	*Physostegia virginiana*	3

Figure 4-5: The perennials in this garden thrive in the heat and summer humidity common to Baton Rouge, Louisiana, or Bombay, India.

❀ By late spring, the icy white petals of 'Little Miss Muffet' (a dwarf Shasta daisy) open to reveal clear yellow centers. 'Coral Gables' is a soft orange variety of the Transvaal daisy.

❀ The golden plate-sized flowerheads of 'Coronation Gold' yarrow first appear in late spring and continue for several months. The starry flowers of 'Sunray' tickseed is a lustrous yellow that stops just short of orange. (Both plants are pictured in this book's color insert.)

❀ If you like really big flowers, you're going to love rose mallows. Their oversized blossoms look like they're made of crepe paper. A daintier flower, showy evening primrose produces frosty pink cups with yellow centers for most of the summer. Always stately and regal, the tall flower spikes of red-hot poker rise dramatically above bold, linear foliage.

❀ Sunshine-colored lemon daylilies brighten the midsummer doldrums. But when silvery velvet sage and rosy rigid verbena begin to bloom, you know that fall is not far off.

Planting Perennials in the Scorching Desert

The southwestern U.S., west-central Australia, South Africa, northern Africa, and southern Asia all have warm deserts. Mild winters distinguish the warm deserts from the cold drylands. Snow isn't unheard of in these regions, but temperatures rarely stay below freezing for long. The mild winters are what attract people to these otherwise-harsh regions (and probably few would stay if they were subjected to a summer without air conditioning!).

Warm deserts share one universal characteristic: *Soil and air temperatures are high.* Summer heat is relentless enough to melt blacktop, at times shutting down major airports. Soil temperature can be 100° F (38° C) — even 4 inches (10 cm) underground. Few habitats on earth seem as inhospitable to the traditional perennial garden as the desert. But these apparent wastelands have another, more exuberant side. Every so often, rain falls at just the right time to produce an unequaled floral display. Local tourist boards and chambers of commerce host wildflower hotlines at peak seasons to track these short-lived events. Admirers from near and far drop whatever they're doing to go witness the desert in a blaze of color.

Although generally perceived as barren and desolate places, warm deserts actually have some of the richest and most diverse floras anywhere on earth. And you can't help but admire the fortitude and endurance of the plants that have evolved in such a seemingly forbidding climate. Learn to adapt to the demands of desert gardening, and you can capture all the excitement and awe of the desert's natural beauty.

Desert soils

Soil types range from pockets of wonderfully fertile soil to nearly pure gravel or heavy clay. Most soils are highly alkaline and some are also quite salty. Desert soils tend to be deficient in decaying organic matter — typically containing only 0.5 to 1 percent. Native vegetation copes with this moisture and nutritional dearth by growing sparsely, spacing themselves widely apart. In the garden — where you want a dense, lush look — amending the soil compensates for the extra competition (see Chapter 11 for tips on amending your soil).

One common type of soil poses a particular problem. *Caliche* is an accumulation of calcium carbonate that can occur several inches to several feet (12 cm to 3 m) deep. In some cases, caliche is granular and drains well, but it can also form a particularly impermeable layer called *hardpan*. You must either break up the hardpan enough to enable plant roots and water to penetrate and drain through the soil, or build raised beds.

Rainfall is scarce and irregular throughout the warm desert regions. None of these areas receives more than 10 inches (25 cm) annually. Moisture evaporates from the soil faster than rain falls. The key to perennial gardening in this arid climate is to shelter the flower bed from the harsh elements so that it doesn't dry out so quickly.

Rain often comes all at once, with one violent storm quickly dumping several inches. In such deluges, most of the water is wasted because it runs off before it has a chance to soak into the parched soil. Strong winds, sandstorms, and intense sunlight all routinely batter unadapted plants, challenging your patience and your sense of humor.

The oasis garden

Reflecting the desert's occasional explosion of color, the oasis garden in Figure 4-6 features a tough and rugged selection of perennials. All are drought tolerant and tough as nails, but they can still use a little help to look their best in this harsh climate.

Place this garden in a courtyard surrounded by a low wall to protect the flowers from sun and drying winds. Or put the garden behind a shelter belt or windbreak of trees and shrubs. Follow these steps to plant and maintain this flower bed:

1. **Plant when the worst of summer's heat is waning.**

   The best time to plant perennials in this climate is early to mid fall.

2. **Amend the soil so that it drains freely but doesn't dry out too quickly.**

3. **After planting, spread several inches of fibrous organic mulch or gravel between the plants.**

4. **Water regularly until the perennials have doubled in size.**

   When the plants are growing strongly, soak the bed once a month in winter and only as often as needed in summer. Always water thoroughly to encourage deep rooting. Water at night or install drip irrigation so that water isn't wasted by evaporation.

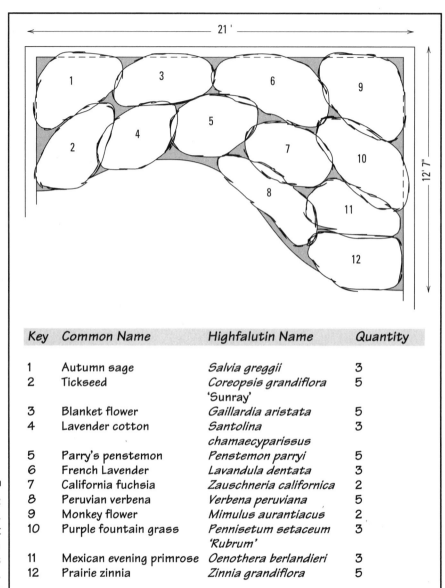

Key	Common Name	Highfalutin Name	Quantity
1	Autumn sage	*Salvia greggii*	3
2	Tickseed	*Coreopsis grandiflora 'Sunray'*	5
3	Blanket flower	*Gaillardia aristata*	5
4	Lavender cotton	*Santolina chamaecyparissus*	3
5	Parry's penstemon	*Penstemon parryi*	5
6	French Lavender	*Lavandula dentata*	3
7	California fuchsia	*Zauschneria californica*	2
8	Peruvian verbena	*Verbena peruviana*	5
9	Monkey flower	*Mimulus aurantiacus*	2
10	Purple fountain grass	*Pennisetum setaceum 'Rubrum'*	3
11	Mexican evening primrose	*Oenothera berlandieri*	3
12	Prairie zinnia	*Zinnia grandiflora*	5

Figure 4-6:
In dry, desert regions, a garden is an oasis.

The vibrant scarlets, purples, and yellows of the following perennials ensure that the intense sunlight of this climate doesn't wash out this garden's brilliance (most of these desert beauties appear in the color insert):

- ❀ As its name suggests, autumn sage blooms in fall and winter and is available in pink, coral, purplish red, red, or white. Any of these choices complement this garden, but choose red if you want to attract hummingbirds.

- ❀ If you pluck off dying blooms regularly, compact 'Sunray' coreopsis overflows with ragged-edged golden daisies for a very long blooming season.

- ❀ Blanket flower, a large burgundy daisy with gilded edges, is set off by the tidy silver mounds of lavender cotton (which appears to be dotted with yellow buttons when in bloom) and the spires of shocking-pink flowers on Parry's penstemon.

- ❀ French lavender sends up purplish flower spikes nearly year-round. As if trying to steal the spotlight, attention-grabbing California fuchsia's showy, tubular, scarlet flowers arch above grayish foliage. In the foreground, clusters of rosy pink Peruvian verbena flowers bloom so profusely that they nearly obscure the plant's foliage.

- ❀ Unlike *Mimulus aurantiacus,* most monkey flowers like plenty of water, so ask for this plant by its botanical name to make sure that you get the one that likes dry conditions.

- ❀ Purple fountain grass adds a sense of grace and movement to the garden. Mexican evening primrose refuses to stay put. It comes up everywhere, but its silky pink cups make it a welcome pest. Next door, prairie zinnia, a native of the American southwest, sports little bright yellow daisies.

Chapter 5
Creating a Color Scheme

· ·

In This Chapter

▶ Two harmonious gardens of pastel colors

▶ An exuberant garden of brilliant, high-volume colors

▶ Two attention-getting gardens with daring, over-the-top colors

· ·

Color is the number one reason why flowers are so universally adored. Sweet fragrance, rich textures, and fascinating shapes all boost flower impact — no question about that. But if flowers only came in shades of gray, they would have about as much appeal as food without flavor.

Fortunately, flowers enjoy a wealth of color diversity, spanning the entire color spectrum. Blossoms occur in an infinite variety of shades and tones. The word *red* gives you only a hint of what to expect. Red may be the insistent red of a traffic signal or the deep, velvety tones of a burgundy wine. The possible shades are unlimited, and each shade has a flower to match.

Combining colors in the garden can be a real outlet for your creative energies. The most talented gardeners elevate garden design to an art form. The rest of us just enjoy fiddling around with color and get a charge out of discovering the impact that different shades have on one another and on our emotions. Does a patch of white flowers soften or highlight companions? Does blue make you feel relaxed, or does it make you feel pensive? Even design authorities disagree; one answer isn't right for everyone. By experimenting with color combinations in your flower garden, you can discover your own garden temperament.

I designed the five plans in this chapter for gardeners in temperate regions. These traditional perennials require winters cold enough to satisfy the need that some varieties have for a period of chilling, but not so cold that winter hardiness greatly limits plant choices. You may also succeed with these plants in sheltered areas in very cold climates or in subtropical regions where nighttime temperatures are cool. Gardeners who live in steamy subtropics, or where winter temperatures routinely fall below –20° F (–29° C), need to take the plans to a local nursery and ask for suggestions for plant substitutions appropriate to their specific climate.

These five gardens are planned around separate color schemes. Color preferences are very personal; most folks have very definite ideas about what colors they like best. Choose whichever plan feels right to you. To build any of these gardens, first decide where it goes and then

1. **Mark the outlines of the flower bed according to the instructions in Chapter 3.**

2. **Clear your site and amend the soil by following the tips in Chapter 11.**

3. **Buy your plants (see Chapter 14 for advice).**

    Ask your local nursery to help you make substitutions for perennials not appropriate for your climate.

4. **Plant the garden as described in Chapter 14.**

5. **Care for your newly installed garden as outlined in Part V.**

6. **Have a party to show off your new garden.**

A Traditional Pastel Garden

Creamy, buttery, and clear yellows; mauve, rose, and sugary pinks; lavenders and blues — these colors capture the freshness of a spring morning and preserve that feeling throughout the gardening season. Pastel color schemes are undemanding, easy on the eye, and never clash. At the end of a long day, these gentle, harmonious colors can quiet and soothe overworked, jangled nerves — just like a martini, but without the calories.

Delicate colors look their best in soft early morning or evening light or in the afternoon shade in hot, sunny climates. They can't stand up to strong light, which gives them the bleached look of faded denim. Pastels have always been popular in places where skies are cloudy and overcast because the delicate colors glow in muted light.

To prevent pale color combinations from becoming dull and insipid, always include a few invigorating accents of white, purple, or hot pink. White brightens and enlivens adjoining colors and becomes reflective to the point of dazzling at dusk and under moonlit skies. Pale pink and soft yellow behave similarly. Both purple and hot pink give strong visual contrast to the gentler pastel tones of lavender and soft pinks. Blues, on the other hand, recede and disappear entirely as evening falls. Also, consider foliage color. Although green generally predominates, the addition of silver, gray, purplish, and multicolored leaves further complements and enhances gentle flower colors.

Plant the pastel flower bed shown in Figure 5-1 in full sun in cloudy regions or in afternoon shade in regions where the sunlight is more intense. These perennials aren't true shade-lovers and need a few hours of direct sunlight to bloom. An open eastern exposure is ideal. Prepare the soil well (see

Chapter 11) and irrigate regularly (see Chapter 15) for best results. The bench provides a comfortable spot for you to sit and let the garden work its calming magic.

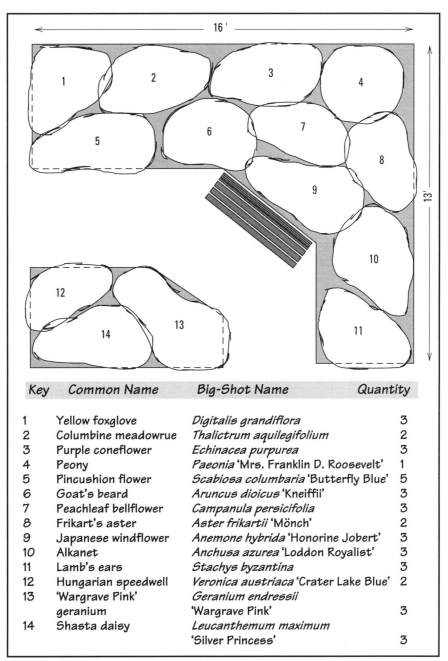

Key	Common Name	Big-Shot Name	Quantity
1	Yellow foxglove	*Digitalis grandiflora*	3
2	Columbine meadowrue	*Thalictrum aquilegifolium*	2
3	Purple coneflower	*Echinacea purpurea*	3
4	Peony	*Paeonia* 'Mrs. Franklin D. Roosevelt'	1
5	Pincushion flower	*Scabiosa columbaria* 'Butterfly Blue'	5
6	Goat's beard	*Aruncus dioicus* 'Kneiffii'	3
7	Peachleaf bellflower	*Campanula persicifolia*	3
8	Frikart's aster	*Aster frikartii* 'Mönch'	2
9	Japanese windflower	*Anemone hybrida* 'Honorine Jobert'	3
10	Alkanet	*Anchusa azurea* 'Loddon Royalist'	3
11	Lamb's ears	*Stachys byzantina*	3
12	Hungarian speedwell	*Veronica austriaca* 'Crater Lake Blue'	2
13	'Wargrave Pink' geranium	*Geranium endressii* 'Wargrave Pink'	3
14	Shasta daisy	*Leucanthemum maximum* 'Silver Princess'	3

Figure 5-1:
A perennial garden plan featuring pastel-colored flowers.

A traditional pastel garden rewards you all season long:

❀ The 'Mrs. Franklin D. Roosevelt' peony is an old-fashioned, springtime favorite with huge, delectably fragrant pink blossoms. Bright blue peachleaf bellflower provides a spiky contrast to the fat peony.

❀ Fluffy lavender flowerheads are carried high above the lacy blue foliage of meadowrue, dainty *Scabiosa columbaria* 'Butterfly Blue' is a compact pincushion flower with a long season of bloom, and *Digitalis grandiflora* is a truly perennial foxglove with snapdragon-like clear yellow flowers. (All three flowers appear in the color insert.)

❀ Dwarf goat's beard features ferny leaves and creamy plumes of delicate flowers that wave in early summer breezes, while alkanet bears a profusion of deep blue blossoms and coarse, hairy foliage.

❀ Across the path, *Veronica austriaca* 'Crater Lake Blue', with its violet blue flowers, repeats the spikes of alkanet in a compact, more refined form.

❀ 'Wargrave Pink' geranium produces clear pink blossoms all summer long on compact mounds of leaves, and crisp white Shasta daisies, with their golden yellow centers, add sparkle to the bed in midsummer.

❀ Lamb's ears is especially appealing for its large, silver, woolly foliage, but its charming little lavender flowers are a bonus. The large, brilliant pink daisies of purple coneflower begin their show in late summer. (Both perennials appear in the color insert.)

❀ The 'Mönch' aster provides a profusion of light blue daisies to the autumn garden. And until the first hard frost, *Anemone hybrida* 'Honorine Jobert' displays large, graceful white blossoms marked by a golden center fringe.

A Soft and Subtle Garden

The garden illustrated in Figure 5-2 features soft and subtle pastels, but it's guaranteed to catch your eye just the same. Look for a photograph of this garden in the color insert. The following list provides some of the highlights of this pastel garden:

❀ Catmint attracts cats and flower-lovers alike with clouds of soft blue flowers that nearly obscure the small, pebbly textured, fragrant foliage. It blooms heaviest in spring and on and off through fall.

❀ In late spring, the brilliant blue blossoms of alkanet contrast softly with pale pink 'Wargrave Pink' geraniums and the brighter pink stars of cheddar pinks.

❀ Steely blue and prickly balls of globe thistles, snow-white sneezewort, and bright pink daisies of purple coneflowers laugh off summer's heat.

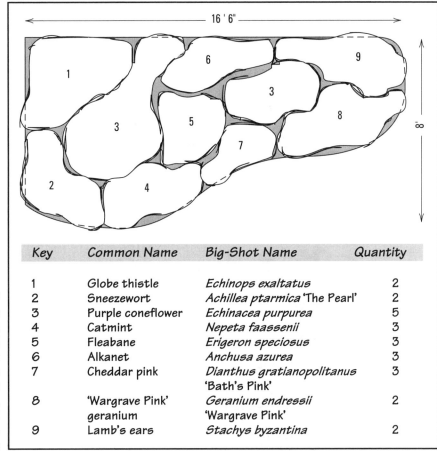

Key	Common Name	Big-Shot Name	Quantity
1	Globe thistle	*Echinops exaltatus*	2
2	Sneezewort	*Achillea ptarmica 'The Pearl'*	2
3	Purple coneflower	*Echinacea purpurea*	5
4	Catmint	*Nepeta faassenii*	3
5	Fleabane	*Erigeron speciosus*	3
6	Alkanet	*Anchusa azurea*	3
7	Cheddar pink	*Dianthus gratianopolitanus 'Bath's Pink'*	3
8	'Wargrave Pink' geranium	*Geranium endressii 'Wargrave Pink'*	2
9	Lamb's ears	*Stachys byzantina*	2

Figure 5-2:
This perennial garden plan highlights soft pastels of pink, blue, and white.

A Jewel-Tone Garden

Take pastel colors, turn up the volume, and you get an attention-grabbing jewel-tone garden. Misty pinks transform to magenta. Grayed blues become sapphire. Muted lavender gives way to purple. Buttery and clear yellows go bright gold. Color roles are reversed from the traditional pastel garden. Instead of bright colors acting as occasional accents for soft, delicate palettes, pastels become subordinate, providing filler and moderating between more exuberant hues.

A formal arrangement brings some sense of order to the joyously carefree group of perennials in the garden plan shown in Figure 5-3. Vibrant color surrounds a centrally placed birdbath, sundial, or sculpture. The bench tucked into the curve gives you an intimate place to sit and absorb the energy radiating from these passionate colors. This garden is best with full sun, good garden soil, and regular watering.

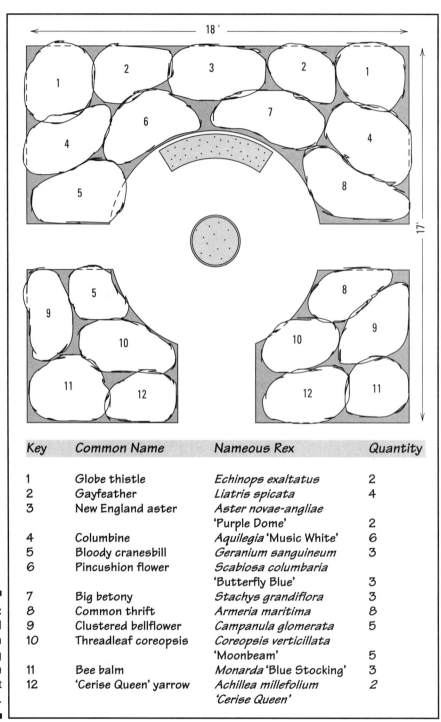

Key	Common Name	Nameous Rex	Quantity
1	Globe thistle	*Echinops exaltatus*	2
2	Gayfeather	*Liatris spicata*	4
3	New England aster	*Aster novae-angliae* 'Purple Dome'	2
4	Columbine	*Aquilegia* 'Music White'	6
5	Bloody cranesbill	*Geranium sanguineum*	3
6	Pincushion flower	*Scabiosa columbaria* 'Butterfly Blue'	3
7	Big betony	*Stachys grandiflora*	3
8	Common thrift	*Armeria maritima*	8
9	Clustered bellflower	*Campanula glomerata*	5
10	Threadleaf coreopsis	*Coreopsis verticillata* 'Moonbeam'	5
11	Bee balm	*Monarda* 'Blue Stocking'	3
12	'Cerise Queen' yarrow	*Achillea millefolium* 'Cerise Queen'	2

Figure 5-3: A perennial garden plan featuring plants with exuberant colors.

Many of the following perennials appear, in all their vibrant beauty, in this book's color insert. Look for them alphabetically, according to their botanical name (refer to Figure 5-3).

❀ In the outer corners of one side of this garden, globe thistle stands impressively with striking, ball-shaped, metallic blue flowers and prickley foliage. Flanking the globe thistle are the substantial white flowers of 'Music White' columbine (which rise, on wiry stems, above lacy foliage) and gayfeather, which forms a lilac pink exclamation point to the summer flower bed with multiple upright spikes that resemble bottle brushes.

❀ In stark contrast to the pure white columbine, the strident, globe-shaped pink flowerheads of common thrift rise above dense grassy tufts of leaves.

❀ Opposite the common thrift resides bloody cranesbill — a bold magenta flower that's not for the faint of heart. Gardeners value this perennial for its rugged disposition and attractive, deeply incised foliage that turns red in the fall. Another pretty thug, clustered bellflower, is sure to spread into areas where you don't want it to go. It carries tight clusters of bell-shaped, intense, purplish blue flowers in early summer.

❀ Behind you, as you rest on the garden bench, is the heavily textured, dark green foliage of big betony. In late spring, this plant produces whorls of delicate, rose red flowers. *Scabiosa columbaria* 'Butterfly Blue' also blooms most heavily in spring, but it continues to send up dainty blue pincushion flowers throughout the growing season.

❀ In early fall, aster 'Purple Dome' creates large mounds covered with so many purple daisies that the blooms completely obscure the foliage underneath.

❀ At the opposite end of the garden, vigorous 'Blue Stocking' bee balm dons fluffy, violet blue flowers that attract every passing bee and butterfly to the garden. Threadleaf coreopsis has clouds of sunny yellow daisies that scintillate the senses and enliven even the brightest companion.

A Garden of Rioting Colors

For the past couple of decades, the pastel color palette has reigned as the epitome of good taste in the flower garden. Whether the popularity of pastels resulted from a reaction to the anything-goes '60s (forever symbolized by neon orange and acid green polyester) or a need to reassert some quiet and harmony to hectic lives, pastels meet the challenge with grace and dignity. Their misty tones are downright impossible to clash and are always peaceful and restful to contemplate.

But pale colors can also start to become a bit tedious and dull, leaving the viewer craving more excitement, more sizzle. Garden fashion has started to reflect this need. Suddenly, garden publications are alive with saturated, flamboyant color. Flowers that were once considered too vulgar for polite company and banished to the alleyway are back in style.

The flower bed in Figure 5-4 is anything but shy, with fiery reds and clear yellows softened only by intermediate tones of orange and creamy yellow. It peaks with a riot of color during the hottest months of summer.

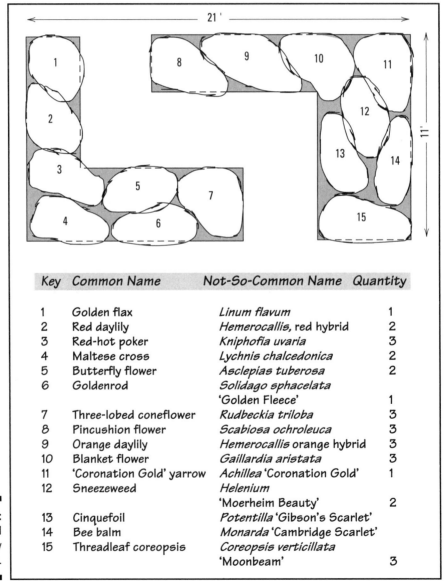

Key	Common Name	Not-So-Common Name	Quantity
1	Golden flax	*Linum flavum*	1
2	Red daylily	*Hemerocallis*, red hybrid	2
3	Red-hot poker	*Kniphofia uvaria*	3
4	Maltese cross	*Lychnis chalcedonica*	2
5	Butterfly flower	*Asclepias tuberosa*	2
6	Goldenrod	*Solidago sphacelata* 'Golden Fleece'	1
7	Three-lobed coneflower	*Rudbeckia triloba*	3
8	Pincushion flower	*Scabiosa ochroleuca*	3
9	Orange daylily	*Hemerocallis* orange hybrid	3
10	Blanket flower	*Gaillardia aristata*	3
11	'Coronation Gold' yarrow	*Achillea* 'Coronation Gold'	1
12	Sneezeweed	*Helenium* 'Moerheim Beauty'	2
13	Cinquefoil	*Potentilla* 'Gibson's Scarlet'	
14	Bee balm	*Monarda* 'Cambridge Scarlet'	
15	Threadleaf coreopsis	*Coreopsis verticillata* 'Moonbeam'	3

Figure 5-4: A hot and brassy garden.

Here's what you can expect from this garden plan (check out the color insert for photographs of many of the following perennials):

❀ A profusion of flat, golden flowerheads of 'Coronation Gold' yarrow stands elegantly over tidy clumps of filigreed, grayish green foliage and continues to send up new blooms for two to three months. Providing a lively counterpoint are the frosty tangerine trumpets of daylily.

❀ Attention-grabbing (just shy of gaudy), good-natured blanket flowers feature red centers and a rickrack edging of gold. Although sometimes short-lived, blanket flowers revel in heat, bloom for up to six months, and leave self-sown offspring to ensure their presence from one year to the next. Pincushion flower adds a tranquil note with buttery yellow pincushions dancing above heavily cut, silvery gray leaves.

❀ On the other side of the bed, 'Cambridge Scarlet' bee balm features explosive red pompoms with all the energy of a fire engine racing through a city street, sirens blaring. 'Gibson's Scarlet' cinquefoil smolders with equal intensity.

❀ Cheerful coreopsis 'Moonbeam' is literally covered with masses of starry, clear yellow daisies on compact mounds from early summer until frost.

❀ Across the walk is another daisy. Three-lobed coneflower is bushy and upright, the flowers golden yellow with dark centers. After the petals fall, these cones persist into the winter months for a whole new season of interest.

❀ Goldenrod creates a late summer fireworks display of — what else? — golden shooting stars.

❀ Easygoing butterfly flower produces radiant flower clusters in mid-summer followed by ornamental seedpods.

❀ Brilliantly scarlet, Maltese cross is a tough old favorite that can be a bit of a pest if allowed to reseed. Removing spent blossoms stops its spread wherever it becomes a nuisance.

❀ Red-hot pokers have a very short period of bloom, but they are spectacular while they last. These flaming torches are worth the fleeting presence.

❀ Mahogany red daisies of sneezeweed contrast attractively with neighboring golden flax.

A Sunny-Side-Up Garden

The garden in Figure 5-5 is one section of a long border that can be used as illustrated for a small space or repeated as many times as needed for a long border.

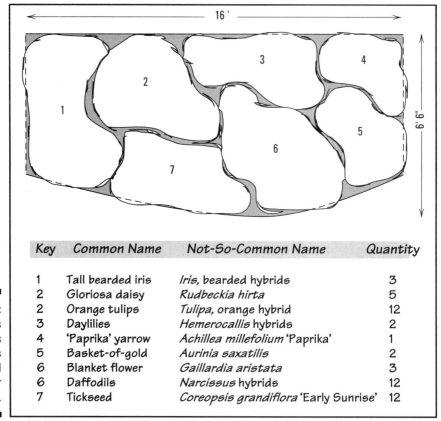

Key	Common Name	Not-So-Common Name	Quantity
1	Tall bearded iris	*Iris*, bearded hybrids	3
2	Gloriosa daisy	*Rudbeckia hirta*	5
2	Orange tulips	*Tulipa*, orange hybrid	12
3	Daylilies	*Hemerocallis* hybrids	2
4	'Paprika' yarrow	*Achillea millefolium* 'Paprika'	1
5	Basket-of-gold	*Aurinia saxatilis*	2
6	Blanket flower	*Gaillardia aristata*	3
6	Daffodils	*Narcissus* hybrids	12
7	Tickseed	*Coreopsis grandiflora* 'Early Sunrise'	12

Figure 5-5: Repeat this section as many times as you need to fill your space.

A description of the sunny-side-up garden follows (see color insert for photos of some of these flowers in bloom):

❀ In spring, elegant tall bearded iris, in either yellow or burgundy tones, and the sweet, golden flower clusters of basket-of-gold, orange tulip, and golden daffodils provide just a hint of the bright color yet to come.

❀ By midsummer, this border reaches full glory — you need sunglasses to behold its brilliance. The annual gloriosa daisies thread their way through the perennial flowers.

❀ Golden 'Early Sunrise' tickseed and blanket flower keep the color going for several months after they first get started.

❀ Pale yellow daylilies soften the flame when they make their brief appearance in midsummer.

❀ Red tones of the blossoms of 'Paprika' yarrow rival the blanket flowers' boldness when they first open, but then they gradually fade to burnished gold for a softer, more subtle effect.

To see what this garden looks like in midsummer, turn to the "Sample flower bed" section in the color portion of this book.

Chapter 6

Potpourri of Perennial Gardens

. . . .

In This Chapter

▶ Creating a warm welcome at the front door

▶ Greeting the mail carrier with flowers

▶ Brightening and lightening a woodland

▶ Tucking flowers against the base of a tree

. . . .

*F*lowers are for sharing. Don't tuck your flower beds out of sight behind the house, only to show them off on special occasions. The first two plans in this chapter break free from the misguided custom of sequestering flowers away in the backyard. These gardens go unabashedly public, bringing a splash of color to the front yard for all to behold and enjoy. After all, nothing says welcome like flowers.

The third and the fourth plans in this chapter are flower beds for the shady property. Shade has a reputation for being incompatible with flower gardening. The trick to transforming a dull and gloomy spot into a romantic woodland glen is selecting the right plants. The shaded flower gardens in this chapter feature bold, luxuriant foliage highlighted by blossoms of uncommon beauty and delicacy — proving that shade can be a genuine asset rather than a challenge.

The perennials in these plans are all acceptable for moderate climates. If you live in a harsh region — be it hot and humid, an arid desert, or where winter temperatures routinely dip well below freezing — some of these choices may not work. You must be prepared to swap some of the perennials from this chapter to choices better adapted to your own region. Ask a local garden center to help you make appropriate substitutions for the few plant selections that aren't right for you. Wherever you live, some of the perennials in these plans are suitable, so you don't need to change every flower in the plan you choose.

Building any of the gardens in this chapter is as easy as 1-2-3 (well, and 4-5). Just follow these basic steps:

1. **Choose your site and mark the dimensions of the plan following the directions in Chapter 3.**

   You can tailor the size and shape of these plans to fit your own site by squashing a bit here or expanding a little there. Add to the total number of perennials to fit a larger space; subtract a few if your spot is smaller than the plan.

2. **Prepare the soil according to the instructions in Chapter 11.**

3. **Buy the perennials.**

   The tables list the numbers of each perennial you need, but these are only suggestions. If you like a "stuffed" look, buy a few more of each or add some annuals the first year for quick fill. If you're on a tight budget, buy three plants wherever five are recommended (and so on) and be patient. Planting fewer perennials simply means that your garden takes longer to completely fill in.

4. **Plant the garden, following the steps in Chapter 14.**

5. **Observe the care and feeding regimen outlined in Part V and prepare to be dazzled.**

   By the next season, your flower display is guaranteed to be the pride of the neighborhood (barring natural disasters and rising creeks).

If You Got It, Flaunt It: Front-Yard Friends

The average front yard is an exceedingly dull place, consisting of a large expanse of lawn, a few foundation shrubs, and a scattering of shade trees. This yard style originated, with the best intentions, as a way to make small suburban properties appear more spacious. Blurring the boundaries between neighbors transforms the whole street into a park-like setting that harks back to the public common green or the park in the center of a small town.

But as family interests and activities have migrated to the private backyard areas, the front landscape has become increasingly impersonal and neglected. The front entrance often isn't the primary entrance because its former role is lost to the more convenient garage or side door. But because new visitors still get their first impression of your home from the front yard, you owe it to them to give your front yard more thought. A flower garden welcomes all with a friendly, cheerful greeting.

If your porch is wide enough, add more color in pots and place a bench or a chair where you can sit and enjoy the garden. Visitors are always grateful to have a place to sit until you can answer the doorbell. And sitting on a bench in front of your house, surrounded by blooming flowers, is a sure way to get to know your neighbors better and rekindle those friendlier times of days gone by.

The simple flower bed in Figure 6-1 is appropriate to any style of architecture and won't clash with the character of even the most conservative (or the most modern) neighborhood. It frames the front walk and entrance porch and adds pizzazz to an area that is too often maddeningly dull.

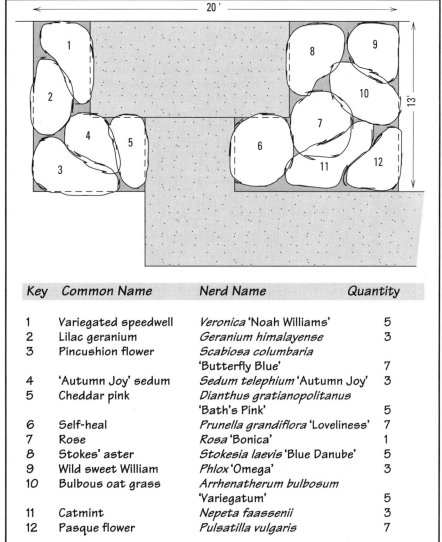

Figure 6-1:
Welcome visitors to your home with an entry garden of perennials.

Key	Common Name	Nerd Name	Quantity
1	Variegated speedwell	*Veronica* 'Noah Williams'	5
2	Lilac geranium	*Geranium himalayense*	3
3	Pincushion flower	*Scabiosa columbaria* 'Butterfly Blue'	7
4	'Autumn Joy' sedum	*Sedum telephium* 'Autumn Joy'	3
5	Cheddar pink	*Dianthus gratianopolitanus* 'Bath's Pink'	5
6	Self-heal	*Prunella grandiflora* 'Loveliness'	7
7	Rose	*Rosa* 'Bonica'	1
8	Stokes' aster	*Stokesia laevis* 'Blue Danube'	5
9	Wild sweet William	*Phlox* 'Omega'	3
10	Bulbous oat grass	*Arrhenatherum bulbosum* 'Variegatum'	5
11	Catmint	*Nepeta faassenii*	3
12	Pasque flower	*Pulsatilla vulgaris*	7

The flowers in this plan prefer a sunny location with at least five to six hours of direct sunlight hitting the spot each day during the growing season. They also require good, deep soil and regular watering.

You can expect the flower garden in Figure 6-1 to reward you in the following ways:

❀ Blooming weeks earlier than many of the spring bulbs, pasque flower gamely shrugs off late snows to send up lovely purple chalice-shaped flowers above finely cut foliage covered with silken hairs. Its fluffy seedheads are equally attractive and add a delicate quality to the late spring garden (see color section for photo).

❀ Catmint produces clouds of tiny lavender blue flowers on spreading mounds of silvery fragrant foliage. It blooms from late spring into summer.

❀ *Dianthus gratianopolitanus* 'Bath's Pink' is a charmer with baby pink stars accented by a maroon center eye and silvery green grassy leaves. Its heady perfume fills the garden from spring to late summer if faded flowers are routinely removed.

❀ 'Bonica' rose is one of the new class of carefree landscape roses. These flowers are deservedly popular because of their vigor and disease-resistance qualities. Blushing pink double flowers are carried in clusters on arching canes all season.

❀ At the foot of the roses, mats of self-heal send up spikes of hooded, deep lavender flowers in summer.

❀ Bulbous oat grass provides a shimmering contrast to nearby pastel flowers. It has white stripes on bluish green blades, creating an overall silvery effect.

❀ Stately 'Omega' phlox has white blossoms with a lilac center. This variety is one of the best of the tall garden phloxes because it's more resistant to mildew than other types of phlox. It flowers in the summer.

❀ 'Blue Danube' aster is a ragged-edged blue daisy with a white center that blooms up to several months if you keep pinching off flowers as they begin to fade.

❀ The striking two-tone green and cream leaves of 'Noah Williams' speedwell are reason enough to include this plant in the flower garden. Spikes of icy white flowers are a generous bonus.

❀ Lilac geranium features lavender blue, five-petaled, open-faced blossoms over bright green bushy clumps of foliage.

❀ Equally attractive in or out of bloom, the fleshy, succulent leaves of 'Autumn Joy' sedum are arranged in whorls on upright stems. Flower buds resemble pale green broccoli heads and open in fall to reveal soft pink, starry clusters, which age to rust and provide interest all winter if left standing.

❀ 'Butterfly Blue' pincushion flower is a charming and easy flower that blooms all through the growing season.

Don't use this garden if you live in an area where watering next to the house can damage the foundation or basement walls.

Planting a Mailbox Garden

The smaller the flower bed, the more difficult it is to keep the color going throughout the whole growing season. Most perennials are at their peak for only two to three weeks at a time.

Think of your flower bed as a botanical version of a relay race. Each combination of perennials sprints through its paces and then rapidly passes the baton to the next in a sequence, marking the rhythm of the seasons. When space is at a premium, you can't always fit in the variety and number of flowers necessary to make this process work effectively. In this case, you need to rely, instead, on a few long-winded marathon performers.

A handful of perennials perform much like annuals, blooming for a month or longer when conditions are favorable. You can help such perennials along by providing rich, well-drained soil, watering at regular intervals, and fertilizing lightly once a month during the growing season. Most important, always cut off flowers when they start to turn brown to encourage the plant to continue blooming.

Many perennials that bloom for several months seem to wear themselves out and may be short-lived as a consequence. But most spread their seeds around the garden with gusto, giving you multiple replacements. Learn to recognize the seedlings and pull the extras and the poorly placed ones. See Chapter 17 for advice on coping with overpopulation problems.

Figure 6-2 shows a plan for a little blue, white, and yellow garden to cheer up that dull patch of your yard by the street. Tucked in between the sidewalk and driveway, this patch of your yard is usually reserved for a mailbox, streetlight, or other functional but less-than-breathtaking item. Often used as a pedestrian shortcut and treated to insults by passing dogs, this hot, dry, and trampled area isn't an easy place to grow grass, either.

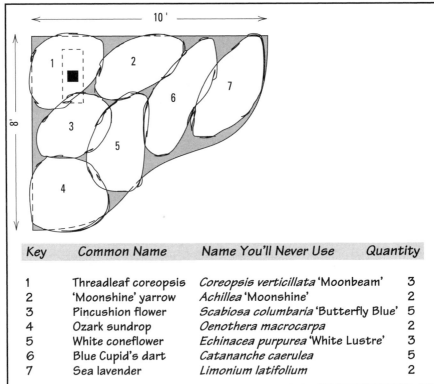

Key	Common Name	Name You'll Never Use	Quantity
1	Threadleaf coreopsis	*Coreopsis verticillata* 'Moonbeam'	3
2	'Moonshine' yarrow	*Achillea* 'Moonshine'	2
3	Pincushion flower	*Scabiosa columbaria* 'Butterfly Blue'	5
4	Ozark sundrop	*Oenothera macrocarpa*	2
5	White coneflower	*Echinacea purpurea* 'White Lustre'	3
6	Blue Cupid's dart	*Catananche caerulea*	5
7	Sea lavender	*Limonium latifolium*	2

Figure 6-2:
Perennials
for a
mailbox
garden.

The perennials in this plan are much tougher than lawn grasses. Replace unhappy grass with a spot of color and brighten up the mail carrier's day. If you don't have a mailbox, you can place this flower garden in any corner that needs livening up.

The flowers in this sample garden don't mind the intense heat reflected off concrete or asphalt, and they stay in bloom for several months. Most don't reach their stride until early summer, so plant some bulbs between and around the perennials for spring color. For best results, choose an orientation that receives a minimum of five to six hours of direct sunlight each day. Here's what you can expect from this garden plan:

 Huge, clear-yellow blossoms of Ozark sundrops look as though they're made from twisted tissue paper. The single blossoms hang over loosely spreading clumps of glossy, green, linear leaves and red stems.

❀ 'White Lustre' is a sparkling white version of purple coneflower, with relaxed, somewhat droopy petals surrounding a prominent bristly orange cone.

❀ 'Butterfly Blue' pincushion flower is an outstanding short perennial with heavily cut foliage and a profusion of lavender blue flowers. It reminds me of an eyelet ruffle around a candlewick center. (Look for a photo of this plant in the color section.)

❀ No garden flower has a more cheerful or sunnier disposition than 'Moonshine' yarrow. Its flat-topped, sulfur-yellow flowerheads are carried high above ferny, silver gray foliage.

❀ Masses of starry, petite yellow daisies cover the green threadleaf foliage of 'Moonbeam' coreopsis from early summer through fall.

❀ Perky cupid's darts feature ragged-edged blue petals, a purple center star, and golden stamens that coordinate with neighboring yellow tones.

❀ Sea lavender produces sprays of thousands of tiny lavender blue flowers, creating an overall effect of delicate sea foam. A good filler in the flower bed, sea lavender is also a florist's favorite, fresh or dried.

Brightening Up Those Shady Spots

Human nature being what it is, gardeners who have an abundance of sunshine eagerly plant trees and impatiently wait for shade, whereas gardeners who are faced with wooded properties complain that they can't get anything to bloom. Although the largest number of perennials prefer sunny sites, dozens more hail from the woodland and forest. Using these plants in shady spots results in a perennial garden every bit as satisfying as one in the sun.

Very few plants can tolerate anything approaching total darkness. Some light is essential for the process of *photosynthesis,* the method plants use to convert the sun's energy to food. Fortunately, many plants are adapted to very low light levels — otherwise, houseplants would only survive in sunny windows.

Problems arise when folks try to grow familiar sun lovers such as marigolds, roses, sunflowers, and petunias in shady locations. When flowers don't get enough light, they rapidly start to look miserable. They signal their distress by stretching toward lighter areas; becoming pale, weak, and spindly; and failing to bloom.

The many shades of shade

You are the garden's matchmaker; your job is to choose plants compatible with the existing conditions. To determine which plants are likely candidates for your yard, first determine the degree of shade in your garden. Shade occurs in infinite gradations and variety, but you can say that it falls loosely into one of three categories, each supporting a different community of plants.

- ✔ **Light shade:** Either the intermittent, dappled light under loosely branched deciduous trees or a relatively bright north- or east-facing exposure receiving as much as three to four hours of direct morning sunlight.

- ✔ **Medium shade:** Areas under a high tree canopy or in the shadow of structures, where some direct and reflected sunlight reaches through the gloom for at least part of the day.

- ✔ **Dense shade:** The shadowy places between tall buildings, alongside high fences, and under mature conifers. Highly restrictive, often dry as well as dark, these areas support very little plant life, including weeds.

In many cases, the only sensible thing to do with dense shade is to cover the area with mulch or, in hot climates, build a patio or deck to take advantage of what is undoubtedly the coolest, most comfortable spot in your yard. Most woodland plants do fine in medium shade. Light shade offers the best of both worlds. It provides enough protection to keep shade-lovers from burning and enough sunlight to satisfy the needs of most sun lovers.

Climate differences can affect the minimum hours of sunlight a particular plant needs to prosper. Where light is really intense and heat is extreme, two or three hours of direct sunlight may be more than adequate. A rose grown in misty Oxford, England, performs best in full sun. The same rose in dry, bright Alberta, Canada, may do better with only marginal amounts. Many flowers that prefer full sun in the north must have a partially shaded site in hot, humid areas or desert climates.

Shade can also be seasonal. Deciduous trees drop their leaves for many months at a stretch, often filtering enough sunlight in to satisfy the needs of spring bulbs and early wildflowers. Also be aware that shadows created by structures lengthen and shorten as the sun changes position in the sky throughout the year. Hostas planted in the shade on the north side of your house in September may find themselves baking in the full sun the following May.

Overcoming the challenges of a shady property

You do have fewer perennials to choose from for the shady garden, but you also have some trade-offs. People benefit from the cooler, more comfortable interior temperatures and reduced air-conditioning costs of shaded properties. Whatever casts a shadow also generally blocks the wind. In very windy locations, this fact increases the comfort level for both you and your perennials. But you can have too much of a good thing.

To let in more light, consider thinning out overcrowded stands of trees or removing a few large limbs. Simply removing some of the lower limbs opens up the area beneath the branches and allows more light to enter from the sides.

Cutting down trees can be a dangerous do-it-yourself project. Call a tree service — a good arborist not only can remove trees and large limbs safely but can also help you decide which trees are too valuable to lose. You may need a permit to cut any tree at all. Check with your local government and, if you live in a covenant-controlled community, also check with the local architectural control committee or homeowners' association.

Most woodland flowers like a rich soil with a high percentage of *humus* — decomposed organic matter such as leaves (see Chapter 11 for tips on amending soils) and even moisture. Tree root competition can become a real problem. Shallow-rooted species such as poplars, maples, beeches, and elms greedily grab all the water and nutrients from the soil before the flowers have a chance to get what they need.

You may be tempted to pile fresh soil on top of the depleted soil or to simply dig out the offending tree roots. But watch out: Piling soil deeply on top of the roots or removing masses of roots can kill a tree. However, you can add a few inches of loose topsoil beneath a tree or dig out a few roots without getting into too much trouble. (The farther you go from the tree's trunk the less likely you are to damage the tree.) Whatever you decide to do, use restraint. Trees can live on stored energy for several years before they die — which can leave homeowners scratching their heads trying to figure out what happened to their lovely tree. A raised bed built three years previously may be what ultimately killed the tree.

A densely leafed tree can also act as a giant umbrella, blocking rainfall from reaching the ground underneath. When irrigating these areas, however, be careful not to water any more than you need to keep your flowers happy. A damp, cool environment encourages mold and mildew to grow as lustily as they do in your refrigerator or shower. Adding any more water than is necessary encourages their spread. See Chapter 15 for watering advice, and turn to Chapter 18 for tips on dealing with mold and mildew.

A sample shade garden

Figure 6-3 shows a good garden plan for a shady yard.

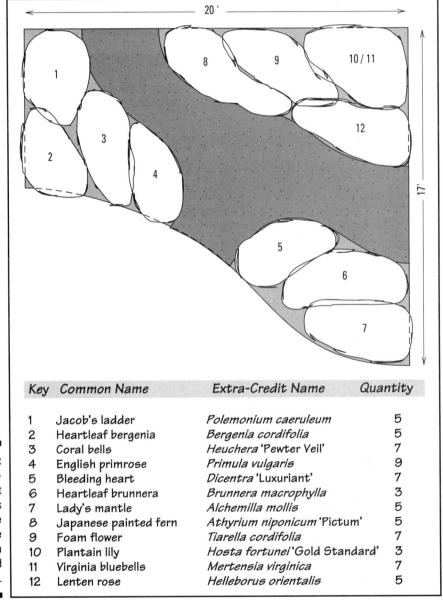

Key	Common Name	Extra-Credit Name	Quantity
1	Jacob's ladder	*Polemonium caeruleum*	5
2	Heartleaf bergenia	*Bergenia cordifolia*	5
3	Coral bells	*Heuchera 'Pewter Veil'*	7
4	English primrose	*Primula vulgaris*	9
5	Bleeding heart	*Dicentra 'Luxuriant'*	7
6	Heartleaf brunnera	*Brunnera macrophylla*	3
7	Lady's mantle	*Alchemilla mollis*	5
8	Japanese painted fern	*Athyrium niponicum 'Pictum'*	5
9	Foam flower	*Tiarella cordifolia*	7
10	Plantain lily	*Hosta fortunei 'Gold Standard'*	3
11	Virginia bluebells	*Mertensia virginica*	7
12	Lenten rose	*Helleborus orientalis*	5

Figure 6-3:
Shade-tolerant perennials form the backbone of a woodland garden.

Place the woodland garden in Figure 6-3 in an area that gets either morning or unfiltered afternoon sunlight if you live in a hot, sunny climate. If you live where summers are overcast and cloudy, this garden can tolerate an unshaded spot in your yard. Add plenty of organic matter to the soil before planting. Woodland flowers like a rich soil (see Chapter 11 for tips on soil preparation). For a smaller space, delete the walk and push the three areas together to create one flower bed.

The following list gives you an idea of what to expect from this garden (many of these perennials appear in the color insert of this book):

❀ Hostas are quite possibly the most popular shade perennial, with hundreds of types available. They form luxuriant rosettes of elongated, heart-shaped leaves in a huge variety of colors, textures, and sizes. 'Gold Standard' is a vibrant yellow form, each leaf edged with an uneven green margin and lavender flower spikes as a pretty bonus.

❀ Heartleaf bergenia is another old-fashioned favorite, prized for its shiny, evergreen foliage topped by pink flower clusters in early spring.

❀ Heartleaf brunnera sends up a profusion of tiny blue forget-me-not flowers. Afterwards, small heart-shaped leaves gradually expand to salad-plate size.

❀ Providing contrast to these large, bold forms is a delicate fern with unusual coloration. Japanese silver-painted fern has silver multicolored fronds on burgundy red stems for a graceful but eye-catching effect.

❀ Foam flower is daintier yet, with a froth of creamy white flowers over ornamental foliage.

❀ Waxy flowers of Lenten rose — each with freckles in shades of wine, rose, and plum — are the first to announce the arrival of spring in the shaded garden. Their handsome, dark green glossy foliage is striking through the rest of the season.

❀ Lady's mantle has uncommonly beautiful leaves resembling a folded cape. The flowers appear to be a chartreuse yellow foam and hover just above the tidy foliage clumps.

❀ In this garden, Virginia bluebells are interplanted with the hostas to take advantage of each other's habits. Following purple-tinged foliage in early spring, Virginia bluebells produce spikes of nodding bells that age to lavender blue. At the first sign of summer's heat, these plants quickly go into decline and look totally dead by mid-summer. Hostas, on the other hand, enjoy sleeping in late and emerge at about the same time the bluebells are passing their prime. By combining the two, you cover the flaws of each and prevent early or late gaps in the flower bed.

❀ Bleeding heart is so named for deeply cut, its red locket-shaped flowers. 'Luxuriant' has unmatched stamina, blooming from spring to the first hard frost. Pink hearts dangle in clusters above elegant blue green clumps of foliage.

❀ Coral bells is another charmer, grown as much for its distinctive leaves as for its delicate flower parts. 'Pewter Veil' is one of the prettiest of all the coral bells, featuring purple red leaves overlaid with metallic frost and dramatic veining.

❀ A popular flower for western and northern climates, Jacob's ladder is intolerant of hot, humid weather. But where adapted, this tough plant produces dainty cup-shaped blue flowers on upright, refined foliage.

❀ Like florist's nosegays surrounded by wrinkled, textured leaves, yellow English primroses are sweet, cheerful flowers that can find a home in every woodland garden.

Dealing with seasonal shade under a deciduous tree

Shade beneath a deciduous tree is seasonal. Tulips get enough hours of sunlight to satisfy their needs before the tree grows its spring leaves, but during the summer months the shade becomes too dense for most lawn grasses. You end up with a ring of exposed soil studded with bedraggled bits of lawn at the base of the tree — not a pretty sight. The garden in Figure 6-4 brings a splash of color to this otherwise difficult area.

The perennials in this group are tough enough to compete with tree roots and can withstand seasonal changing of light and shade patterns.

❀ Bright red tulips trumpet beside steel blue spikes of Spanish bluebells. To hide their dying foliage, interplant the bulbs with daylilies and Japanese windflowers.

❀ White bleeding hearts dangle from gracefully arching stems and mirror the white edge of neighboring plantain lilies.

❀ Low-growing woodland phlox features masses of star-shaped flowers. If you can find it, use the blue variety with reddish centers to echo the red of the tulips and the blue of the Spanish bluebells.

❀ For attractive foliage throughout the growing season, plantain lilies, purple bugleweed, and lady's mantle are hard to top. All three provide lovely flowers as a bonus.

❀ Bloody cranesbill's name gives you some idea of what to expect — its bright magenta blossoms are impossible to ignore.

❀ 'Kneiffii' is a petite goat's beard with fluffy white flower spikes.

❀ Daylilies ensure midsummer color. Red is a good choice for a partially shaded sight that's protected from fading and hot afternoon sun.

❀ This garden's color continues in fall with soft coral flowers of plume poppy and silky cup-shaped blossoms of Japanese windflower.

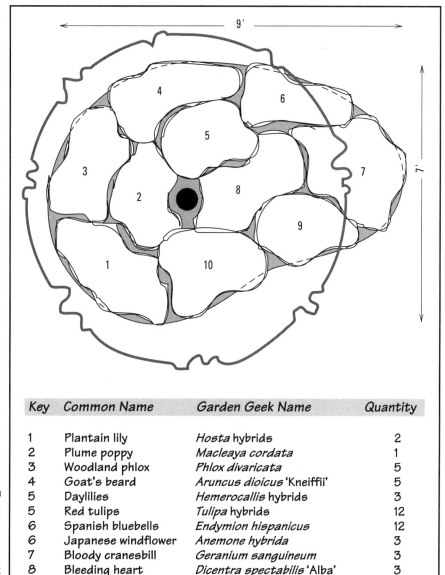

Key	Common Name	Garden Geek Name	Quantity
1	Plantain lily	*Hosta* hybrids	2
2	Plume poppy	*Macleaya cordata*	1
3	Woodland phlox	*Phlox divaricata*	5
4	Goat's beard	*Aruncus dioicus* 'Kneiffii'	5
5	Daylilies	*Hemerocallis* hybrids	3
5	Red tulips	*Tulipa* hybrids	12
6	Spanish bluebells	*Endymion hispanicus*	12
6	Japanese windflower	*Anemone hybrida*	3
7	Bloody cranesbill	*Geranium sanguineum*	3
8	Bleeding heart	*Dicentra spectabilis* 'Alba'	3
9	Bugleweed	*Ajuga reptans* 'Catlin's Giant'	5
10	Lady's mantle	*Alchemilla mollis*	3

Figure 6-4:
A garden plan for a tough-to-plant spot under a tree.

See the color section of this book for a photo of this garden in late spring.

Part III
Cast of Characters

The 5th Wave   By Rich Tennant

In this part . . .

You could fill your yard with new perennials every year and never come close to planting all the different kinds of perennials that are available. Fortunately, nature narrows your choices for you. The amount of sun your garden gets, your climate, the composition of your soil, and many other factors all determine which perennials your garden can sustain (for more than a week, that is). And because a balanced garden is more than just flowers, this part also contains profiles of perennials with great foliage, as well as lists of shrubs, annuals, and bulbs that make nice companions for your perennial garden.

Chapter 7

Easy-Going Favorites with Sunny Dispositions

. . . .

In This Chapter

▶ The scoop on sun — how much is enough? Can you have too much?

▶ Loads of easy-going, sun-loving perennials

▶ Miscellaneous tips and tidbits for choosing the best perennial for you

. . . .

*F*lowers and sunshine are natural friends. After all, plants need sun to make their food. (Remember *photosynthesis,* from high-school biology?) Although plants that hail from woodland habitats prefer a shady location and perhaps some SPF–14 sunblock, the majority of common perennials love to bask in the sun. This chapter concentrates on these common, sun-loving perennials. (For more on gardening in shade, see Chapter 8.)

Combing through the hundreds of sun-loving perennials to decide which ones to include in this chapter was not an easy task. I grow every flower I can get my hands on, and choosing among them is about as difficult as picking a favorite child. I'm crazy about all my perennials, even though, on different days of the week and at different seasons, some stand clearly above the rest. To narrow down the selection process, this chapter includes only the following (with a few exceptions):

> ✔ **Perennials that grow in a wide variety of conditions and climates:** Every perennial is easy to grow somewhere, but that *somewhere* may be very exacting (see the nearby sidebar, "Catering to your climate"). A plant that grows like a weed in a desert region is probably impossible to grow in a cool, damp climate without a greenhouse. But the flowers in this chapter have a wide range of tolerance, as far as climate is concerned. Daylilies, yarrows, Shasta daisies, tall bearded iris, and black-eyed Susans are just a few of the flowers that grow almost anywhere, short of the tundra and the tropics.

✔ **Perennials that are easy to grow:** The most widely adapted perennials, the old favorites that I call *traditional perennials,* have long ago had their fussiness bred out of them. You don't have to do somersaults and handsprings to keep the plants in this chapter alive and performing up to reasonable expectations.

✔ **Perennials that are easy to locate:** You can find most of the plants in this chapter at your local nurseries and garden centers. All are available through the mail-order catalogs listed in the appendix.

Too Much of a Good Thing?

Perennials that are considered to need "full sun" exposure don't necessarily require sunshine all day long. In hot, desert climates, for example, even the most sun-loving plant may need a bit of afternoon shade to cool down. If you live in a very hot, dry region, try to plant these perennials where they can get plenty of sunshine in the morning, but where a wall, tree, or other structure casts sufficient shade to protect them from the intense afternoon heat.

Subtropical climates can be tricky because of humidity. Hot, muggy climates tend to be much more restrictive than hot, dry regions. In a hot and arid region, you can place a plant that requires cool temperatures in the shade and water it often, but you can't do much to reduce high humidity coupled with intense heat. I've indicated in the text which perennials are most sensitive to heat combined with humidity. In some areas, these plants are grown as annuals, planted in the fall to bloom the next spring. Check with local nurseries and gardeners in your own region to find out their experience with any plant you're uncertain of.

Catering to your climate

When you get to the extreme climate limits of perennial gardening — the subtropics and regions with permafrost and polar bears — the number of *traditional* perennials you can grow is considerably reduced, compared with the more moderate areas.

Perennial gardening has its roots in England, Western Europe, and the northeastern United States, so the flowers that are most compatible to these regions are the ones that have become part of the heritage. The bulk of the

plants listed in this chapter reflect this trend, but I have included a few perennials from off the beaten path. Some are subtropical plants that are often grown as annuals in cooler climates. A few are desert relatives of familiar flowers, and a number are plants newly introduced to the nursery trade.

See Chapter 4 for a discussion on the particulars of how climates and temperatures affect what perennials you can grow.

Sun-Loving Perennials

An average of five to six hours of sun a day keeps the perennials in the following list fit and healthy, although most will settle for less sunlight without making too much of a fuss. Look for the term *partial shade* to find perennials that may need a bit more protection from intense afternoon sun.

 If you have as much trouble choosing from among the following perennials as I do, pick the ones that most pique your interest and then pare down your "wish list" to a dozen or so of your very favorites. Use the design tips in Chapter 2 to help make these difficult cuts.

Because the common names of perennials vary so much from place to place, the following list is arranged alphabetically according to the more specific (if clunkier) botanical name. Paragraphs with a Photo Op icon discuss plants that appear in this book's color insert, also arranged by botanical name. (Refer to Chapter 1 for an explanation of botanical versus common names.)

- **Common yarrow** *(Achillea millefolium):* This perennial is absolutely easy-care, except for its wandering tendencies. The flowerheads are large, flat clusters of tiny daisies on long, straight stems — excellent for cutting or drying. The foliage is dark green, very fine, ferny, and aromatic when crushed. 'Cerise Queen' is bright, rosy red. 'Paprika' opens red and fades to burnished gold. The Galaxy Series includes soft pastels, such as pale yellow and salmon tones.

 Common yarrow grows in spreading mats and can be a bit of a pest if you let it overrun less aggressive companions. The plant is less floppy and better behaved in dry, well-drained, infertile soil. Fertilize it infrequently and lightly. Divide it annually to control spread or to propagate (see Chapter 19).

Cut the stems down to within a few inches of the ground after blooming is finished. No winter protection is necessary. Common yarrow is short-lived in hot and humid areas. It enjoys hot daytime temperatures but prefers cool nights. Common yarrow can withstand average wintertime temperatures as low as −40° F (−40° C).

 A relative of common yarrow, 'Coronation Gold' yarrow (*Achillea* 'Coronation Gold') grows 2 to 3 feet (60 to 90 cm) tall; has ferny, gray green foliage; and produces dozens of deep yellow flowers over several months.

- **Blue star flower** *(Amsonia tabernaemontana):* This bushy plant has upright, arching stems and long, narrow, willowlike leaves. In the spring, each stem bears a cluster of steely blue, star-shaped flowers. Very few perennials offer much in the way of fall color, but blue star is an exception. It turns a glowing yellow around the same time the pumpkins are ripening.

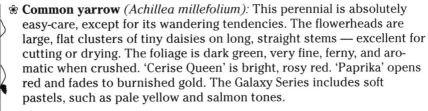

Blue star accepts any well-drained soil in full sun or partial shade. It's not fond of pH over 8. My plants always become pale and yellowish, which I remedy with a few doses of iron to keep them from yellowing before fall. I cut mine back in half after they've finished blooming just to restrict their ultimate height. Blue star grows well in all climates and can withstand wintertime lows averaging as cold as −40° F (−40° C).

❀ **Japanese windflower** *(Anemone hybrida):* Japanese windflowers prefer partial shade, except in cool climates, where they can withstand full sun. In autumn, sprays of delicate pink, deep rose, or sparkling white flowers dance above light- to dark-green grapelike foliage. 'Honorine Jobert' is bright white with yellow centers and dependably produces many flowers. 'September Charm' is rose pink on the inside of the petals, darker on the reverse.

All parts of Japanese windflower are poisonous if eaten in large amounts.

Plant Japanese windflowers in deep, fertile soil with plenty of moisture. In cold regions, protect these plants over the winter with a heavy layer of mulch. They can become invasive, especially in sandy soils. Taller varieties can flop without support. This plant isn't a good choice for hot, humid, mild-winter climate. But it is handy where wintertime averages don't dip below −30° F (−34° C).

❀ **Common thrift** *(Armeria maritima):* This plant looks like a cluster of drumsticks. In the springtime, tubular blossoms are packed into tight balls and held upright on stiff, straight stems above a tussock of grassy foliage. Diverse varieties are available, from little rock garden miniatures to robust, 1-foot-tall 'Ruby Glow' and 'Splendens'. The pink shades vary from soft and delicate to screaming magenta to almost red.

This plant's only requirement is fast drainage; common thrift is otherwise tough as nails. It tolerates salt, pure sand, and drought.

The foliage of common thrift is evergreen except in extreme cold. In hot and humid climates, this plant appreciates shade from afternoon sun. Remove spent flowerheads to the ground to encourage continued blossoming. My plants bloom on and off all summer after their initial spring burst. Common thrift grows in any region and can withstand average wintertime temperatures as low as −40° F (−40° C).

❀ **Butterfly flower** *(Asclepias tuberosa):* When men first walked on the moon, I'm surprised that they didn't find butterfly flower growing there. This flower adapts anywhere without complaint. Bees and butterflies love it. Although unfashionably orange, butterfly flower (also called butterfly weed) is so pretty that the anti-orange crowd overlooks this so-called flaw. The 'Hello Yellow' variety offers an alternative to orange, for the faint of heart.

Butterfly flower is late to break dormancy in spring. Mark the plant's location so that you don't accidentally dig into the crown before it emerges. This plant is difficult to transplant, so you may kill several before you get one to take. After settling, though, they are tough and durable. Well-drained soil is essential in wet climates. Heavy clay is fine elsewhere as long as it is not water-logged. This plant is absolutely drought tolerant and is hardy to an average wintertime low of –40° F (–40° C).

Eating butterfly flower can cause a stomachache.

Frikart's aster *(Aster frikartii):* An international celebrity, this aster was developed in Switzerland early in the 20th century. It produces masses of blue daisies from midsummer until frost. Butterflies love it. Individual plants are long-lived and carefree. Two varieties are widely sold: 'Mönch' has darker blue flowers and never needs staking; 'Wonder of Staffa' is almost indistinguishable from its sibling.

This plant is not fussy about soil — mine is happy in heavy clay — and is tolerant of both heat and humidity. Most sources report limited winter hardiness. Plants in my Colorado garden have survived –20° F (–28° C) through several winters without damage. However, wet winters may be fatal at much higher temperatures. My plants don't get a winter mulch, but this may actually improve hardiness by insuring that they dry out completely. A winter mulch may be helpful if the soil is well-drained.

A relative of Frikart's aster, New England asters *(Aster novae-angliae)* 'Alma Potschke', 'Hella Lacy', 'Purple Dome', and 'September Ruby' are big plants that give a spectacular fall show (New England aster 'Purple Dome' appears in the color insert). These varieties are prone to developing "bare legs," so place them behind other, shorter perennials for camouflage.

Peachleaf bellflower *(Campanula persicifolia):* The bellflower family is a huge one with at least a dozen good garden perennials readily available. Most are easy and charming. Peachleaf bellflower is a European native but handles all climate extremes in stride. Individual bells are large and open, carried on stiff, upright stems above linear evergreen basal leaves.

This perennial does best where night temperatures don't stay above 70° F (21° C). It's hardy to an average wintertime low of –40° F (–40° C). Give peachleaf bellflower any well-drained soil. Cut the finished flower stalks to the ground to encourage rebloom later in the summer or fall. The clumps increase and spread but not invasively. Peachleaf bellflower self-sows, but not to the point of becoming a pest.

A cousin of peachleaf bellflower, clustered bellflower *(Campanula glomerata)* has tight clusters of deep blue bells in early spring, and its foliage has a sandpapery texture. It can be an aggressive spreader.

❀ **Tickseed** *(Coreopsis grandiflora):* Tickseed is the perfect choice for anyone who can't get enough daisies. This one blooms its head off if regularly deadheaded. The flowers have a casual air. Each petal is ragged-edged and arranged around a golden center. Many fine varieties are available — 'Sunray', 'Early Sunrise', and 'Goldfink' (a variety of *Coreopsis lanceolata*) are just a few, with various flower forms, sizes, and heights.

Individual plants are generally short-lived, but self-sown seedlings are positively guaranteed. Halfway through the growing season, shear the whole plant in half to tidy it up. It recovers quickly and starts blooming again. Any well-drained soil is fine. Tickseed tolerates drought and extreme heat and humidity and is hardy to an average wintertime low of –20° F (–29° C). If yours get floppy, cut back on water and fertilizer.

A relative of tickseed, threadleaf coreopsis 'Moonbeam' *(Coreopsis verticillata)* grows as a low, spreading compact mound. It bears a profusion of pale yellow daisies and blooms for months on end. 'Zagreb' (pictured in the color insert) is more upright and has stronger yellow flowers. Both prefer good garden soil. 'Moonbeam' is reportedly drought tolerant, but Colorado tests its endurance. My plants require regular watering.

❀ **Summer daisies** *(Dendranthema):* Like The Artist Formerly Known as Prince, summer daisies used to be called chrysanthemums until the botanists needed something to do and got busy changing their names. To confuse things further, they don't really have a proper common name and are usually referred to by their variety names. The best known variety, 'Clara Curtis', is pink; 'Mary Stoker' has buff-colored daisies. (You can find photographs of both varieties in the color insert.) All varieties have grayish green, strongly aromatic foliage.

Touching the leaves can cause a skin rash in sensitive individuals.

Give summer daisies full sun in any soil except soggy. The fragrant flowers are great as cut flowers. Cut a few inches from the tips of each stem several times before midsummer to create more compact plants and later blooms. This plant grows in any climate but the very coldest; it's hardy to an average wintertime low of –30° F (–34° C).

My only complaint with summer daisies is that they spread like wildfire in fertile soil and need dividing annually to stop them from taking over the whole flower bed. But *tough* is an asset in some situations, and no chrysanthemum is tougher.

❀ **Purple coneflower** *(Echinacea purpurea):* Large, purplish pink daisies with bristly orange centers contradict the old adage that pink and orange always clash. Foliage is large, coarse, and dark green. Purple coneflower is a good cut flower, and butterflies find it irresistible. It blooms for a very long period, from early summer to frost. After the petals fall, the cone is attractive in dried arrangements.

Unaffected by heat and humidity or winter cold, these tough plants are very adaptable, and you can grow purple coneflowers successfully almost anywhere. They're hardy to an average winter low of –40° F (–40° C).

Don't fertilize the soil too much, or the plants may flop over and require staking. Grow them in any soil except wet and poorly drained. Although purple coneflower tolerates short periods of drought, it is happier with regular watering.

❀ **Queen-of-the-prairie** *(Filipendula rubra):* Masses of pink cotton candy plumes are an impressive sight when this regal perennial is in bloom. It's tall and sturdy, forming large clumps of dark green, jagged leaves. 'Elegans' is a white variety of *Filipendula purpurea.* 'Venusta' has deeper pink flowers than the original. This plant usually doesn't bloom until the second season after transplanting.

Queen-of-the-prairie requires moist, deep, rich soil that doesn't dry out. It persists through drought but becomes very sorry-looking and develops scorched leaf margins. Mine is fairly invasive, overtaking but not smothering everything in its path. Give it room to spread and divide it to limit its spread (see Chapter 19). Water and fertilize regularly. Place in full sun in cool climates and in afternoon shade in hot, humid regions. Queen-of-the-prairie is hardy to an average wintertime low of –40° F (–40° C).

❀ **Blanket flower** *(Gaillardia aristata):* In colors so loud they'll rattle your windows, blanket flowers bloom from spring to fall with concentric circles of red and yellow. But like most perennials that bloom for a very long season, blanket flowers tend to be short-lived. They strew their seeds around, but their progeny are usually quite changed in appearance from mom and dad. I replace dead plants each spring and am grateful when any of the previous season's crop survive the winter.

Handling the leaves of this plant may cause skin rashes in sensitive individuals, so wear gloves as a precaution.

Blanket flowers grow anywhere — even on sand dunes in Florida. They are cold-hardy practically to the Canadian tundra (withstanding wintertime lows of –50° F [–46° C]) and appear everywhere in between. In addition, this plant is completely drought tolerant in any climate. Plant blanket flowers in any well-drained soil in full sun — it blooms the first year from seed.

❀ **Appleblossom grass** *(Gaura lindheimeri):* Appleblossom-like flowers dangle on long, willowy stems. The flowers are white with shrimp-pink anthers, lower petals, and stems — from a distance, the overall effect is a pink cloud.

Increasingly popular, this delicate and airy plant has a really rugged constitution. Appleblossom grass is hardier than anyone first suspected, surviving temperatures well below 0° F (–18° C) in well-drained soil and full sun or dappled shade. It's native to regions with plentiful rainfall but is also completely drought tolerant in the driest part of my xeric garden. When other desert natives wilt and dry up, appleblossom grass is still going strong. This plant also tolerates extreme heat and humidity.

❀ **Bloody cranesbill** *(Geranium sanguineum):* Very long-blooming and adaptable, bloody cranesbill grows in a loosely mounded form and sports attractive leaves that turn crimson in fall. The simple, open-faced flowers are a strident magenta, held several inches above the foliage. If magenta is too strong a color for your tastes, choose one of the softer varieties. 'Album' is white; *Geranium sanguineum striatum* (pictured in this book's color insert) is pale pink with dark veining.

Plant bloody cranesbill in any soil except the wettest. It can spread far too rapidly in fertile, moist soil and is generally better behaved when kept a little stressed. Thoroughly drought tolerant, bloody cranesbill is also successful in subtropical climates. Although it does grow in dry shade, it produces more blooms in a sunny location. Flowering is heaviest in the spring, but bloody cranesbill blooms sporadically throughout the summer. This plant is hardy to –30° F (–34° C).

A relative of bloody cranesbill, lilac geranium *(Geranium himalayense)* sports violet blue flowers and foliage that turns orange in autumn.

❀ **Transvaal daisy** *(Gerbera jamesonii):* Tender daisies grown as annuals outside their hardiness range, Transvaal daisies perform best in hot, humid regions where rainfall is high. They come in a rainbow of colors — white, cream, yellows, apricot, orange, pink, and red — in single and double forms. Each flower is held singly on a strong stem, poised elegantly above low foliage rosettes.

Buy the small seedling size for transplanting into the garden. The large, lush florists' pots don't have a good survival rate.

Transvaal daisies like plenty of water and well-drained soil. Plant in sandy soil well-amended with humus or in raised beds. Let the soil dry out briefly between waterings. This plant may die to ground when temperatures dip below freezing, but it usually returns in spring. Average wintertime lows down to 10° F (–12° C) are acceptable.

❀ **Common sneezeweed** *(Helenium autumnale):* Featuring pretty daisies on upright tidy plants, common sneezeweed is also tough and adaptable. It starts blooming during the midsummer slump when most of the garden is taking a siesta. The flowers resemble badminton shuttlecocks with a raised center knob and a frill of notched petals. 'Butterpat' is a clear yellow. 'Moerheim Beauty' is mahogany red with burgundy centers, and it fades to gold as the flowers age.

Although adaptable to most climates and soils, common sneezeweed may need support to stay upright in rich soils and light shade. It tolerates wet soils and heavy clay. *Pinch* in spring, removing the top few inches of each stem to create a bushier plant and delay blooming. Cut the stems back to within a few inches of the ground after flowering wanes. Divide every two to three years to renew vigor (see Chapter 19). Common sneezeweed is hardy to −40° F (−40° C).

❀ **Daylily** *(Hemerocallis* hybrids): The daylily's dazzling trumpets are open for only one day, but are indispensable for the midsummer garden. Daylilies send up new flowers every day for two to three weeks. Hundreds of varieties are available, from pale yellow and orange to red, pink, and purple. All but the deep reds and purples have sherbety undertones. Size is variable, from 12-inch (30-cm) tall miniatures to 4-foot (1.2-m) tall giants, and everything in between. The foliage is green and grasslike, and the flowers are sometimes fragrant.

Most varieties prefer full sun, but reds and purples fade less if they have afternoon shade in hot regions. Give daylilies rich, fertile soil and plenty of water. They happily grow in soggy soils in cold climates. In hot, humid regions, too much water promotes diseases.

Daylilies face the sun, so always place them where you can see their faces. Pick evergreen types for hot, humid, warm-winter climates. Where winters are severe, choose dormant varieties. Check with local daylily societies for the best selections for your area.

❀ **Shasta daisy** *(Leucanthemum maximum):* An indispensable old-fashioned favorite, Shasta daisies are impressive, large white daisies with golden yellow centers. Many forms are available, from simple, rather formal daisies to shaggy doubles. 'Alaska' is the hardiest selection, 'Cobham Gold' is creamy yellow, and 'Alaya' is heavily fringed. (See the photo section of this book for a picture of 'Shasta Snow'.)

Grow this plant in fertile, well-drained soil. It needs regular water during the growing season but is intolerant of winter wet. Tall varieties flop over if they aren't staked. Cut stems back to within a few inches of the ground when blooming stops. Divide annually in hot, humid climates (see Chapter 19) and pinch stems early in the season to create a bushier plant. Shasta daisy is hardy to −40° F (−40° C).

❀ **Gayfeather** *(Liatris spicata):* This plant is a real attention-grabber when in bloom. It looks like a bouquet of rosy purple exclamation points. Each individual flower is tiny, but the flowers are densely clustered on upright spikes. The foliage is dark green and grassy. Gayfeather flowers are good for cutting and attract butterflies. White forms are also available. 'Kobold' is shorter than the regular gayfeather.

Gayfeather has tuberous roots that don't mind being treated like bulbs and shipped through the mail. They're a real bargain purchased this way — you can buy several for the price of one potted plant.

Plant gayfeather in any well-drained soil — it prefers ample moisture in the growing season but doesn't tolerate winter wet. Cut spikes to the ground when they're finished flowering to promote additional blooming. The plant withstands occasional periods of drought and is hardy to −40° F (−40° C).

❀ **Sea lavender** *(Limonium latifolium):* You wouldn't guess what a tough constitution this plant has by looking at it. A delicate haze of tiny lavender flowers fills the air above substantial, dark green foliage. The flowers dry on their stems and hold up almost indefinitely. Sea lavender is a florist's favorite, cut or dried. Leave some stems uncut for winter interest.

Sea lavender is undaunted by salty soils or salt spray. It grows in any soil in cool climates but must have fast draining soil where it's hot and humid, or it may succumb to crown rot. It's equally happy with regular water or very little. Full sun is best in cold climates; afternoon shade is better in hot, humid regions. Cut it to the ground in spring. This plant is hardy to −40° F (−40° C).

❀ **Lupine** *(Lupinus* hybrids): Reliable and easy in cool climates, lupine is unfortunately finicky elsewhere. This perennial comes in a wide array of colors — white, yellow, orange, red, blue, lavender, purple, pink, and two-tones. The substantial flower stalks are 1 to 2 feet (30 to 60 cm) tall over bushy clumps of dark green palm-shaped leaves. It blooms for eight to ten weeks if you cut the spent flower stalks back to the basal rosette.

Eating any part of a lupine plant can cause vomiting, irritation of the mouth and throat, and abdominal discomfort.

Although lupines are utterly intolerant of heat, whether humid or dry, they are definitely worth growing as an annual in hot, humid, mild-winter climates. Plant in late fall for spring blooms. Lupines in my garden are occasionally spectacular, and a real disappointment other years. The successful years are worth the wait. Give them well-drained, moist soil that you've amended with plenty of humus. Lupines are hardy to −30° F (−34° C).

❀ **Maltese cross** *(Lychnis chalcedonica):* An old-fashioned cottage garden favorite, Maltese cross has brilliant scarlet flowerheads. The individual flowers are cross-shaped and carried in rounded clusters at the top of tall, stately stems. It's easy to grow but is usually short-lived. Maltese cross scatters its seeds around, and some of the seeds do grow into new plants. White, pink, and salmon forms are also available.

Give Maltese cross any well-drained soil in full sun. The lower leaves may become brown during dry spells. Hide these "bare legs" behind other flowers. Deadhead routinely to promote continuous blooming and divide clumps every two to three years to maintain vigor. This plant may become a nuisance if all the flowerheads are allowed to set seed. Maltese cross is hardy to −40° F (−40° C).

❀ **Monkey flower** (*Mimulus* hybrids): Often grown as annuals in cold climates, these showy flowers come in a wide variety of colors — cream, yellow, gold, red, orange, and burgundy — sometimes with contrasting freckles and dark blotches. They are good choices for mild-winter climates. The dry varieties must have well-drained soil and occasional watering during the summer months.

Water requirements vary greatly by variety, but most are happiest in really wet, even swampy conditions. This trait makes them the perfect choice for wet, humid regions. Most are hardy to 0° F (–18° C).

❀ **Bee balm** *(Monarda didyma):* Available in varieties of pink, white, blue, violet, purple, and scarlet, bee balm's flowers look something like raggedy, mop-head daisies. All parts of the plant are deliciously aromatic, with a scent reminiscent of Earl Grey tea. The green foliage is mintlike, slightly toothed, narrow, and pointed. Clumps can spread invasively, but the runners are shallow and easy to pull out. (Look in the color section of this book for a photograph of *Monarda* 'Cambridge Scarlet' bee balm.)

Bee balm prefers cool climates and is not a good choice for hot, muggy, or desert regions. (Bee balm can withstand wintertime lows as cold as –30° F [–34° C].) Give it regular, even moisture and rich soil. Spread a thick blanket of organic mulch beneath the plants to help maintain these conditions. Bee balm always comes down with powdery mildew late in the growing season. When the mildew becomes more than you can bear to look at, cut the plants down to the ground. They always recover and grow healthy new foliage for me.

❀ **Ozark sundrop** *(Oenothera macrocarpa):* The huge-but-delicate, clear yellow, four-petaled blossoms of Ozark sundrop appear to be twisted from tissue paper. They fairly glow in both harsh and soft light. The plant has a relaxed spreading form, red stems, and waxy, long, narrow leaves. It flowers for most of the summer. The four-winged papery seedpods are also interesting and are so huge that they don't appear to come from the same plant.

Give Ozark sundrop any well-drained soil. It may rot if its roots stay too wet, so let the soil dry out between waterings.

Ozark sundrop is drought tolerant with an occasional deep soaking, but it doesn't like heat combined with humidity. The blooms continue without regular deadheading, making it a good plant for the lazy gardener. Cut it back to the ground annually in winter, and this plant asks for nothing more. It's hardy to –30° F (–34° C).

❀ **African daisy** *(Osteospermum barberae):* These are rugged plants. The flowers are lavender with pink and blue shadings and dark blue centers. They bloom fall through spring and on and off throughout the summer in coastal or Mediterranean climates. The flowers close on cloudy days. 'Compactum' is a newly introduced form that should significantly extend the hardiness range to at least –20° F (–29° C).

African daisies prefer good garden loam and regular watering, but they can also grow in poor soil and withstand drought after they're well-established. Pinch back the tips several times a season to create fuller, bushier plants. Cut back the stems by half if the plants become over-grown and floppy. These make good container plants outside of their hardiness range, which is to 20° F (–7° C).

❀ **Common beardtongue** *(Penstemon barbatus):* With scarlet tubular flowers on tall, graceful spikes over basal rosettes of shiny green, lance-shaped leaves, common beardtongue is a true hummingbird magnet. The tiny birds come from miles away when these flowers are in bloom. The seedheads are stiff, reddish brown teardrops and are attractive in winter or cut for dried arrangements.

As a rule, penstemons don't like hot, humid weather. But common beardtongue and its hybrids are more tolerant of a wider range of conditions than most penstemon kin. All penstemons are short-lived, even in the best of circumstances, but common beardtongue persists for three to five years in my garden. Full sun is best. Give it well-drained soil, sand, or gravel in wet climates. You can grow this plant in clay if you don't overwater it. It's hardy to –50° F (–46° C).

A cousin of common beardtongue, Parry's penstemon *(Penstemon parryi)* is a Sonoran desert native with pink flowers on 2- to 3-foot (60- to 90-cm) stalks. It likes drought and heat but not humidity and is hardy to 0° F (–18° C).

❀ **Wild sweet William** *(Phlox carolina):* Not as well-known as its cousin, garden phlox, wild sweet William phlox (or spotted phlox) is more adaptable and mildew-resistant. It produces plump clusters of delicate, five-petaled blooms for many weeks. Strong, upright stems support whorls of glossy, narrow leaves. 'Alpha' is rose with a dark eye. 'Miss Lingard' is clear white. Among the hybrids, 'Alpha' is rose with a dark eye, and 'Omega' is palest pink with a violet eye. All are highly fragrant and make good cut flowers.

Plant wild sweet William in well-drained, moist, humus-amended soil. Spotted phlox is the best tall phlox for hot, humid climates, but it's also very cold-hardy. Deadhead finished flowers for reblooming (see Chapter 17) and fertilize and water regularly. Seedlings that pop up here and there usually revert to the mauve pink of the unimproved form. Phlox likes afternoon shade in hot, dry climates and full sun elsewhere. It's hardy to –40° F (–40° C).

A relative of wild sweet William, woodland phlox *(Phlox divaricata)* is a lovely trailing plant for woodland sites. It comes in pale blue, white, purple, and blue varieties, some with a dark eye. Space these fragrant plants to allow for air circulation and — to help prevent the growth of mildew — don't water the foliage. I just ignore the mildew and cut the plants to the ground when the mildew gets too unsightly (see Chapter 18).

❀ **Obedient plant** *(Physostegia virginiana):* As its name implies, obedient plant is generally easy to grow — although I have killed a few by letting them get too dry. When it's happy, obedient plant forms expanding colonies of upright stems and lance-shaped fresh green leaves. Its tubular flowers are tightly arranged in rows at sharp right angles to one another. 'Vivid' is a dwarf deep pink. 'Summer Snow' is white. 'Variegata' is pink with white leaf margins.

Obedient plant can spread very quickly in rich soil, so you may need to divide it annually to control its expansion (see Chapter 18). Most sources recommend acidic soil, but my plants are perfectly fine in highly alkaline clay. Fertilize and water it regularly. Drier soil is acceptable with afternoon shade. The blooms persist for several weeks and are an outstanding cut flower. The seedheads are attractive in winter. Obedient plant is hardy to –40° F (–40° C).

❀ **Strawberry cinquefoil** *(Potentilla nepalensis* 'Miss Willmott'): The dark green, heavily textured, five-part leaflets of strawberry cinquefoil are arranged in a casually sprawling form. Cheerful pink flowers with dark centers are borne in loose clusters at the ends of arching stems for most of the summer. Strawberry cinquefoil likes cool nights and dislikes heat combined with humidity. The name *strawberry cinquefoil* refers to the strawberry-like foliage.

Cut back leggy stems by half to keep the plant compact. This plant needs well-drained but not overly fertile soil, so let it dry out between waterings. Strawberry cinquefoil is intolerant of wet soil in winter and may be short-lived. In really hot climates, provide afternoon shade. It's hardy to –20° F (–29° C).

❀ **European pasque flower** *(Pulsatilla vulgaris):* One of the first flowers to announce the arrival of spring, pasque flower often appears well before tulips and daffodils are up. Large, chalice-shaped purple blossoms open while the foliage is still furry little tufts. The leaves are soft, silky, and finely divided. The seedheads, which look like silvery feather dusters, are as charming as the flowers. Many colors are available.

Pasque flower may cause skin irritation and blistering, so use gloves when handling it. This plant may also cause nausea, vomiting, and diarrhea if you eat it.

Plant pasque flower in well-drained soil in full sun in cool climates but in partial shade where summers are hot and dry. It needs regular water in the spring. The plant goes dormant and its leaves disappear in midsummer. Where it's really happy, pasque flower provides abundant seedlings. Combine it with early bulbs for a show that continues right through late snowstorms. It's hardy to –30° F (–34° C).

❀ **Orange coneflower** *(Rudbeckia fulgida sullivantii):* Easy, cheerful, uncomplaining, and long-blooming from midsummer through the first frost, coneflowers grow happily almost anywhere. Their large golden daisies are accented with flat, dark brown center disks. Standing straight and upright, they form dense colonies 2 feet (60 cm) tall and feature handsome dark green foliage. *Rudbeckia fulgida* 'Goldstrum', pictured in the color section of this book, is a popular variety developed in Germany.

Orange coneflower is not particular about climate, soil, or moisture, but it performs best in fertile soil with ample moisture and full sun. Deadhead the spent blooms until late in the season and leave the last wave of flowers to dry on the stalks for winter interest. The flowers are good for cutting. If you grow them in partial shade, the plants lose their compact form and get a bit leggy. They're hardy to –40° F (–40° C).

A cousin of the orange coneflower, three-lobed coneflower *(Rudbeckia triloba)* is short-lived but self-sows with abandon, so its progeny pop up here and there. This is a big plant with masses of tiny, golden, black-eyed daisies. Hardy from the harsh winter to hot, humid climates, this plant grows in sun or partial shade and prefers some moisture.

✿ **Violet sage** *(Salvia nemorosa): Salvia* is a large family of garden perennials that are popular for their showy flowers, attractive and usually aromatic foliage, and ease of care. Violet sage is a very long-blooming hybrid with spikes of deep purple flowers and wrinkled, grayish green foliage. 'East Friesland' and 'May Might' are similar with dark violet blue flowers. 'Blue Hill' is true blue. 'Rose Queen' is pink and less vigorous than the blue varieties.

Sages like any well-drained soil. They aren't a good choice for hot, humid regions. Very drought tolerant, they require only an infrequent deep soaking to perform well. Moist, fertile soil can cause the stems to flop, so cut back spent flower spikes to keep the form compact and to encourage continued bloom. My plants flower for nearly six months. They are supposedly sterile, but plants in my garden self-sow like mad. Violet sage is hardy to –30° F (–34° C).

Violet sage has a number of cultivated cousins. Velvet sage *(Salvia leucantha)* has lavender and white flowers and woolly, aromatic foliage. It's hardy only to 20° F (–7° C) but is equally adapted to dry or humid heat. Azure sage *(Salvia azurea* 'Grandiflora'*)* has tall, willowlike stems and deep blue flowers in autumn. It tolerates dry or humid heat. Cold-hardy to –20° F (–29° C), *Salvia verticillata* 'Purple Rain' is an outstanding new introduction with compact clumps of soft mauve flowers. It's very long-blooming and hardy in my Colorado garden to –15° F (–26° C) so far. (Both 'Purple Rain' sage and velvet sage are pictured in the color pages of this book.)

✿ **Pincushion flower** *(Scabiosa caucasica):* The handful of perennials with pincushion-style blossoms are especially valuable for the contrast they provide against other, more familiar flower shapes. With pincushion flowers, a fluffy center tuft is surrounded by a lacy, ruffled row of petals. The flowerheads are held gracefully on long stems and come in many shades of blue, lavender, pink, and white. The leaves are long, narrow, and pointed.

Pincushion flowers are easy to grow in well-drained, fertile soil with regular watering. They prefer alkaline conditions and benefit from added lime where soil pH is low (see Chapter 11). The plants bloom for months if you regularly deadheaded them (see Chapter 17). They prefer climates with cool summer nights. Winter wet can be fatal; use a loose winter mulch to protect crowns in really cold regions. These flowers are hardy to −50° F (−46° C).

A relative of *Scabiosa caucasica*, *Scabiosa columbaria* 'Butterfly Blue' and 'Pink Mist' are dwarf plants that bloom all summer and attract butterflies (look for *Scabiosa columbaria* in the color section of this book). *Scabiosa ochroleuca* has the softest butter-yellow flowers and is extremely vigorous and drought tolerant.

❀ **Goldenrod** (*Solidago rugosa* 'Fireworks'): The attention-grabbing, golden yellow starburst flowers of goldenrod look very much like exploding sky rockets. The individual flowers are small, but their numbers make up for their size, forming graceful plumes over compact clumps of red-tinged foliage (see color pages for a photo). The flowers are good for cutting or drying and are attractive to butterflies. They bloom for several weeks. In spite of the rumors you may have heard, goldenrod does *not* cause hay fever.

Dwarf goldenrod (*Solidago glomerata* 'Golden Baby') is 2 to 2¹/₂ feet (60 to 75 cm) tall, golden yellow, and quite drought tolerant. Look for a photo of this little bruiser in the color section of this book.

Goldenrod is native to the southeastern U.S. and appreciates an open site with fairly fertile soil and plenty of moisture. It slowly expands into a good-sized clump. You can leave the flowers to dry on the plant late in the season for fall texture — cut them off after snow has smashed down the stems. Goldenrod is hardy to −30° F (−34° C).

❀ **Lamb's ears** (*Stachys byzantina*): Lamb's ears is everyone's favorite silver-foliage perennial. The leaves are as soft as flannel and invite touching. In fact, few people can resist feeling the lamb's ears. The plant grows in loose rosettes that expand outward into mats. The flower stalks are as heavily felted as the leaves. The flowers, a delicate purplish pink, are a good choice for cut flowers — fresh or dried. 'Silver Carpet' is a non-flowering variety for those who don't want the flower.

Lamb's ears likes any fairly well-drained soil, moist or dry, but may rot in hot, humid climates. 'Helen von Stein' is a large-leafed form that is less likely to melt down. These plants are hardy to −30° F (−34° C).

If the plants die out in the center, dig up the whole mat and replant a few pieces. It spreads quickly and can be a bit of a nuisance, but (I think) a pleasant one. I'm always digging up plants that are busily consuming paths and putting them back where I want them to be.

❀ **Stokes' aster** (*Stokesia laevis*): Though it breaks my heart, I just can't seem to please these lovely flowers. They grow just fine for other local gardeners, but appear to have thirst and good drainage requirements that I can't easily accommodate. The starry flowerheads resemble huge pink, blue, or white shaggy dandelions over narrow, long, dark green leaves. Butterflies love them, and they're a good cut flower.

Stokes' asters demand well-drained soil, especially in winter. Otherwise, they're not fussy about soils. Water them regularly. They bloom most of the summer if the spent flowers are routinely deadheaded. They are especially successful in hot, humid climates. In cold climates, cover the plants with a thick, loose mulch to protect the crowns over the winter. They're hardy to –20° F (–29° C).

❀ **Rose verbena** *(Verbena canadensis):* A vigorous and freely-blooming plant, rose verbena forms relaxed, spreading clumps. Its stems root wherever they touch the ground. The bright pink flowers form rounded clusters that last all summer; the foliage is crisp and evergreen. Many color variations exist — you can find lilac, red, white, and rose. 'Homestead Purple' is an outstanding bright purple.

Rose verbena's winter hardiness is variable, and not one variety has ever survived a winter in my Colorado garden. But I replant it every year, give it a winter mulch, and cross my fingers. Plant it in any well-drained soil; rose verbena rots if it's kept too wet, but it's quite drought tolerant. Cut the stems in half if they get too tall and leggy. This plant attracts butterflies and is hardy to –20° F (–29° C).

❀ **Spiked speedwell** *(Veronica spicata):* Hard to beat for late summer color, speedwell comes into its own when most of the perennial garden is having a heat-induced snooze. For nearly two months, speedwell produces dense spires of deep blue flowers over tight mats of shiny green or soft gray leaves, depending on variety. 'Minuet' is pink with silvery foliage. 'Blue Charm', pictured in the color section of this book, is a good lavender blue. 'Red Fox' is dark rose.

Speedwell likes any well-drained soil with regular waterings. Poor drainage combined with hot, humid weather is a certain killer. To keep the plants compact, don't over-fertilize. Its clumps increase slowly, never invasively. 'Goodness Grows' tolerates hot, humid climates better than most. Remove the spent flowers for continued blossoming. Speedwell are hardy to –30° F (–34° C).

❀ **Prairie zinnia** *(Zinnia grandiflora):* Most folks know the popular annual zinnias, but gardeners in arid regions have become better acquainted with a charming little wildflower cousin, the prairie zinnia, which brings a splash of bright yellow to the dry-climate garden. Low mounds of tiny, narrow foliage spread to create solid colonies. The flowers are golden yellow, sometimes with red centers, and dry to a papery texture.

Prairie zinnia can be difficult to transplant. You must water it whenever the soil dries out until the plants are growing strongly. Give it well-drained, infertile soil in arid and semiarid regions. Individual plants are long-lived and slow to spread. Prairie zinnia can survive on desert rainfall, but the plants grow more strongly with a good soaking once or twice a month. Late to break dormancy in spring, prairie zinnia is hardy to –30° F (–34° C).

Chapter 8

Made for Shade

*I*f you garden in shade, you may be disappointed on your first trip to your local garden center to find that the number of shade-loving plants is considerably smaller than the selection of perennials for sunny gardens. The list in this chapter reflects this reality as well. But don't despair. Take a closer look, and you discover that most of the sun-loving flowers I list in Chapter 7 can also handle at least partial or dappled shade. These plants may not flower as freely in the shade as they would in full sunlight, but the large majority of them can cope with some shade.

If you're dealing with extremes — for example, very dense shade with either soggy wet or very dry soils — the number of adapted perennials you can choose from is quite limited. If at all possible, give serious thought to moving your flower bed to a more suitable place. Alternatively, you may choose to thin out a few trees to bring in more light or to install drainage tiles or a watering system. If none of these solutions appeals to you, just enjoy the selection of perennials that *can* tolerate such extremes — and be sure to give them lots of encouragement and praise for their adaptability.

Making Perennials at Home in the Shade

A recurring theme among shade-loving perennials is a woodland origin. Most perennials that do well in the shade appreciate the typical conditions found in the forest.

- ✔ Give them a loose, porous soil, deeply dug, with plenty of added humus to get them off to a strong start. (See Chapter 11 for more on soils.)

- ✔ After planting, re-create the leaf litter found on the forest floor by spreading 2 to 3 inches (5 to 8 cm) of a light, airy, organic mulch, such as pine needles, between the plants. (Turn to Chapter 13 for tips on mulch.)

- ✔ When experimenting with flowers that normally fancy more abundant sunlight, give each plant plenty of elbow room so that it can take full advantage of whatever light reaches it. Spacing plants more widely in shade also creates better air circulation, which helps prevent foliage diseases.

You can easily measure whether a particular perennial is adapting to its shady environment by watching its performance. When a flower fails to bloom or starts to look pretty darn pathetic — with anemic, yellowing leaves on spindly, weak, and sprawling stems — it's time to admit defeat. Put the poor thing up for adoption to a sunnier home and try another plant.

On the other hand, when a shade plant is getting too much sunlight, it also lets you know that it's unhappy. The leaves generally bleach out and become papery thin, or they may actually sunburn and develop scorched patches and brown margins. Plants are every bit as efficient at showing their displeasure as my pet spaniel — after you learn to read their signals.

Planning a Flower Bed in the Shade

Designing a shade garden is no more complicated than designing any other flower bed. (See Chapter 3 for tips on planning your flower bed.) As always, the key to successful gardening is choosing plants that are compatible with your site or modifying the site enough to accommodate the flowers that you're bound and determined to grow.

For a shady location, you can either plant shade-lovers or cut down the trees that are blocking the sun. Planting shade-lovers is much less work. Besides, if the shade is cast by a structure, you don't have the second option — unless your neighbors agree to knock over their house or garage so that you can have a nice, sunny garden.

In some respects, designing for shade is simpler and more satisfying than designing for sun, because the focus on flowers is automatically diminished. Flower color is only one part of putting together an outstanding garden. Foliage shape, color, and texture are all equally essential elements. Shady perennials win hands-down over their sunny counterparts in this respect.

Where light is low, catching sunlight becomes more important than conserving moisture loss through evaporation. The result is plants (such as hostas and heart leaf bergenia) with massive leaves. Add a few ferns, and you certainly don't need to worry about texture.

If you close your eyes and imagine a forest glen, you probably picture lush green. But your woodland garden doesn't have to be endlessly green. You can add extra sparkle by choosing varied foliage colors. Green hostas are pretty, but you can also select varieties with leaves of golden, glowing yellow, and elegant blue. Other varieties of hostas come in a seemingly limitless spectrum of two-tones with yellow, cream, or white markings. Play off the dull green of perennial forget-me-nots against the shine of heart-leaf bergenia. Throw in a splash of purple with some of the vibrant coral bells. Now that's a flower bed!

Getting More Blooms with Less Sun

To be fair, I must admit that the shaded garden doesn't flower as freely as the flower bed in full sun. Most of the perennials in this chapter bloom in spring and then are unobtrusive for the rest of the year.

To add flower appeal to your shady garden, leave space among the perennials for a few annuals to keep the flowering season going longer. Ageratums, browallias, fuchsias, tuberous begonias, coleus, impatiens, baby-blue-eyes, cinerarias, Canterbury bells, monkey flowers, flowering tobacco, and wishbone flowers all do well in shade. Where tree roots interfere with planting annuals, grow them in pots and set them beneath the tree. Or hang baskets of annuals from lower limbs for another splash of color.

Many bulbs have woodland ancestors and do well in the shade, giving you the opportunity to add more color. If your garden is shaded by deciduous trees and has unobstructed sunlight during the winter months, you can likely grow any of the early sun-loving spring bulbs such as tulips, daffodils, and crocuses. These flowers bloom before the trees don their spring leaves.

Other spring-blooming bulbs prefer some shade. Tuck any of these bulbs here and there in between the other flowers:

- ❀ Windflowers *(Anemone blanda)*
- ❀ Camass *(Camassia)*
- ❀ Glory-of-the-snow *(Chionodoxa)*
- ❀ Spanish bluebells *(Endymion hispanicus)*

✽ Winter aconites *(Eranthis hyemalis)*

✽ Dog-toothed violets *(Erythronium dens-canis)*

✽ Snowflakes *(Leucojum)*

✽ Grape hyacinths *(Muscari)*

✽ Squill *(Scilla)*

TIP

For additional summer foliage color, pop in a few fancy-leafed caladiums or coleus. They come in a huge number of bright — even flamboyant — colors. Although both caladiums and coleus have insignificant blossoms, their foliage is so extravagant that you probably won't miss the flowers.

Refer to Chapter 6 for detailed plans of a woodland garden and a garden surrounding a tree. The designs bring many of the plants listed in this chapter together into attractive shade gardens. Chapter 6 has additional information for gardening in shade, and Chapter 9 lists many other foliage plants for the shaded garden.

Perennials Made for the Shade

The following list is just a handful of the hundreds of true shade-loving perennials in circulation. Some of these plants absolutely *insist* on shade. Others don't mind direct sunlight in varying degrees, depending on your climate and light intensity. You can plant many of them in full sun if you live in a region where summers are generally cool and overcast.

Some of the plants in this chapter can grow in dappled, intermittent, or open shade with either a brief period of uninterrupted sunlight each day or plenty of bright light reflected from light-colored walls or sidewalks. When a plant is adapted to this kind of *partial shade,* I say so in the text. Other plants can adapt to a greater degree of shadow, and I point out this trait as well. Use these recommendations as guidelines, not hard and fast rules. You need to experiment a bit to discover what works in your garden. (Refer to Chapter 6 for information on different types of shade.)

PHOTO OP

✽ **Lady's mantle** *(Alchemilla mollis):* Lady's mantle is perfectly content in full sun in cloudy, overcast climates, but its leaves get badly scorched by intense sunlight. Called lady's mantle because each leaf resembles a pleated cape, this is a luxuriant plant with foliage every bit as attractive as the flowers. The flowers, a froth of chartreuse yellow, bloom from spring through most of the summer and are outstanding when cut. This plant can withstand average wintertime lows to –30° F (–34° C).

Lady's mantle thrives in woodland conditions with moist but not sopping wet soil. It's more tolerant of dry soil in shade than in sun. This plant can be quite invasive, spreading into large patches and also seeding some distance away. Remove spent flowers to slow down spreading. Lady's mantle does best in regions with cool overnight temperatures and can withstand extreme winter cold, but it isn't tolerant of heat combined with humidity in subtropical regions.

❀ **Japanese painted fern** (*Athyrium niponicum* 'Pictum'): Ferns are synonymous with shade. But if you automatically picture green foliage when you think ferns, this one comes as a complete surprise. The fronds are grayish green overlaid with silver. To add more complexity to this color combination, the mid-ribs are burgundy red. The foliage is heavily cut and filigreed for a delicate and graceful texture.

This fern is more rugged than its appearance suggests; it grows easily in well-drained, humus-enriched soil in either shade or partial shade. Early to emerge in spring, the Japanese painted fern goes dormant if you allow it to get too dry during the growing season. Protect and preserve moisture with several inches of light organic mulch. It sends up new fronds throughout the summer, but its deciduous fronds die back to the ground in winter. This plant is a good choice for any climate except subtropical — it's hardy to −40° F (−40° C).

❀ **Pigsqueak** (*Bergenia cordifolia*): You probably haven't heard the name *pigsqueak* unless you live in Colorado. This plant is usually called by its botanical name, *bergenia,* but pigsqueak is more memorable and certainly more descriptive. If you pinch a leaf in your moistened fingertips, you can produce a very pig-like squeal (and liven up those dull parties). Pigsqueak has large, thick, glossy leaves in open rosettes and pink flower spikes very early in the spring.

This plant's evergreen foliage turns red during wintertime in mild climates. In climates with colder winters, pigsqueak is deciduous — or ratty enough that you wish the foliage would take a winter vacation. Although pigsqueak tolerates a full sun position in cloudy, cool regions, it prefers shade everywhere else. Any soil is fine, but too much fertilizing makes this plant floppy. It's fairly drought tolerant in dry shade. Slugs can do a great deal of damage to this plant (see Chapter 18 for tips on dealing with these slimy critters). Pigsqueak is hardy to −40° F (−40° C).

❀ **Heartleaf brunnera** (*Brunnera macrophylla*): In early spring, dainty clusters of tiny blue forget-me-not flowers make their appearance above small, emerging leaves. The leaves quickly expand into their full size of 6 to 8 inches (15 to 20 cm) across. They are somewhat heart-shaped, rough to the touch, and heavily veined. 'Hadspen Cream' and 'Variegata' have creamy white leaf margins and must be sheltered from sun or wind to look their best.

This plant prefers moist, fertile woodland conditions. Heartleaf brunnera, also called *perennial forget-me-not,* needs cool nights. It withstands full sun in overcast climates and is somewhat drought tolerant in shade, especially in heavy clay soils. This plant self-sows but doesn't make a pest of itself. To preserve moisture and keep the soil cool, use several inches of an organic mulch around the plants. Protect it from slugs (see Chapter 18). This plant is intolerant of heat combined with humidity but can withstand wintertime lows to −40° F (−40° C).

* **Bleeding heart** (*Dicentra* hybrids): The hybrid bleeding hearts are unbeatable. They are the ideal perennial — blooming for six months, long-lived, adaptable, easy-care, and possessing beautiful foliage. Clusters of charming, locket-shaped flowers hang over deeply cut, ferny foliage. 'Luxuriant' is deep pink, 'Snowdrift' is white, and 'Bountiful' is rosy red. All are hardy to −40° F (−40° C).

All parts of bleeding hearts, if eaten, are toxic to both you and your pets. The roots contain the largest concentration of poison, so be especially careful when these plants are out of the ground.

Bleeding hearts can be placed in full sun in cool climates, but they prefer shade anywhere else. They want a humus-enriched, moisture-retentive but not wet soil. But because I don't have such a site, mine have to make do in heavy clay under a pine tree. They don't seem to object. The clumps expand slowly and are never invasive. This plant is not a good choice for hot, humid subtropical gardens.

* **Lenten rose** *(Helleborus orientalis):* If you don't already have a shady spot on your property, Lenten roses are enough of an incentive to plant a tree. Dramatic and elegant, they are among the first non-bulb flowers to bloom in the spring. The foliage is handsome, glossy, and evergreen except in the coldest winters. The flowers are open bells of cream to soft rose, often with purple freckles and a touch of the palest green.

Lenten roses are long-lived and easy to grow in any climate with wintertime lows above −30° F (−34° C). The clumps mature and increase very slowly, so buy large plants, or you may wait several years to see these lovely flowers for the first time. They like plenty of moisture and soil enriched with organic matter but also tolerate dry shade well in my garden. Some years the foliage and first flowers are zapped by cold temperatures. Cut them off, and the plants readily bounce back. Mulch plants heavily to preserve soil moisture.

* **Coral bells** *(Heuchera sanguinea):* Amazing things are being done to your grandmother's coral bells. They are currently undergoing extensive selection and hybridization. Every year a few more of these beauties hit the market.Varieties with attractive flowers come in shades of red, pink, coral, and white. The types chosen for outstanding foliage usually don't offer much in the flower department, but what an amazing array of leaf colors! Speckled and splashed, washed in silver, deep purples and subtle reds — each more fetching than the last.

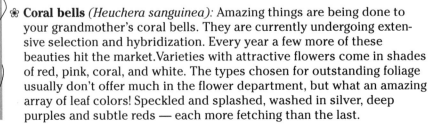

Plant coral bells in a woodland-type soil, fertilize with plenty of humus, and provide consistent moisture. Full sun works in cloudy climates, but not where sunlight is truly intense. This plant is intolerant of wet soil in winter, so provide good drainage. Use an organic mulch year round and cover with pine boughs or other lightweight winter protection in bitterly cold regions. The foliage is evergreen in mild climates.

Coral bells are best in cool climates (withstanding wintertime lows to −40° F [−40° C]) but are also quite comfortable in dry heat. Breeding for hot, humid climates is a current focus, so expect more of these coming soon.

❀ **Plantain lily** (*Hosta* hybrids): Another collector's plant, the plantain lily (also called *shade lily*) has hundreds of varieties to suit every taste. Tough and reliable, it's the ultimate shade perennial. Some forms have impressively immense foliage rosettes; other types are only a few inches tall. They come in every shade of green, steely blues, and translucent yellows; in solid colors; and every conceivable pattern of variegation in cream, white, or chartreuse. The purple or white flowers are often deliciously fragrant.

Plant the plantain lily in any soil, but it performs best with generous amounts of humus mixed in before planting. Although some varieties can withstand full sun (especially in cool, overcast regions), most scorch and burn when either exposed to strong sunlight or allowed to dry. These are late emergers in spring, so don't panic when they aren't up with the tulips. Protect them from slugs and snails unless you like the "cut-work" look. (Chapter 18 has advice on fending off unwanted plant munchers.) Plantain lilies are hardy to −40° F (−40° C).

❀ **Virginia bluebells** (*Mertensia virginica*): Wherever you grow hostas or ferns, you must throw in a few Virginia bluebells. They are easy-care, long-lived wildflowers that put up with neglect and mistreatment without complaint and are hardy to −40° F (−40° C). The leaves, green with purple tints, emerge in late winter or early spring. The flowers are nodding clusters of tubular bells, opening pink and aging to lavender blue.

Bluebells go dormant with the beginning of hot weather, so always place them where other perennials hide their death throes. After the yellowing foliage starts to brown, cut it off — the only care these low-maintenance flowers ever need. They do best in fertile, moist soil, especially in spring when they're just coming out of dormancy. The plants slowly spread to fill all the barren spaces in the shade garden.

❀ **Jacob's ladder** (*Polemonium caeruleum*): This plant features loose clusters of five-petaled, soft blue flowers on spikes above ladder-shaped leaflets. The blossoms are ornamented with prominent yellow stamens. Jacob's ladder is long-blooming, especially if faded flower spikes are removed. It's also available in a white form. 'Apricot Delight' is lavender with apricot centers. *Polemonium reptans* 'Blue Pearl' is bright blue.

Unfortunately, this plant is not adapted to hot, humid climates. Jacob's ladder is hardy to –50° F (–45° C), but if you live in a subtropical climate, this plant isn't a good choice for you. Where nights are cool and dry, it's dependable and easy to grow. My plants struggled for years until I moved them to a shaded spot to within a few feet of a rock wall base in heavy clay soil. They do well in full sun only in cooler, cloudy climates. For best results, water regularly.

❀ **Auricula primrose** *(Primula auricula):* Neat and tidy as a florist's nosegay, auricula primrose is also extremely cold-hardy and more drought-enduring more than most of its moisture-loving clan. The species is yellow, but just about every color imaginable has been developed from it.

The flowers often have contrasting eyes, and some have a coating of *farina* (a dense white fuzz), although they generally lose this coating when grown outdoors.

Place this plant in fertile, well-amended, humus-laden soil and provide consistent moisture throughout the growing season. This primrose grows in full sun in cool summer climates, but needs afternoon shade elsewhere. It's not well-adapted to hot, humid subtropical climates. In my garden, these primroses accept dry shade in heavy clay soil. Sometimes they die back in midsummer and I think that I've lost them, but they return in cooler fall weather. The foliage is evergreen to at least –20° F (-29° C), the plant is hardy to –50° F (–45° C).

❀ **Foam flower** *(Tiarella cordifolia):* A relative unknown, foam flower has suddenly become increasingly popular as hybridizers play around with leaf shape and color and flower color. The original plant has toothed, heart-shaped leaves with burgundy veining and attractive, bronze red fall color. The flowers are delicate and starry. New varieties feature deeply cut, ruffled, and brightly-colored foliage and fragrant pink, coral, or white flowers.

The foliage is evergreen in mild areas. These flowers are best in cool shade, but they can stand heat as long as they are kept well-watered. Amend the soil with plenty of organic matter and plant in partial to full shade. Use an organic mulch to keep the soil cool and moist. Water before the soil dries out completely. Although foam flower isn't adapted to the muggiest subtropical regions, it is fast-growing and quickly forms good-sized colonies elsewhere. Foam flower can withstand average wintertime lows of –40° F (–40° C).

Table 8-1 lists other shade-loving perennials that are worth a try in your garden.

If a picture's worth a
thousand words, then
the following pages of
photographs are saving
me from writing (and
you from reading) over
130,000 words! Look up
the perennial you want to
know more about — the following
flowers are arranged alphabetically
according to their botanical names
(see Chapter 1). Or browse through
the pages until you find a plant you
like — just remember that not every
kind of perennial can grow in every
kind of yard (see Chapter 4 for
climate recommendations).

Yarrow: *Achillea* 'Coronation Gold' (Chapter 7)

Monkshood: *Aconitum napellus* (Chapter 9)

African lily: *Agapanthus* hybrid (Chapter 4)

Bugleweed: *Ajuga reptans* 'Burgundy Glow', 'Silver Beauty', and 'Purple Torch' (Chapter 9)

Lady's mantle: *Alchemilla mollis* (Chapter 8)

Japanese windflower: *Anemone hupehensis* 'September Charm' (Chapter 7)

Columbine: *Aquilegia* 'McKana Giants' (Chapter 9)

Common thrift: *Armeria maritima* 'Dusseldorf Pride' (Chapter 7)

Goat's beard: *Aruncus dioicus* (Chapter 11)

Butterfly flower: *Asclepias tuberosa* (Chapter 7)

New England aster: *Aster novae-angliae* 'Purple Dome' (Chapter 7)

False spirea: *Astilbe* hybrids (Chapter 8)

Japanese painted fern: *Athyrium niponicum* 'Pictum' (Chapter 8)

Basket-of-gold: *Aurinia saxatilis* (Chapter 4)

Blue wild indigo: *Baptisia australis* (Chapter 4)

Heartleaf brunnera: *Brunnera macrophylla* (Chapter 8)

Fancy-leafed caladium: *Caladium bicolor* (Chapter 10)

Feather reed grass: *Calamagrostis acutiflora* 'Stricta' (Chapter 9)

Clustered bellflower: *Campanula glomerata* (Chapter 7)

Peachleaf bellflower: *Campanula persicifolia* (Chapter 7)

Canna lily: *Canna* hybrid (Chapter 10)

Red valerian: *Centranthus ruber* (Chapter 9)

Tickseed: *Coreopsis grandiflora* 'Sunray' (Chapter 7)

Threadleaf coreopsis: *Coreopsis verticillata* 'Zagreb' (Chapter 7)

Montbretia: *Crocosmia 'Lucifer'* (Chapter 10)

Delphinium: *Delphinium Pacific Giant Strain* (Chapter 4)

Summer daisy: *Dendranthema 'Clara Curtis'* (Chapter 7)

Summer daisy: *Dendranthema 'Mary Stoker'* (Chapter 7)

Bleeding heart: *Dicentra spectabilis* (Chapter 8)

Fortnight lily: *Dietes vegeta* (Chapter 10)

Yellow foxglove: *Digitalis grandiflora* (Chapter 5)

Purple coneflower: *Echinacea purpurea* (Chapter 7) and **Globe thistle:** *Echinops exaltatus* (Chapter 5)

Epimedium: *Epimedium versicolor* 'Sulphureum' (Chapter 8)

Sulfur flower: *Eriogonum umbellatum* (Chapter 4)

Joe-pye weed: *Eupatorium maculatum* 'Gateway' (Chapter 11)

Cushion spurge: *Euphorbia polychroma* (Chapter 23)

Blue fescue: *Festuca glauca* (Chapter 9) with **African lily:** *Agapanthus* (Chapter 4)

Queen-of-the-prairie: *Filipendula rubra* (Chapters 7)

Blanket flower: *Gaillardia* 'Kobold' (Chapter 7)

Appleblossom grass: *Gaura lindheimeri* (Chapter 7)

Gazania: *Gazania* hybrids (Chapter 4)

Lilac geranium: *Geranium himalayense* (Chapter 6)

Bloody cranesbill: *Geranium sanguineum striatum* (Chapter 7)

Baby's breath: *Gypsophila paniculata* (Chapter 9)

Blue oat grass: *Helictotrichon sempervirens* and **Coral bells:** *Heuchera* 'Palace Purple' (both in Chapter 9)

Sunflower heliopsis: *Heliopsis helianthoides* 'Summer Sun' (Chapter 23)

Lenten rose: *Helleborus orientalis* (Chapter 8)

Lemon daylily: *Hemerocallis lilioasphodelus* (Chapter 7)

Daylily: *Hemerocallis* hybrids (Chapter 7)

Coral bells: *Heuchera sanguinea* (Chapter 8)

Coral bells: *Heuchera* 'Pewter Veil' (Chapter 9)

Rose mallow: *Hibiscus moscheutos* 'Disco Red' (Chapter 4)

Plantain lilies: *Hosta* 'Francee', 'Krossa Regal', 'Sum & Substance', 'Francis Williams' (Chapter 8)

'Spreckles' bearded iris: *Iris* 'Spreckles' (Chapter 5)

Red-hot poker: *Kniphofia uvaria* (Chapter 4)

Yellow archangel: *Lamiastrum galeobdolen* 'Herman's Pride' (Chapter 9)

Spotted dead nettle: *Lamium maculatum* 'Beacon Silver' (Chapter 9)

English lavender: *Lavandula angustifolia* (Chapter 9)

French lavender: *Lavandula dentata* (Chapter 4)

Tree mallow: *Lavatera thuringiaca* (Chapter 9)

Shasta daisy: *Leucanthemum maximum* 'Shasta Snow' (Chapter 7)

Gayfeather: *Liatris spicata* (Chapter 7)

Lily: *Lilium* 'Black Dragon' and 'Gold Eagle' (Chapter 10)

Lily: *Lilium* 'Star Gazer' (Chapter 10)

Sea lavender: *Limonium latifolium* (Chapter 7)

Golden flax: *Linum flavum* 'Cloth of Gold' (Chapter 5)

Blue flax: *Linum perenne* (Chapter 4)

Cardinal flower: *Lobelia cardinalis* (Chapter 9)

Lupine: *Lupinus* hybrid (Chapter 7)

Maltese cross: *Lychnis chalcedonica* (Chapter 7)

Rose campion: *Lychnis coronaria* (Chapter 9)

Plume poppy: *Macleaya cordata* (Chapter 9)

Virginia bluebells: *Mertensia virginica* (Chapter 8)

Maiden grass: *Miscanthus sinensis* 'Morning Light' (Chapter 9)

Bee balm: *Monarda* 'Cambridge Scarlet' (Chapter 7)

Maiden grass: *Miscanthus sinensis* (Chapter 9)

Daffodil: *Narcissus* hybrids (Chapter 10)

Catmint: *Nepeta faassenii* (Chapter 6)

Mexican evening primrose: *Oenothera berlandieri* (Chapter 7)

Golden oregano: *Origanum vulgare* 'Aureum' (Chapter 23)

Peony: *Paeonia* 'Legion of Honor' (Chapter 23)

Switch grass: *Panicum virgatum* 'Heavy Metal' (Chapter 9)

Oriental poppy: *Papaver orientale* (Chapter 23)

Purple fountain grass: *Pennisetum setaceum* 'Rubrum' (Chapter 9)

Parry's penstemon: *Penstemon parryi* (Chapter 7)

Pineleaf penstemon: *Penstemon pinifolius* (Chapter 7)

Russian sage: *Perovskia atriplicifolia* (Chapter 9)

Sticky Jerusalem sage: *Phlomis russeliana* (Chapter 9)

White woodland phlox: *Phlox divaricata alba* (Chapter 7)

Woodland phlox: *Phlox divaricata* (Chapter 7)

New Zealand flax: *Phormium tenax* 'Sundowner' (Chapter 9)

Obedient plant: *Physostegia virginiana* (Chapter 7)

Balloon flower: *Platycodon grandiflorus* (Chapter 23)

Solomon's seal: *Polygonatum odoratum* (Chapter 8)

English primrose: *Primula vulgaris* (Chapter 8)

Bethlehem sage: *Pulmonaria saccharata* 'Mrs. Moon' (Chapter 9)

European pasque flower: *Pulsatilla vulgaris* (Chapter 7)

Matilija poppy: *Romneya coulteri* (Chapter 4)

Orange coneflower: *Rudbeckia fulgida* 'Goldstrum' (Chapter 7)

Three-lobed coneflower: *Rudbeckia triloba* (Chapter 7)

Silver sage: *Salvia argentea* (Chapter 9)

Autumn sage: *Salvia greggii* (Chapter 10)

Velvet sage: *Salvia leucantha* (Chapter 7)

Golden common sage: *Salvia officinalis* 'Icterina' (Chapter 9)

'Purple Rain' sage: *Salvia verticillata* 'Purple Rain' (Chapter 7)

Lavender cotton: *Santolina chamaecyparissus* (Chapter 9)

Pincushion flower: *Scabiosa columbaria* 'Butterfly Blue' (Chapter 7)

'Autumn Joy' sedum: *Sedum telephium* 'Autumn Joy' (Chapter 9)

Checker-bloom: *Sidalcea malviflora* (Chapter 23)

Goldenrod: *Solidago glomerata* 'Golden Baby' (Chapter 7)

Lamb's ears: *Stachys byzantina* (Chapter 7)

Stokes' aster: *Stokesia laevis* (Chapter 7)

Feverfew: *Tanacetum parthenium* (Chapter 9)

Columbine meadowrue: *Thalictrum aquilegefolium* (Chapter 5)

Thyme (several kinds): *Thymus* (Chapter 9)

Foam flower: *Tiarella cordifolia* (Chapter 8)

Spiderwort: *Tradescantia* 'Innocence' (Chapter 8)

Mullein: *Verbascum chaixii* (Chapter 9)

Rose verbena: *Verbena canadensis* (Chapter 7)

Spiked speedwell: *Veronica spicata* 'Blue Charm' (Chapter 7)

Culver's root: *Veronicastrum virginicum* (Chapter 9)

California fuchsia: *Zauschneria californica* (Chapter 4)

Prairie zinnia: *Zinnia grandiflora* (Chapter 7)

Although looking at individual perennials can be useful in planning your garden, complete flower beds give you a better idea of the impact you can achieve by varying color, texture, and height. When choosing various perennials for your garden, select flowers that bloom during different seasons to maintain an attractive flower bed year-round. Be sure to pick a combination of plants that have similar climate, sun, and soil requirements.

Under a deciduous tree: Colors and textures of spring at the Missouri Botanical Garden include *Hosta*, leaves of plume poppy, and late-blooming red tulips. The blue flowers are Spanish hyacinths. See the plan for this garden in Chapter 6.

Soft and subtle: Purple coneflower *(Echinacea purpurea)* is accented in shape and color by ball-like blue globe thistle *(Echinops exaltatus).* See the plan for this garden in Chapter 5.

Sunny-side up: Hot yellows and golds of tickseed (*Coreopsis grandiflora* 'Early Sunrise'), gloriosa daisy
(*Rudbeckia*), and blanket flower (*Gaillardia aristata*) combine here to make a river of daisies.
See this garden plan in Chapter 5.

Raised bed with perennials of varying heights: 'Husker's Red' beardtongue (*Penstemon digitalis* 'Husker Red') — Chapter 4 — with Delphinium — Chapter 9. Chapter 12 discusses raised beds, and Chapter 2 explains the importance of choosing perennials of varying heights.

Backyard beauty: Flowering Jerusalem sage, *Phlomis fruticosa,* adds the informal appeal of shrubbery to this backyard garden. Chapter 10 suggests other shrubs you can use to accent your perennial flower bed.

Cottage garden: This cottage garden features easy-to-care-for English lavender. See Chapter 9 for a full plant description.

Sunny summer blooms: Yarrow (*Achillea millifolium 'Paprika'*) and lady's mantle (*Alchemilla mollis*) both bloom in midsummer. See Chapters 7 and 8, respectively.

A touch of grass: Blue oat grass, *Helictotrichon sempervirens*, adds texture as well as color to this perennial garden. See Chapter 9 for more about this and other grassy additions for your flower bed.

Table 8-1	More Perennials for Shade			
Common Name	*Botanical Name*	*Flower Color*	*Season*	*Low Temp.*
Common bear's breeches	*Acanthus mollis*	White, purple	Spring	−20° F (−29° C)
European wild ginger	*Asarum europaeum*	Brown	Spring	−30° F (−34° C)
False spirea	*Astilbe arendsii*	Assorted	Spring to summer	−30° F (−34° C)
Great masterwort	*Astrantia major*	White, pink	Summer	−30° F (−34° C)
'Blue Panda' corydalis	*Corydalis flexuosa* 'Blue Panda'	Blue	Spring	−20° F (−29° C)
Bleeding heart	*Dicentra spectabilis*	Pink, white	Spring	−50° F (−45° C)
Leopard's bane	*Doronicum columnae*	Yellow	Spring	−30° F (−34° C)
Autumn fern	*Dryopteris erythrosora*	No flowers	n/a	−30° F (−34° C)
Longspur barrenwort	*Epimedium grandiflorum*	Pink	Spring	−20° F (−29° C)
Epimedium	*Epimedium versicolor* 'Sulphureum'	Yellow	Spring	−20° F (−29° C)
Cardinal flower	*Lobelia cardinalis*	Red	Summer	−50° F (−45° C)
Woodland forget-me-not	*Myosotis sylvatica*	Blue	Spring	−40° F (−40° C)
Cinnamon fern	*Osmunda cinnamomea*	No flowers	n/a	−50° F (−45° C)
Fragrant Solomon's seal	*Polygonatum odoratum*	White	Spring	−40° F (−40° C)
English primrose	*Primula vulgaris*	Assorted	Spring	−20° F (−29° C)
Common spiderwort	*Tradescantia virginiana*	Blue, pink, white	Spring to summer	−20° F (−29° C)

Chapter 9
Foliage Follies

*W*hen most folks picture a flower garden, they think of flowers — naturally enough. In a typical parking-lot display of annuals, flower color is all you get. Who can recall what the foliage of any of these blobs of color looks like in such a flower bed? But, perhaps in self-defense, the perennial garden takes another slant. Because perennials generally bloom for only a few weeks at a stretch, foliage is all you have to look at for the rest of the growing season.

If you remember the 1960's terrarium craze, you know how pretty a garden composed completely of foliage can be. Many gardeners expand the terrarium idea into a larger scale, intermingling diverse foliage sizes, colors, and textures into a satisfying weave.

A garden of flowers and no foliage is not a pleasant thought. Imagine a musical score consisting only of the melody. When you add harmony, you get a rich blend of tones. Leaves can be the bass notes, the accents, or the whole supporting orchestra behind the soloist flowers. The perennials in this chapter give you beautiful flowers *and* better than average foliage — you get the best of both worlds.

The Grass Menagerie

Flowers and grass are natural partners, occurring together wherever ample sunlight is available — in fields, meadows, and prairies. No other foliage plant surpasses grasses for the texture and beauty they bring to the flower garden. Still, if you've ever battled either weedy grasses or lawn grasses growing where they aren't wanted, you may question the sanity of intentionally introducing grass into the flower bed.

Granted, a few of the ornamental grasses are every bit as tenacious and aggressive as crabgrass or quackgrass. These invasive grasses do have landscape applications for extremely difficult sites, and you can use them as ground covers for interesting alternatives to traditional lawn grasses. But for the flower garden, you want to seek out the better-behaved members of this large and diverse group of plants. Look for clump-forming grass varieties or slow-spreading *rhizomatous* types (those with creeping roots).

If you want the best of both worlds in your flower bed (the invasive ornamental grasses without the invasions), bury a large pot or a section of sewer pipe and plant the "attractive nuisance" inside the barrier, where you can confine its traveling ways. Vigilance is still prudent — check for escape attempts every so often. Some rhizomes inevitably try to go over the wall. Be sure to pull these run-away grasses out before they attempt to take over your flower bed.

Not all grasses are what most people think of as grass. Reeds, rushes, sedges, cereal grains, and bamboo are all lumped together in the same extended family with ornamental grasses. All grasses do share a few distinguishing physical traits. The most obvious is the foliage — long, narrow blades with parallel veins running the vertical length of each leaf. Their understated blooms aren't flowers in any traditional sense. Grass flowers are feathery or spiked affairs.

Grasses can do a lot to enliven the flower bed, including

- Lend an unrivaled sense of grace and movement, swaying softly in the slightest breeze.
- Make attractive fillers when you plant them in groups or drifts, and dramatic accents when you plant them singly.
- Step in to help compensate for the seasonal failings of most perennial flowers. Many grass varieties provide fall color and winter texture.
- Create seedheads that attract songbirds and are also great for dried flower arrangements.

A grass type exists for every possible site, from the swamp to the desert. The following list includes six of the best grasses for a wide variety of conditions (all are hardy to –20° F [–29° C] or colder). Dozens more are currently in cultivation. Grasses are enjoying a real surge in popularity, so you're likely to find several types to choose from at your local nursery.

Caring for grasses

When choosing grasses on the edge of their winter hardiness range, plan to transplant them in spring to give the roots a chance to grow strongly before winter. For example, when planting a maiden grass that's supposed to be hardy to −20° F (−29° C) in a climate that really does get that cold, get it in the ground early for a better chance of success.

Grass maintenance is simple: Cut down each clump to within 3 to 6 inches (7 to 15 cm) of the ground in late winter or early spring. Even evergreen types benefit from an annual haircut.

Use sharp scissors or pruning shears, or better yet, tie up the top of the clump (I use a bungee cord) and cut the whole thing down — carefully — with a chain saw or handsaw.

You can also burn off the dead foliage, if doing so is safe and legal where you reside. Grass clumps can make an impressive bonfire, so you must use extreme caution if you plan to burn grass clumps. You don't want to meet the local firefighters or become a neighborhood legend.

❀ **Feather reed grass** (*Calamagrostis acutiflora* 'Stricta'): This grass, severely vertical in form, is one of the toughest of all the grasses. It's highly adaptable, growing well in wet, heavy clay and being fairly drought tolerant in arid regions with an occasional deep soaking. It blooms in early summer. The narrow flower cluster is purplish red in early summer, dries to buff, and persists throughout the winter if early snows don't crush it.

❀ **Blue fescue** (*Festuca glauca*): The little tufts of blue fescue resemble inverted shaving brushes. The blades are intense steel blue and are very fine, almost needlelike. Stiff and upright in the center of the clump, the blades arch slightly around the outside. Blue fescue blooms in summer. The seedheads are pretty initially but deteriorate quickly and are not particularly showy when dry.

❀ **Blue oat grass** (*Helictotrichon sempervirens*): The blades are graceful and arching, very thin and curved slightly inward at the edges. The flower cluster doubles the height of this grass in early summer, emerging silvery and drying to straw color. The blossoms hold up well the entire summer and into the winter. Blue oat grass is good singly (as an accent) or in groups.

❀ **Silver-variegated maiden grass** (*Miscanthus sinensis* 'Morning Light'): Even though this grass can grow quite tall, it still has a delicate, graceful air about it. The leaf blades are very fine, with silver variegation. The form is narrowly upright and somewhat arching. The reddish bronze flowers are feathery and beautiful, either cut for flower arrangements or left to add texture and elegance to the winter garden.

❀ **Switch grass** *(Panicum virgatum):* This plant is a bit more wild in appearance than most of the other grasses featured in this section. Its form is open and arching. The leaf blades are wide and long, appearing at intervals along a stiff, rounded stem. The seedheads are the crowning glory of this grass. They are open and airy, holding individual reddish purple grains. Switch grass has a golden orange fall color and is a wonderful addition to dried floral bouquets. 'Heavy Metal', a steely blue variety, is pictured in the color section.

❀ **Dwarf fountain grass** *(Pennisetum alopecuroides):* Dwarf fountain grass creates a soft, graceful open mound. The foliage is clear green, very long, and deeply bowed. The flowers open green with mauve tones in midsummer and age to buff, making a good cut flower, fresh or dried. The flowerheads persist and add winter interest. Nursery labels promote this plant as hardy to –20° F (–29° C), but I've never been successful leaving this grass in my garden through the winter.

A relative, *Pennisetum setaceum* 'Rubrum' (pictured in the color section), is a purplish red color. Purple fountain grass is a tender perennial grown as an annual in cold climates.

Big and Bold Herbaceous Perennials

When you come across a perennial listed at 10 feet (3 m) tall, you may find yourself wondering whether you are seeing a typographical error or the effects of nuclear fallout, steroids, or mega-doses of vitamins. In fact, what you're looking at are the Incredible Hulks of the flower bed — herbaceous perennials who die back to the ground in winter to return each spring and quickly grow to the proportions of a large shrub.

Appeal of the big ones

Some folks are bound to feel intimidated by perennials towering skyward like Jack's enchanted beanstalk. But these plants can work magic on even the smallest garden. Large perennials are real attention-grabbers. Even motorists driving by at high speeds are compelled to slow down and take another look. These plants have the same attraction as a large advertising balloon. Everyone is fascinated by a flower as big as a dinner plate.

Many garden designers caution against including really massive perennials in the small garden. They fear that small spaces are too easily overwhelmed and dominated by such an imposing presence. But whether or not you include these big beauties in your little flower bed depends entirely on the look you're after. Large foliage makes a good accent and provides contrast to the fine texture. If all the flowers are shorter than waist high and have refined, subtle forms, your garden can easily become awfully dull. A few big and bold perennials are guaranteed to break up the monotony.

Where to put the giants

If you want a tropical, luxuriant air to your garden, use a large percentage of perennials with big blooms and dramatically oversized foliage. For more of a cottage garden ambiance, use only a few as accents, either standing alone or arranged in small groups of two or three. Keep in mind that the more large foliage you include, the less of an impact it has.

Gardeners traditionally place large-scale perennials at the back of the flower border or along the spine in the center of an island bed. This arrangement is logical enough — you don't want anything bulky blocking the view to all the flowers behind it. But you can make things more interesting by bringing some large plants forward to the mid-range or, in some cases, to the front row. Silver sage, for example, has a large, low rosette of magnificent silvery foliage. Place this plant at the front or in a corner of the flower bed where it has space to spread out completely unobstructed. The flower spikes are 4 to 5 feet (1.2 to 1.5 m) tall, but they are open-branched and candelabra-like, creating an attractive veil that enhances but doesn't upstage the shorter neighbors standing behind them.

King-sized perennials

This list contains examples of the many forms that big and bold perennials can take. Some are large and hulky; others are tall, slender, and airy. All promise to make a strong statement in the flower garden. All the plants in the following list appear in this book's color photo section.

❀ **Monkshood** *(Aconitum napellus):* A stately plant with regal bearing, monkshood produces spires of deep, velvety purple flowers on sturdy upright stems. The foliage is dark green and deeply divided. 'Album' is a pinkish white variety; 'Blue Valley' is dark blue; 'Rubellum' is a soft rose.

All parts of this plant are extremely toxic if eaten, even in small quantities.

❀ **Columbine** *(Aquilegia* hybrids): The flower form of the columbine is unique, with five fat, rounded petals inside a traditional star of pointed petals and long *spurs* behind the flowerhead, like tails on a comet. Individual flowers are held on long, graceful stems, and nod and gambol on the slightest breeze. The hybrids capture every color but orange. Columbine's foliage is light and airy, greatly resembling a maidenhair fern. The widely available 'McKana Hybrids' are pictured in the color insert of this book.

❀ **Tree mallow** *(Lavatera thuringiaca):* As big as a shrub, tree mallow dies back to the ground in winter. Like all the mallow family, this is a good-natured, reliable plant. Little used, tree mallow ought to be in every garden within its hardiness range.

The 2- to 3-inch (5 to 7 cm) pink blossoms resemble hibiscus and carry on several months from summer to first frost without deadheading. Foliage is sage green and lobed. *Lavatera* 'Barnsley' is even prettier than the original; the flowers are the palest pink with a darker center eye.

✿ **Plume poppy** *(Macleaya cordata):* This plant towers to really great heights but is airy and graceful in stature. The leaves are bluish green and irregularly lobed, resembling giant oak leaves. The tiny flowers, held in feathery plumes, are creamy white to soft coral. The seedheads are as ornamental as the flowers; leave them uncut until the first frost.

✿ **Sticky Jerusalem sage** *(Phlomis russeliana):* A big, rough-and-tumble plant, sticky Jerusalem sage bears elongated, heart-shaped leaves that are 6 to 8 inches (15 to 20 cm) long and densely hairy. The foliage is medium green on top and dull green on the underside. Heavy, square-stemmed flower spikes bear tiers of the softest yellow flower clusters. Sticky Jerusalem sage isn't very well known yet in North America, but it's a popular plant in Colorado because of its drought tolerance.

✿ **New Zealand flax** *(Phormium tenax):* A tender perennial in most regions, New Zealand flax is invaluable where it's winter hardy. Sword-shaped leaves stand stiffly upright in a fanlike clump. Tubular red or yellow flower clusters rise on sturdy stalks high above the foliage. Infinite leaf color variations and sizes are available — variegated with yellow, pink, purple, cream, and white or solid gray green, purple, or bronze. New Zealand flax is only hardy to 10° F (–12° C).

✿ **Silver sage** *(Salvia argentea):* With huge, heavily wrinkled, silver white felted foliage, silver sage is very striking when grown either as an accent or planted in groups. The foliage rosette is low to the ground, so this plant needs to be sited near the front of the flower bed so that it isn't hidden from view, despite the height of the flower stalks. The flowers are white on branched, open stems.

✿ **Mullein** *(Verbascum chaixii):* A stately, elegant plant, nettle-leafed mullein has either solitary or candelabra-like flowering stalks. The basal rosette is composed of large, soft green leaves with a red mid-rib. The leaves become smaller as they climb the flower spike. The flowers are small but profuse, soft yellow with a purple eye. The flowers open in the morning and close at midday.

✿ **Culver's root** *(Veronicastrum virginicum):* A stately and elegant plant, culver's root is tall and stiffly upright. The foliage is arranged in whorls on sturdy stems. Each leaf is long and narrow, shiny, crisp green, heavily veined, and toothed. The flowers are tiny, pale blue or white, arranged bottlebrush-like on slender, tapering spikes. Culver's root extends the blooming season in late summer, when most of the flower garden is in a resting state.

A Rainbow of Foliage Colors

Foliage colors are as varied as the paint chip selections in your hardware store. This section lists only a few of the best in each color category.

A case of the blues

Blue foliage tones in the garden have a similar effect on the senses as the greens do. They never clash with stronger colors and actually have a neutralizing, calming effect. Planting blue foliage is a safe means to expand the foliage color palette, only slightly departing from the ever-present green. Most of the blues lean toward bluish green, so the transition is usually a gentle one.

The blues in the following list range from the steely blue of hosta 'Elegans' to the near-silver blue of the horned poppy. They range in hardiness from −20° F to −40° F (−29° C to −40° C).

❀ **Red valerian** *(Centranthus ruber):* Red valerian is a short-lived perennial that can be a reseeding pest. But this plant also has some attributes to recommend it. It's adaptable to really difficult sites and blooms from spring through the last frost. The flowers are rosy red; the leaves are long, narrow, and blue green. The flowers are also available in white, brick red, and maroon variations. Red valerian attracts bees and butterflies and makes a good cut flower.

❀ **Sea kale** *(Crambe maritima):* The perfect all-purpose perennial, sea kale is an old-fashioned, long-lived vegetable in the cabbage family. It's still most often included with the corn and radishes in seed catalogs, but it's far too ornamental to exclude from the flower bed. The plant forms an unstructured rosette of large, gray blue, succulent, deeply ruffled foliage. The flowers, small, white, and fragrant, are carried in clusters on thick stalks.

❀ **Cheddar pink** *(Dianthus gratianopolitanus* 'Bath's Pink'): This perennial forms low, evergreen mounds of silvery blue green foliage. Flowers are soft pink and very fragrant, with a sweet, spicy scent. The leaves are small and needlelike. The blossoms are fringed and so profuse that they almost obscure the foliage. Many other fine varieties are available: 'Tiny Rubies' is dark rose; 'Splendens' is red.

❀ **Horned poppy** *(Glaucium flavum):* Silvery blue rosettes with long, ruffle-edged, felted leaves make a striking accent in or out of bloom. But when these plants send up branched stems of yellow or apricot tissue-paper-thin flowers, visitors are inevitably stopped in their tracks. The seedheads are also attention-grabbing — the long, thin horns somewhat resemble a silvery green bean.

❀ **Baby's breath** *(Gypsophila paniculata):* If you've ever bought a rose, you're already familiar with this plant. It's the froth of tiny white flowers that florists traditionally pair with rose buds. In the garden, baby's breath is a large plant, creating clouds of fragrant, dainty flower sprays. The bluish green foliage is quite small and unimposing. Baby's breath is the ultimate "filler flower" to complement larger blooms, and it makes an outstanding cut flower, fresh or dried. 'Bristol Fairy' is one of the best of the white variations; *Gypsophila repens* 'Pink Star' is a good pink form.

❀ **Shade lily** *(Hosta sieboldiana* 'Elegans'): The blue leaf varieties of hostas are really magnificent plants. Individual leaves are immense and heart-shaped, with deep ribs running their length. They are substantial, textured, and steel blue. The foliage turns golden in autumn. The pale lavender flowers are sometimes hidden by the leaves. Many other fine blue hosta varieties are available.

❀ **Showy oregano** *(Origanum laevigatum* 'Herrenhausen'): This light and delicate plant is showy from the time it first starts to bloom in summer until you cut the seedheads down the following spring. The leaves are small, blue green ovals on wiry, reddish stems. Each flower is a tiny violet tube, but they're carried in rich profusion on branched and arching sprays. When the flowers fall, they leave behind reddish purple *bracts* (small leaflike structures) that hold their color indefinitely if you cut them before the sun bleaches them to brown. Just be sure to leave a few stems standing to provide winter texture.

❀ **Rue** *(Ruta graveolens):* For a flower garden, rue's foliage is unbeatable. It's lacy and blue on a shrubby, upright form. Rue also comes in a yellow variegated selection.

Traditionally grown as a medicinal herb, rue is much safer when considered strictly ornamental. This plant is toxic if eaten in large amounts and can also cause skin rashes if handled without gloves.

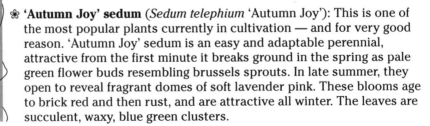

❀ **'Autumn Joy' sedum** *(Sedum telephium* 'Autumn Joy'): This is one of the most popular plants currently in cultivation — and for very good reason. 'Autumn Joy' sedum is an easy and adaptable perennial, attractive from the first minute it breaks ground in the spring as pale green flower buds resembling brussels sprouts. In late summer, they open to reveal fragrant domes of soft lavender pink. These blooms age to brick red and then rust, and are attractive all winter. The leaves are succulent, waxy, blue green clusters.

Purples and reds

Purple and red foliage has a moody, sultry quality. It emboldens pastel color schemes or dampens the flames of red and orange companions to an exquisite smolder. The foliage tones in this section vary from bronze over green to solid dusky purple, crimson red, or almost black. Some are further complemented by red or purple stems. Few of the leaves are a single, solid hue; most are complex layers of multiple tones, changing entirely when viewed from another angle and at different times of the day.

❀ **Coral bells** (*Heuchera* 'Pewter Veil'): An outstanding new introduction, coral bells make a soft mound of large, rounded, slightly lobed, and toothed foliage. Each leaf is overlaid with pewter patina. The veining is prominent and dusky purple. The undersides of the leaves are a solid reddish purple. The flowers are inconspicuous, odd, and greenish, but who needs flowers with leaves like these? 'Pewter Veil' is only one of many red- and purple-leafed varieties currently available. Another very popular variety is 'Palace Purple' (see the color section for a photo). Expect newer and better varieties each year.

❀ **Cardinal flower** (*Lobelia fulgens* 'Queen Victoria'): With very showy flowers for a woodland habitat, you can grow cardinal flower in a pond as a bog plant. The combination of scarlet red flowers and bronze leaves is really striking — probably not for the timid. The plant is upright in form with loose spikes of asymmetrical, starry flowers, attracting hummingbirds and butterflies. The leaves are long and cigar-shaped.

❀ **Black mondo grass** (*Ophiopogon planiscapus* 'Niger'): A very striking and unique color, this plant really is nearly black. It isn't really a grass but rather a member of the lily clan. The foliage is narrow and very grasslike, and the dainty pink flowers are little nodding bells on short spikes. Glossy black berries further ornament this plant in the fall. Use it in drifts of three or more for impact. Hardy only to –10° F (–24° C).

❀ **'Husker Red' beardtongue** (*Penstemon digitalis* 'Husker Red'): This is a handsome plant with wine red foliage and sugar pink flowers. It forms a basal rosette of slender, pointed leaves that become increasingly short and stout as they progress up the flower stalk. The flowers are nearly white with a hint of pink, resembling tiny snapdragons. They form a pink haze at their peak. (And, sports fans, it does hail from Nebraska!)

❀ **Purple stonecrop** (*Sedum telephium maximum* 'Atropurpureum'): A dark and moody plant, purple stonecrop has bronzy red, succulent leaves on darker, purplish red stems. It's attractive from the moment the brussels-sproutesque buds first push out of the soil in spring. The flowers are dense, softly mounded clusters of dusty pink stars. The seedheads slowly ripen to rust color and can be left standing to grace the winter garden until new growth starts the following spring. 'Mohrchen' is a similar purple-leafed variety.

Silvers and grays

Your taste in jewelry may be a clue to your reaction to silver and gray leaves. Those who prefer silver over gold are likely to find this same bias spilling over into their perennials selections. Though many garden designers consider silvers and grays good mediators to calm harsh, jarring factions, their methods are certainly unconventional. Instead of creating neutral tones, these shimmering beauties call your attention to themselves and away from any warring colors nearby. With only a few exceptions, silver or gray foliage indicates at least a degree of drought tolerance and a need for full sun.

❀ **'Moonshine' yarrow** (*Achillea* 'Moonshine'): Most sources describe 'Moonshine' as a soft yellow. But in my experience, this plant's flower color is about as bright and intense as yellow gets. The combination of sunny yellow flowers with a hint of gold and silver filigreed leaves makes this yarrow a favorite perennial. The flowers are flat clusters of tightly packed tiny daisies. The flowerheads stand tall above the foliage clumps.

❀ **Wormwood** (*Artemisia absinthium* 'Lambrook Silver'): Even though I'm terribly allergic to this large family of plants, I can't resist their ethereal beauty. Fortunately, the flowers aren't much to look at anyway, so dodge their pollen by shearing them off well before they open. 'Lambrook Silver' is one of the best of the clan with lacy, silver foliage on branched but upright stems. The flowers are inconspicuous.

❀ **English lavender** *(Lavandula angustifolia):* Well-loved all over the world for its aromatic foliage and flowers, lavender forms dense clumps of silvery gray foliage, needlelike and upfacing on stiff stems. Bluish purple flowers appear in whorls on short spikes. Cut the flowers before they are fully open. 'Hidcote' has purple flowers; 'Jean Davis' is pink; 'Munstead' is 12 inches (30 cm) tall.

❀ **Rose campion** *(Lychnis coronaria):* A short-lived perennial or biennal, rose campion is especially valuable as one of the few silver-leafed flowers for shady locations. The foliage is softly felted and grows in attractive rosettes. The flowers are borne on branched stalks and are a deep magenta, shaded gradually lighter to white in the center. Closely related s Maltese cross *(Lychis chalcedonica),* of which 'Abbotswood Rose' is soft pink, and 'Angel's Blush' is white with a pink center bleaching to pure white in full sun.

❀ **Russian sage** *(Perovskia atriplicifolia):* A tall, upright plant, Russian sage is airy and graceful. Its silver green leaves are heavily cut and strongly pungent when crushed. The flowers have a similar but not as sharp aroma and make a good cut flower. The flowers are multiple spikes of lavender blue that start in summer and bloom tirelessly for several months. Leaf shape can be quite variable within the species.

❀ **Lavender cotton** (*Santolina chamaecyparissus*): This plant is a shrublet that's way too small to line a stately drive but that is just the right size to fit into the flower garden. Lavender cotton forms dense, spreading mounds of fine, woolly gray foliage. The flowers are solitary, bright yellow buttons at the top of each stem. The whole plant is evergreen, except in really cold winters when the tops may die back and brown out badly. This aromatic plant is reported to repel mosquitoes.

Variegated

Usually, *variegation* (having multiple colors) is a natural mutation, showing up as mottling on an otherwise solid-colored leaf. These markings may be white, silver, cream, chartreuse, or yellow on a background of green, blue, silver, or red. The variegation may be dots, freckles, stripes, or blotches of contrasting color. Some foliage has more than two colors, such as 'Burgundy Glow' bugleweed, with various shades of pink, purple, ivory, and green. Others have only a slight brushing of white on the leaf edges.

These oddities are especially valuable for lightening and brightening shady gardens. Combine variegated foliage cautiously; too many patterns arranged too closely together can easily become clownish. (All the plants in the following list are hardy to −40° F [−40° C].)

❀ **Bugleweed** (*Ajuga reptans* 'Burgundy Glow'): Taking variegation to the extreme, 'Burgundy Glow' bugleweed is probably too garish for some tastes. The sage green leaves are splashed variously with cream, pink, and reddish purple. The flowers are blue. Not as vigorous as most of its relatives, this variety slowly spreads into restrained mats and forms a striking accent when placed at the feet of either green- or red-leafed companions. (Several varieties of bugleweed appear in the color section of this book.)

❀ **Yellow archangel** (*Lamiastrum galeobdolon* 'Florentinum'): The pattern of white variegation on yellow archangel has a distinctive metallic sheen. The leaves are softly triangular in shape with toothed margins and a sparse covering of coarse hairs. In my English garden, this plant gave me fits, aggressively spreading and climbing everything in its path. It's much better behaved in my Colorado garden. 'Herman's Pride' is a more refined selection, a restrained spreader, and a better choice overall for flower gardens (look for this variety in the color pages).

❀ **Spotted dead nettle** (*Lamium maculatum*): Some of the prettiest variegated perennials for the front of the lightly shaded flower bed, the spotted dead nettles include a wide selection of variegation patterns and flower colors. All are equally attractive. Choose whichever strikes your fancy. 'Shell Pink' has pale pink flowers and a white stripe down the center of green leaves. 'White Nancy' has white flowers and frosted leaves with green only at the edges. 'Beacon Silver' (pictured in the color pages) has similar leaves and pink flowers. 'Beedham's White' has white flowers and glowing yellow foliage with white stripes.

❀ **Fragrant Solomon's seal** (*Polygonatum odoratum* 'Variegatum'): This plant forms a loose colony of arching stems carrying stout, oval-shaped pointed leaves. In the variegated variety, the foliage is very lightly brushed with white. The flowers are delicate, fragrant white bells that dangle along the stem beneath the leaves. They're easy to miss, so make sure you watch for them in the spring.

❀ **Bethlehem sage** (*Pulmonaria*): A must for the shaded flower garden, Bethlehem sage has neat rosettes of large, lance-shaped leaves that are variously speckled, splotched, or dusted with bright white, depending on which variety you choose. The flowers appear very early in the spring, before the leaves have fully emerged. Clusters of pink buds open to reddish pink upright bells and then age to blue. They last up to two months. 'Mrs. Moon' (pictured in the color section) has spotted leaves and blue flowers. 'Sissinghurst White' has irregular dapples and white flowers. 'Roy Davidson' has even spots and blue flowers. 'Pink Dawn' has pink flowers.

Yellows

Exceedingly popular at present are the rare and unusual yellow, chartreuse, and golden-leafed perennials. I have to admit that I've been slow to be won over to these plants. Due to the high alkalinity of my garden soil, I expend a good deal of effort fending off the sickly yellow of *chlorosis* — a disease caused by nutrient deficiencies — so I'm predisposed to wrinkle my nose at yellow foliage. Still, when these plants are used effectively, they can be very beautiful indeed. They are particularly desirable for bringing a luminescent glow to the shaded flower garden.

The following plants can withstand average wintertime lows to between –20° F and –40° F (–29° C and –40° C), depending on the plant.

❀ **Creeping Jenny** (*Lysimachia nummularia* 'Aurea'): The first time I ever laid eyes on this plant was when it had taken over and strangled out most of a mature garden. I vowed never to let it loose to wreak havoc in my garden. But I've become smitten with the less rampant yellow-leafed variety. It has round, penny-sized leaves and fragrant, clear yellow flowers.

❀ **Golden lemon balm** (*Melissa officinalis* 'All Gold'): Traditionally grown as an herb, lemon balm is just as valuable in the flower garden, especially the golden-leafed varieties. Leaves are pale golden yellow, small, wedge-shaped, and heavily textured with toothed margins. Flowers are tiny and a honeybee magnet. Every part of the plant is aromatic, smelling sweetly of lemons when bruised or brushed against. 'Aurea' is another gold form. 'Variegata' has golden yellow variegation.

❀ **Golden sage** (*Salvia officinalis* 'Aurea'): An aromatic herb used in cooking, the sage species is quite cold-hardy, but most of the more colorful varieties are much less so. Treat them as annuals where they don't overwinter. Golden sage is a subshrub in warmer regions, deciduous where snow falls. Leaves are oval, green in the centers, and edged with yellow. Flowers grow in whorls on loose spikes and are very attractive to honeybees.

'Icterina', pictured in the color section of this book, is another good yellow variegated form.

❀ **Golden feverfew** (*Tanacetum parthenium* 'Aureum'): A short-lived perennial, golden feverfew's chartreuse-yellow foliage in early spring turns green by midsummer. The leaves are lacy and pungent. The flowers, dense clusters of dainty white daisies with yellow centers, are excellent long-lasting cut flowers. For maximum impact, plant in drifts of at least five plants. A photo of feverfew appears in the color section.

❀ **Lemon thyme** (*Thymus citriodorus* 'Aureus'): A low, creeping plant for the front of the flower bed, 'Aureus' is a golden-leafed variety of popular lemon thyme. It makes a carpet of fresh, lemon-scented foliage. The individual leaves are tiny and round. The flowers are dainty little lavender clusters so profuse that they nearly obscure the foliage. Use in cooking for a lemon flavor. 'Bertram Anderson' is chartreuse. 'Nyewoods' has green leaves that are broadly edged in creamy yellow.

All varieties of thyme suffer in heavy shade. Place them along a walkway or a wall where the fragrance can be enjoyed. They tolerate light foot traffic without complaint. Cut the plants back by half in spring and whenever needed throughout the growing season to prevent legginess (or to add to the stew pot).

Chapter 10
Perennial Companions

· ·

In This Chapter

▶ The mixed border

▶ Bulbs in the flower bed

▶ Annuals among the perennials

▶ Shrubs for year-round structure

· ·

*C*ombining perennial flowers with a few annuals, bulbs, and shrubs can
transform the commonplace flower garden into a sublime outdoor
retreat, always filled with fragrance and color. The difference between a
mixed flower bed and one that's composed solely of perennial flowers is like
the difference between mixed nuts and plain peanuts. Peanuts by themselves can satisfy the appetite, but by adding just a few fancy cashews,
filberts, and almonds, you change an ordinary snack into a gourmet party
treat.

The philosophy behind the mixed flower bed is to boost the flower garden
so that its beauty spans the whole calendar year. Why be content with only
three months of color when you can easily extend the flower season into
late winter by adding early-blooming bulbs? Annuals pinch-hit for slow-
maturing perennials and guarantee a continued midsummer performance
when many perennial flowers are taking a break from the heat. Shrubs
provide fall color, year-round structure, and winter interest when all the
flowers are indulging in their seasonal naps.

Bring on the Bulbs!

Gardeners and nurseries tend to treat bulbs as a unique class of plant, but
bulbs are actually just regular perennials with special coping skills. Like any
other perennial flower, bulbs come back every year, provided that you grow
them in the proper conditions. What *is* unique about bulbs is their capacity
to store food and water for long periods. This capability enables gardeners
to harvest and ship bulbs without pampering or caring for them much at all
while they're out of the ground.

Every climate and every season has a bulb suited to it. Tulips may be the first bulbs that come to your mind, but tulips are not the only spring bulb, and spring is not the only bulb season. Many other varieties of bulbs are available to brighten your garden in the summer or fall. In subtropical and coastal regions, many bulbs bloom in midwinter, as well. Some bulbs are *evergreen* (the leaves live year-round); others are *deciduous* (the leaves die back and the bulb indulges in a rest period). Some bulbs bloom as fleetingly as spring snowfalls; others flower for several months.

GARDEN JARGON

Sorting through bulbs

When you flip through the pages of a bulb catalog, many of the bulbs you see aren't really bulbs at all. They're perennials that have developed a wide variety of storage methods.

The following list describes a few of the most common types of perennials that are sold as bulbs:

✔ **True bulbs:** Cut a tulip bulb in half, and packed inside you find a perfect, miniature tulip plant surrounded by layers of scales exactly like a cooking onion. In tulips, daffodils, and onions, these scales are pressed together tightly to form a solid mass. In contrast, lilies have loose scales. True bulbs usually have a papery covering and are generally teardrop-shaped, with a point at the top and roots coming from a flat area at the base.

✔ **Corms:** Crocuses, freesias, and gladiolas are all *corms.* They look much like true bulbs but are formed from modified stem tissue. When you cut into a corm, you find solid tissue instead of rings. Like true bulbs, corms also come wrapped in a papery covering. The pointed side goes up, and the base has either a small, round depression or what looks like a snap.

✔ **Rhizomes:** Rhizomes are swollen stems that creep horizontally along or just below the surface of the soil. Roots grow from the underside; leaves and flowers grow from the expanding tip of the rhizome. Tall bearded iris and cannas are examples of rhizomes.

✔ **Tubers:** Potatoes are probably the best-known tuber. Similar to corms but without the depressed circle at the base or the papery covering, tubers are enlarged stem tissue with *eyes* (indented depressions on the surface) that grow roots or shoots. Some tubers look like dried spiders when you open the package; others are wrinkled, shapeless lumps. Guessing which side is up is often impossible (imagine trying to figure out which side is up on a potato!). If I can find roots, I place those down. Otherwise, I just bury the thing and let it right itself.

✔ **Tuberous roots:** Tuberous roots are seriously swollen roots. They have ordinary-looking roots sprouting from the enlarged portion. Dahlias are tuberous-rooted perennials.

In this chapter, I use the term *bulbs* to refer to true bulbs, corms, and tubers. Other than their capability to survive above ground for a time, perennials with rhizomes and tuberous roots are treated no differently than other perennials.

Buying bulbs

You can buy bulbs through mail-order catalogs or in garden centers.

- ✔ When comparing mail-order prices, compare bulb sizes as well. Large bulbs mean larger flowers.

- ✔ Shopping for healthy bulbs at a nursery is just like shopping for potatoes and onions at a grocery. Choose solid and firm bulbs with no rotten or discolored spots.

I've had good luck with potted bulbs that I've rescued from florists' trash bins. I just plant them in the garden, like I plant any other bulbs. A year or two may pass before these discarded bulbs gather enough strength to bloom again (maybe they need that much time to recover their dignity), but most of them do come back.

Planting bulbs

By using bulbs, you can pack more bloom into a small garden. They are compact, don't require much space, and don't greedily grab nutrients and water from neighboring plants. You can squeeze bulbs in between perennials or plant them right under other perennials.

You can plant bulbs individually, but an easier approach is to plant more than one bulb in a single hole — each a few inches apart from its hole-mates. (See the Cheat Sheet in the front of this book for recommended bulb spacing.) If you're planting a group of large bulbs, simply dig one large hole, drop in several large bulbs, and cover them with soil. If you're planting bulbs of various sizes, plant them in layers, placing smaller bulbs directly on top of larger ones (see Figure 10-1) with a layer of soil in between.

Because most bulbs produce only a few flowers (maybe only one), always arrange them in groups:

- ✔ For the largest bulbs (such as lilies or crown imperials), plant at least three bulbs together.

- ✔ Tall tulips, daffodils, and hyacinths look best in clusters of five to seven.

- ✔ The really little bulbs, with flowers under 12 inches (30 cm) tall, should be planted in large numbers to make an impact, 25 at a bare minimum. A hundred is better yet. These small bulbs are usually inexpensive, so you can afford to splurge. (Don't try to cram all 100 in the same hole. Even little bulbs need space between them.)

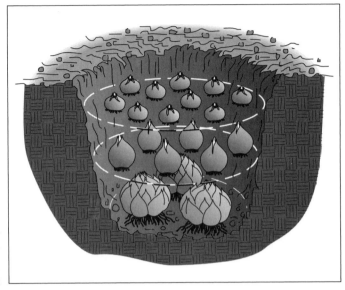

Figure 10-1:
When planting layers of bulbs in the same hole, place the larger bulbs at the bottom and the smaller ones closer to the top.

Some bulbs have special planting instructions, so always read the package or ask the nursery people for advice. The general steps for planting most bulbs are as follows:

1. **Plant the other perennials first and then add the bulbs to reduce your chances of chopping a dormant buried bulb in half.**

   For example, if you plant your perennials in the spring, add tulips in the fall. Or if you plant your perennials in the fall, get them in the ground first and then plant the bulbs in the spaces between the flowers.

2. **To plant large bulbs, put a bucket next to where you're digging the hole and then shovel the dirt directly into the bucket.**

3. **Dig a hole two to three times deeper than the height of the bulb — use a ruler to measure the depth of the hole.**

   For example, plant a 2-inch (5-cm) tall tulip bulb in a hole 4 to 6 inches (10 to 15 cm) deep. In cold climates, you can plant bulbs deeper so that their flowers come up later and are less subject to damage from a late freeze.

4. **Mix a fertilizer especially formulated for bulbs into the soil at the bottom of the hole, according to the package instructions.**

   This fertilizer is usually available wherever you buy your bulbs. (See Chapter 16 to find out everything you ever wanted to know about fertilizer but were afraid to ask.)

5. **Place the bulbs right side up in the pit.**

   Generally, the roots go down and the pointy part goes up. Don't worry if you can't tell which end is up, though, because the bulb will right itself.

6. **Dump the bucketful of soil back into the hole.**

7. **After planting all the bulbs in the flower bed, set up a sprinkler and soak the whole area until the soil is wet as deep down as you planted the bulbs.**

You may want to mark the spots where you plant your bulbs. When you're hard at work planting, you can't believe that you'll ever forget what you've put in the ground, but six months later, you probably won't have a clue. Use any sort of a plant label — a friend of mine uses plastic swizzle sticks. He uses model paint to color the tips of the sticks the same color as the bulb's flower. That way, he knows where to expect the red tulips or yellow crocuses.

Caring for bulbs

Many bulbs are very forgiving of abuse and don't even seem to notice if you leave them out of the ground for several months. Others, however, need to be replanted as soon as possible so that they don't dry out. The trick is knowing which is which. The type of packing material is probably your best clue. If the bulbs are sold loose and dry, you're usually safe storing them for a few weeks until you have time to plant them. Bulbs packed in damp peat moss need to be put into the ground quickly.

Many bulbs reproduce by forming new bulbs. Wait to move or divide an evergreen bulb until its non-flowering stage. Transplant other bulbs when they are *dormant* — that is, after their leaves turn brown. Dig up the whole clump and gently pull the bulbs apart; replant each bulb separately. Repeat this process every few years, and you can reap hundreds of plants where you originally planted only a dozen bulbs.

Always cut off the bloom as soon as it dries out so that the bulb doesn't waste energy trying to convert the dead blossom into seeds. Instead, the bulb gets to work storing energy for a new bloom.

The ripening leaves of dormant bulbs can be a real trial after the flowering is long finished. You must steel yourself to let the process run its full course. If you want the flowers to repeat their performance, you have to give the bulbs enough time to store energy for the following year. Place large bulbs behind bulky perennials whenever you can to hide their ugly phase. If the yellowing foliage is really getting on your nerves, you can safely cut it off six weeks after the bulb stops flowering.

Many factors can make bulbs that should be hardy in your region fail to come back. For example, most tulips are absolutely intolerant of wet soils, especially during their dormancy period. In areas with high summer rainfall, you must dig up your tulips after their leaves turn brown and store them in a cool, dry location to prevent rotting. Or you can treat tulips as annuals and replant new bulbs each year.

Mice and squirrels may also be responsible for missing bulbs. If you suspect that these culprits have eaten your bulbs, plant the bulbs in wire cages so that the flowers and leaves can grow out but the little gourmands can't get in. Line the bottom of the hole with a piece of chicken wire, place the bulbs in the hole, bring the wire up over the top of the bulbs, and cover the whole contraption with soil.

Bulbs for every occasion

The following is a representative sampling of just a few of the hundreds of bulbs available for your flower garden.

- ❀ **Fancy-leafed caladium** *(Caladium bicolor):* One of the few plants to thrive in dense shade, caladium features arrowhead-shaped leaves in shades of red, pink, white, and green and in every imaginable pattern and variegation. Grow these plants for their striking foliage, not for their unremarkable flowers.

- ❀ **Canna lily** *(Canna hybrids):* The canna lily's dramatic foliage and showy flowers bring a touch of the jungle to the temperate flower garden. The leaves are large, with prominent veining. Some varieties have bronze, purple, or variegated foliage. The flowers are available in pink, red, salmon, yellow, white, and orange. The blooms are carried in dense, floppy-petaled clusters at the top of sturdy stalks.

- ❀ **Spider lily** *(Crinum bulbispermum):* Spider lily forms large clumps of dark green, arching, grasslike leaves. The flowers are long pink or white trumpets with vertical bands of darker pink. These fragrant blossoms dangle in loose clusters atop a sturdy, leafless stem.

Although many bulbs don't mind at all when you dig them up for the winter, the reclusive spider lily prefers not to be disturbed. If your winters are too cold for the spider lily, plant the bulbs in pots so that you can simply dig up the pot and bring the plant in, undisturbed, during winter.

- ❀ **Montbretia** *(Crocosmia crocosmiiflora):* An elegant and imposing plant, montbretia has upright, sword-shaped foliage clumps in dense fans. Wiry, arching stems hold triangular sprays of brilliant flowers that are most commonly scarlet but also are available in salmon, yellow, maroon, and orange. Where this plant is hardy, it rapidly spreads, forming large colonies. 'Bressingham Beacon' is the most winter-hardy strain. Another favorite, 'Lucifer', appears in the color section of this book.

❀ **Dahlia** (*Dahlia* hybrids): Dahlias are available in a bewildering assortment of shapes, from cheerful little daisies to tight pompoms to fireworks-inspired clusters of pointed petals.

❀ **Fortnight lily** (*Dietes vegeta*): The fortnight lily is a stately iris relative with clumps of upright, grassy foliage. The blooms are white, marked with yellow on the lower petals and lavender on the upper. The blooms are open for only one or two days, but in a succession lasting two weeks. Then the plant rests for two weeks, flowering on and off most of the year in warm-winter climates.

❀ **Gladiola:** (*Gladiolus* hybrids): Gladiolas form very erect, straight fans of sword-shaped foliage from which arise large flower spikes of openfaced, six-petaled blossoms arranged in a triangle-on-triangle fashion. The blooms come in many different sizes and every color except true blue.

❀ **Lily** (*Lilium* hybrids): Many wonderful selections of lilies are available, and the best vary by climate. Check with local nurseries to find out which types are best suited to your region. Some varieties are deliciously fragrant, all make outstanding cut flowers, and most can be grown in pots. The blooms are variously trumpet-shaped flowers, and myriad colors are available. (Turn to the color section to see 'Black Dragon', 'Gold Eagle', and 'Star Gazer' varieties.)

❀ **Daffodil** (*Narcissus* hybrids): Hundreds of varieties of these cheerful, old-fashioned garden favorites are available. Most have the typical center trumpet with a ruffle of petals at the base, but you can also find star-burst double forms. Daffodils come in yellows, oranges, apricots, and white.

❀ **Tulip** (*Tulipa* hybrids): Tulips come in a rainbow of colors and with widely variable flower shapes and sizes. A few varieties have lovely white or cream variegation or dark specks and streaks on the foliage. Some types are sweetly fragrant, and most make excellent cut flowers, although a few close up in low light.

Annual Frenzy

In some parts of the world, spring is a gentle season. Its arrival is announced by the first cherry blossoms, crocuses, or the emerging spears of asparagus. But on the plains of Colorado, where I live, winter reluctantly surrenders its chokehold, and these events simply mark the intervals between late snowstorms.

When spring finally does come to Colorado, an odd ritual takes place at local supermarkets. Sometime during the first or second week in May — weather permitting — thousands of trays of annual flowers are unloaded from semitrailers. These flowers are displayed on massive rolling racks that are set up right smack in the middle of the parking lots. Hoards of winter-crazed shoppers descend upon the trays, mesmerized by the kaleidoscope of brilliant color. The flower-seekers are not fazed by the automobiles careening around them; fender-benders and traffic tie-ups create temporary chaos as shoppers fill their carts with dozens of four-packs and six-packs of flowers. Then, just as suddenly, these racks are withdrawn. Within one or two weeks, the flowers are gone and order is restored.

Annual flowers can do a great deal to enhance your perennial bed. Perennials may take several years to mature and fill their allotted space. In the mean-time, why stare at expanses of dirt and mulch when you can plunk down a few annuals to fill the gaps?

Switching gears — all about annuals

An *annual* is a plant that goes through its entire life cycle — starting from seed, blooming, and setting seed — in a single growing season. This structure is nature's built-in safeguard for avoiding bad growing conditions, whether long periods of drought or extreme cold. Annuals ride out the hard times as seed, always ready to germinate and take advantage of good circumstances whenever they can. Instead of expending energy on growth, annuals throw themselves into seed production. As a result, many annuals die after they set seed, because they've accomplished their mission. By removing the faded flowers before they form seeds, you fool the plant into continuing to send up new flowers instead.

Although all annuals complete their life cycle in a single year, different types germinate at different seasons. This difference divides annuals into general categories — *warm season* and *cool season*. Because many annuals originate in tropical and desert climates, where the temperature seldom (if ever) reaches freezing, annuals are further classified as *hardy* or *tender*. To confuse matters even more, another class of flowers is called *biennials*. Most flowers fall into more than one category.

✔ **Warm-season annuals:** These plants wait until the late spring or early summer, when weather is relatively warm, to germinate. You can't rush them. Seeds or transplants put into the garden too early often rot or *stunt*, never quite catching up with their brothers who were planted at the proper time. Most warm-season annuals are also tender, blackening at the first hint of cold weather. In warm-winter climates, warm-season annuals are often planted in spring and in fall for a second bloom season. Flossflower is an example of a warm-season annual.

✔ **Cool-season annuals:** Whether tender or hardy, all these annuals prefer cool weather. The hardy types, such as love-in-a-mist and bachelors' buttons, often germinate in the fall and spend the whole winter as a clump of leaves. The following spring, they rush into bloom the minute the weather warms up. The tender ones germinate while the soil is still cool and damp early in the spring. Cool-season annuals perform best in climates where summer evenings are below 70° F (21° C). Both types set seed and die when the weather really heats up. In hot, humid, mild-winter areas, they're usually planted in fall for winter color.

✔ **Hardy annuals:** An annual that can withstand frost is called *hardy*. These plants are often the first annuals that nurseries offer in the spring, because you can safely plant them outside while late snows are still a strong likelihood. Many hardy annuals, such as bachelor's button, may be sown outside in the fall. Their winter hardiness is relative, of course. Those annuals hardy in England are not necessarily going to survive a Canadian winter. Some varieties of hardy annuals may continue to bloom late in the fall through several light frosts.

✔ **Half hardy:** Seed catalogs may use the term *half hardy* to describe annuals that can tolerate some cold, wet weather and possibly a very light frost. This hardiness is variable by climate. Many of these plants, such as snapdragons, are fully hardy in moderate weather regions.

✔ **Tender:** Tender annuals are intolerant of any frost at all — don't even give them a cold stare. Marigolds are examples of tender annuals.

✔ **Biennials:** These flowers (including canterbury bells and hollyhocks) need two growing seasons to complete their life cycle. They form a rosette of leaves the first year; in the second year, they bloom, set seed, and die. Occasionally, biennials don't bloom for several years, waiting for ideal conditions. Sometimes, biennials persist for a third year, growing off-sets from the crown and acting much like a perennial, but you can't count on such good luck. Most biennials don't come back.

To keep biennials in the garden, you need to plant seeds or seedlings every year so that you always have a crop of rosettes to form the next season's flowers. Many biennials self-sow and eventually take over the task of planting seeds.

✔ **Tender perennials:** A perennial that you're growing outside of its hardiness limitations is considered *tender*. Many perennials that are long-blooming and bloom the first year from seed are treated as annuals. Snapdragons are tender perennials that only occasionally survive the winter in my very cold climate. African daisies are annuals in my garden, but fully perennial in coastal climates.

✔ **Bedding annuals:** These flowers can be cool- or warm-season, hardy or tender. They are annuals chosen for their capacity to stay in bloom for a long time; their ease of propagation; their short, stout stature; and their conformity in appearance. Many public flower displays use bedding annuals as blocks of color that can be organized into shapes such as clocks or a city name. Most of the annuals sold in multiple plastic packs are bedding types.

Caring for annuals

In the world of gardening, *deadheading* has nothing to do with wearing tie-dyed T-shirts or idolizing Jerry Garcia. Rather, deadheading is the practice of pinching off blooms that have passed their prime, as shown in Figure 10–2. (Of course, if you want to listen to the Grateful Dead while doing so, be my guest.)

Not all annuals need deadheading to stay in bloom, but even annuals that don't require it look better when you routinely clean up the spent flowers. Most annuals benefit from being sheared in half about midway through the growing season. Pinch back the top few inches of tall, spindly plant stems anytime to keep the plants bushy and strong. A few annuals, such as hollyhocks, need staking even after you've pinched them back.

Annual popularity

Anyone who says that bedding annuals have lost their popularity hasn't witnessed the spring phenomenon in Colorado. You may as well leave room for a few annuals in your perennial garden, because you're probably going to give in to the temptation and buy some. Besides, annual flowers have much to offer:

✔ They can fill in the gaps while you're waiting for that 1-foot tall peony to expand to its allotted 3 feet of space.

✔ They temporarily shelter young perennials from sun and wind.

✔ They bridge the period of scorching summer heat, when very few perennials send up flowers. Many annuals peak in the hottest months of summer.

The well-planned perennial display is constantly evolving and changing, but adding a few long-blooming annuals can help create a sense of continuity throughout the season. Self-seeding annuals also bring serendipity to the garden by scattering themselves far and wide, forming unlikely but striking combinations that you may not have considered. In my garden one fall, an orange California poppy put itself next to a wine-red chrysanthemum. The effect was *fabulous.* I never would have learned this lesson in color had I been a tidier gardener and pulled out the errant seedling.

You may also use frost-intolerant perennials as annuals in cold climates, so you can enjoy heliotrope even if your winters are too cold for it to come back year after year.

Figure 10-2:
Deadhead faded flowers to tidy up your annuals and encourage them to continue blooming.

Fertilize annual flowers once a month throughout the growing season to promote strong growth. For more on fertilizing, see Chapter 16.

Annuals are most economical when you grow them from seed (see Chapter 19 for how-to instructions). You can also collect and save your own seed. But be aware that many bedding types are sterile, and seedlings from hybrids usually don't resemble the flower from which you saved the seed. (The seed catalogs or seed packages generally tell you which annuals are hybrids.) *Different* doesn't necessarily translate to *unattractive,* though. I let my hybrid snapdragons seed themselves, and I end up with many pretty shades of pink. I also get a small percentage of ugly colors, which I promptly pull and compost.

You can buy seed for annuals in mixed colors or in single shades. The separate colors tend to be more expensive and harder to locate. Often seed catalogs are a better source than nurseries when you're trying to find something out of the ordinary.

A parade of annuals

The following list contains many different types of annuals, biennials, and tender perennials. Some annuals bloom only briefly; others are grown for their foliage rather than for their flowers. Choose the ones that suit your climate and needs.

❀ **Flossflower** (*Ageratum houstonianum* 'Blue Horizon'): You may be familiar with the low-bedding version of this plant, with little blue or white puffballs in tidy mounds. 'Blue Horizon' is a better plant for intermingling with perennials. It's tall and narrowly upright and can be easily tucked in to fill gaps in the flower bed. The foliage is dark green, modified heart-shaped, wrinkled, and scalloped around the edges. The flowers are clusters of furry, lavender blue sputniks that make good cut flowers.

❀ **Hollyhock** (*Alcea rosea*): Large, showy flowers on spires are available in singles (a single row of petals), semi-doubles (a double row of petals), or doubles (which look like the tissue flowers that kids make). Colors range from pinks, reds, salmon, cream, white, and yellows.

❀ **Snapdragon** (*Antirrhinum majus*): What child can resist sticking a finger in the dragon's mouth? A charming, nostalgic flower, the snapdragon comes in a wide assortment of colors and heights. Taller varieties fit well inside the flower bed, and dwarf clump forms make good edging plants.

❀ **Blue-eyed African daisy** (*Arctotis stoechadifolia grandis*): The blue-eyed African daisy has large, graceful white flowers with steely blue center discs and a yellow ring at the base of the petals. The blooms have an annoying habit of closing up on cloudy days and in the afternoon, but, otherwise, it's a spectacular plant. This one blooms straight through early frosts until the first hard frost. The foliage is felted gray with a bushy habit.

❀ **Pot marigold** (*Calendula officinalis*): Not as well-known as the true marigold, the pot marigold is a very useful annual that's grown as a cool-season annual in hot, humid climates. The flowers are yellow, orange, apricot, or cream daisies, with a single row of petals or layers of overlapping petals, and are long-lasting cut flowers.

❀ **Canterbury bells** (*Campanula medium*): A must for the cottage garden, these charming old favorites produce plump, nodding bellflowers on lax stems. Canterbury bells come in a wide variety of heights and colors. These biennials form a rosette of leaves the first season and bloom early the following spring. True annual forms are also available for spring planting and same-year flowering.

❀ **Sunflower** (*Helianthus annuus*): The same flowers that are responsible for the seeds and oil, sunflowers are also currently a very popular decorative motif, showing up just about anywhere — from T-shirts to kitchenware. Many outstanding forms besides the familiar bright yellow are available. 'Italian White' is white with only a hint of yellow. 'Velvet Queen' and 'Prado Red' are dark, velvety mahogany red. All varieties make great cut flowers, and birds love the seeds.

❀ **Rose mallow** (*Lavatera* hybrids): This plant brings a reliable splash of color to the late summer garden when most of the perennials are taking a time-out. Delicate, silky rose, cerise, and clear white varieties of hibiscus-like flowers sit on bushy mounds of dark green foliage.

❀ **Love-in-a-mist** *(Nigella damascena):* The individual plants of love-in-a-mist are in flower only briefly, but because the seeds germinate unevenly, a new crop is usually starting tirelessly throughout the growing season. The flowers are starry and surrounded by a veil of threadlike green leaves for an other-worldly effect. The foliage is ferny, and the seedpods make wonderful additions to dried flower arrangements.

❀ **Castor bean** *(Ricinus communis):* A big, bold plant, castor bean is excellent for quick, temporary fill, or you may want to leave a space in the flower bed so that you can fit it in every year. It comes in solid green, cut leaf, and red forms. My favorite is 'Carmencita', which has huge reddish leaves. Pink buds open to insignificant, fluffy white flowers. The seedpods are attractive, bright red studded balls with deep reddish purple stems. Castor bean imparts a tropical, exotic air to the temperate garden.

The beans contained inside the castor bean seedpods are deadly poisonous. They resemble edible dried beans when they're ripe, which makes them especially dangerous to small children. If you decide to grow this plant where children have access to it, cut off the flower spikes so that the seeds can't form. If you harvest pods for next year's seed, store them out of reach of children, just as you store any household poison.

Shrub Starters

Unless you're starting from scratch with a brand-new landscape, the one thing that you probably feel that you already have enough of on your property is shrubs. So right now you're probably wondering why a book on perennials would advocate planting more shrubs or leaving a few in place in the flower bed. But shrubs have many benefits:

✔ They provide year-round structure.

✔ They shelter the flowers (and you) from the sun and wind.

✔ They create a permanent privacy screen.

✔ They make a neutral background for your perennials.

Many shrubs also produce flowers and seedheads that are every bit as attractive as the perennials themselves. They may add the constant of evergreen foliage or the fascinating tracery of bare twigs to the winter garden. In fall, their changing leaf colors round out and echo the reds, yellows, and oranges of the surrounding landscape.

You can treat some shrubs like herbaceous perennial flowers, cutting them to the ground once a year to keep them small and compact. These shrubs — sometimes called *subshrubs* or *prubs (perennial* and *shrub)* — must be fast growers that form their flower buds on the current season's new growth. Don't try this trick on lilacs or other shrubs that form new flower buds immediately after blooming, or you won't get any flowers next year.

Pruning particulars

Pruning is simply the act of cutting off unwanted growth. To keep shrubs blooming strongly and in scale with the flower bed, prune them whenever they get too big for their space. Always make cuts just above outward-facing buds.

Use one of these three methods for pruning:

- ✔ Cut the branches to within a few inches of the ground (see Figure 10-3).
- ✔ Shorten each stem by approximately one-third.
- ✔ Remove all three-year-old branches to the ground.

Figure 10-3:
One method of pruning shrubs involves cutting the branches to within a few inches of the ground.

Shrubs for show

A good shrub for the perennial flower bed is one that does all the following:

- ✔ It pays its dues in all four seasons. For example, variegated dogwood blooms for several weeks in the spring. In the summer, it produces pretty berries. Its already-attractive foliage turns a magnificent red in the fall. The berries hang on into the winter, rounding out a full year of beauty.

- ✔ It's small enough at maturity that it stays in scale with the rest of the flower bed. In other words, small flower beds need small shrubs.

- ✔ It doesn't *sucker* too badly — sending up new stems far away from the parent plant. After all, you don't want the shrubs to form a thicket inside the flower bed.

- ✔ It has upright or only slightly arching branches, so that it's less likely to overwhelm neighboring flowers.

- ✔ It tolerates root competition and crowding without complaint.

The shrubs that are described in the next few pages satisfy these requirements and make excellent additions to your garden.

- ❀ **Japanese barberry** *(Berberis thunbergii):* Especially worthy for the flower garden are the Japanese barberry varieties with red, yellow, or variegated leaves. The leaves are small, and the overall form is densely rounded and slightly spreading. The spring flowers are cute, though not remarkable. But the flowers are followed by bright red, teardrop-shaped fruits that hang on into the winter after the leaves drop and all varieties exhibit brilliant fall color.

  This shrub is thorny, so place it with low-maintenance flowers so that you don't get any bloodier than is absolutely necessary.

- ❀ **Butterfly bush** *(Buddleia davidii):* A butterfly bush can easily outgrow flower-garden size in mild-winter climates, so choose dwarf varieties or plan to chop it down to the ground once a year. In cold climates, winter kills this shrub to the ground, keeping all varieties manageably small. This plant forms an open shrub with long, arching stems and sprays of sweetly fragrant flowers from midsummer until first frost. The foliage is dark green or silvery gray, varying by variety.

- ❀ **Blue mist spirea** *(Caryopteris clandonensis):* A good four-season shrub, blue mist spirea is traditionally grown in the flower bed and cut down to the ground annually. It has a twiggy, loosely rounded form with narrow, lance-shaped, slightly toothed gray green leaves that are silver green on the reverse side. This shrub produces a mist of soft blue flowers in late summer. The seedheads fade from green to golden beige and persist all winter.

This shrub attracts bees, so don't place it next to a walk or a patio if bees frighten you, or if you're allergic to them.

❀ **Variegated dogwood** (*Cornus alba* 'Argenteo-marginata'): Beautiful at every season, the variegated dogwood is deciduous, but the bare stems turn bright red in winter, contrasting attractively with dried grasses, seedheads, and evergreens. The leaves are soft, grayed green with creamy, uneven leaf margins that turn purplish red in fall. Showy, flat clusters of ivory flowers are followed by blue-tinted berries.

❀ **'Carol Mackie' daphne** (*Daphne burkwoodii* 'Carol Mackie'): An elegant, graceful shrub, the 'Carol Mackie' daphne makes a real statement in the flower border. Each leaf is small and oval-shaped with soft gray green outlined in gold. This shrub fairly shimmers in soft light. It's evergreen in all but the harshest winters. The flowers are tight, starry little nosegays, opening white and aging to pink. Their knock-your-socks-off fragrance carries great distances across the garden.

❀ **Jerusalem sage** (*Phlomis fruticosa*): An easy, good-natured, informal shrub for cool, mild-winter, and coastal climates, the Jerusalem sage tolerates cooler areas of hot, humid climates. It has a lax, somewhat sprawling form and wrinkled, gray green leaves covered with white down on their undersides. The flowers are bright yellow and are carried in dense, heavy whorls at the end of each stem.

❀ **'Bonica' rose** (*Rosa* 'Bonica'): This variety blooms all summer and forms attractive red fruits in the fall. 'Bonica' is a lovely pink rose, but it's only one representative of the many outstanding shrub and land-scape roses compatible with perennial flowers. If you're interested in growing roses, pick up a copy of *Roses For Dummies* by Lance Walheim and the National Gardening Association (published by IDG Books Worldwide, Inc.).

❀ **Autumn sage** (*Salvia greggii*): A bushy, evergreen shrub, autumn sage has upright stems covered with flowers from spring through frost. The leaves are dark green, oval, glossy, and aromatic when bruised or crushed. The flowers are somewhat tubular, with asymmetrical open-ings. This shrub is available in many colors — rose, salmon, red, purple, and white — and attracts hummingbirds.

❀ **Bumold spirea** (*Spiraea bumalda*): With showy flowers, bumold spirea is similar to pink yarrow, but without the aggressive spreading tenden-cies. It forms small shrubs with dark green foliage and flat clusters of fuzzy flowers. 'Anthony Waterer' and 'Froebelii' both produce bright pink blossoms. The leaves of 'Gold Flame' emerge rusty red in the spring and fade to yellow by summer. All varieties have bright fall color, from soft orange to purplish red.

Part IV
Making Your Bed

In this part . . .

1f you spent your childhood playing with erector sets and building blocks, you're going to like this part best. Here begins the building phase of gardening — ideas on paper actually become a reality as you follow the steps in this part.

Chapter 11 shows you how to identify the peculiarities of your soil and how to compensate for its shortcomings. Chapter 12 introduces you to structural elements you can build to make your garden more comfortable, practical, and enticing. Then explore the benefits of a protective blanket of mulch in Chapter 13. Finally, I show you how to shop for perennials and put them in the ground in Chapter 14.

Chapter 11

The Dirt on Dirt

*O*ther mortals dream of wealth, fame, and riches, but gardeners are a different sort. What they yearn for is the elusive *perfect soil.* Good soil makes all the difference between a garden that prospers and one that struggles and sulks. When you begin to recognize soil as a living, breathing, and evolving entity that needs as much monitoring and care as the flowers themselves, you've cracked the code to successful gardening.

The ideal soil for most perennials is deep and porous, neither holding too much water nor drying out too quickly. Perennials also prefer soils rich in plant nutrients and *humus* — decomposed organic matter.

Unlike vegetable gardens, where gardeners recharge the soil between crops, flower beds are more permanent features. Initially digging fertilizer and such into the ground to correct deficiencies in your soil (a procedure called *amending soil*) is hard work, but all your sweat and blisters are repaid many times over. If you prepare and maintain a flower bed correctly, you may never need to dig it again.

Getting to Know Your Soil

Soil is a mixture of decaying organic matter, air, water, living organisms, and various types of weathered rock. Factors such as the bedrock composition, climate, and topography unique to each area can cause soil ingredients to vary dramatically from one region to the next.

Testing texture

A soil's *texture* (that is, its fineness or coarseness) has nothing to do with organic-matter or nutrient makeup. Soil texture is defined by its relative volume of three types of mineral particles:

- **Sand:** The stuff of beaches and sandboxes, sand is coarse and gritty. It drains well, but it dries out too quickly for most perennials. Sandy soil doesn't compact and is easy to cultivate, but nutrients wash out of it too readily.

- **Silt:** Silt is similar to sand, but the individual particles are much smaller. When silt is dry, it feels like flour. Silt holds water longer than sand, but not as tightly as clay.

- **Clay:** Clay is so fine that each particle can be seen only with an electron microscope. Clay soils are sticky to the touch and drain slowly. Some clays liquefy when wet and then dry to the consistency of concrete. Clay cakes on shoes and tools. It's high in nutrients, but these nutrients often occur in forms unavailable to plants.

Fortunately, few soils are composed of only one of these mineral particle types — most soils are a combination of all three.

When the mineral particles occur in ideal proportions, the soil is called *loam*. Loam contains 10 to 20 percent clay, 25 to 70 percent silt, and 20 to 60 percent sand. Very few gardeners get loam. You probably have to make do with soil that contains too high a percentage of either sand or clay for the perennials you plan to grow. Determining your soil's texture is critical, because each type has distinct characteristics and management requirements. You may also find that you have several types of soil. Probably more than one truck load of fill dirt was used to contour your property, and each load may have originated from many different sources.

You can get a fairly accurate measure of your soil's texture by using one or both of the following simple tests. Get ready to re-live your seventh grade science class.

The feel test

To conduct the feel test, grab a fistful of moist — not squishy wet — soil and squeeze it into a ball. Examine the results:

- Sand doesn't hold together very well and feels gritty and coarse.

- Silt can hold a shape fairly well and feels smooth but not sticky. If you roll silt between your palms, it forms a fat clump but doesn't hold a rope shape.

- Clay feels slippery, and you can roll it between the palms of your hands into an elongated rope shape.

If your handful of soil holds its shape briefly and then slowly crumbles apart to look like chocolate cake crumbs, congratulations! You've won the soil lottery! You have loam or a soil with a large percentage of organic matter. Either soil is perfect for a wide range of perennials.

The jar test

The jar test is a low-tech version of the soil lab's texture test, one that you can do at home. It tells you the basic character of your soil — whether your soil is predominantly sand, silt, or clay.

1. **Add 1 inch (2.5 cm) of dry soil to a quart jar.**

   Mayonnaise and peanut butter jars do nicely.

2. **Fill the jar two-thirds full of water.**

3. **Add one teaspoon of non-sudsing detergent or water softener.**

4. **Screw on the lid and shake the jar vigorously.**

5. **Set the jar where it can be left completely undisturbed for at least three days.**

6. **After three days, measure each layer that settles out.**

   The layers are quite distinct, as shown in Figure 11-1.

7. **Multiply the depth of each layer by 100 and then divide the result by the total depth of all three layers.**

   The number that you calculate is the percentage of each particle type. Sand is the heaviest and forms the bottom layer. Silt forms the middle layer, and clay is on top. (Some clay particles are so light that they float in suspension indefinitely.)

Figure 11-1:
The jar test
in action.

Water

Clay

Silt

Sand

Complete soil testing

For a more accurate, complete soil test, contact your state's cooperative extension service, usually located at the state agricultural college or a private laboratory. Or call the Green Gems Company at (800) 431-SOIL. This company works with several professional soil labs and tests for 15 essential soil elements. It sends reports back to you by mail, fax, or e-mail. The cost is $23, including shipping and handling.

A soil test isn't essential unless you're experiencing problems or you suspect that your soil is high in salt, but knowing the availability of the various soil nutrients can guide you to more efficient fertilizer use. You don't need to add elements that the soil test indicates already exist in your soil in sufficient quantities. The soil test results include recommendations for improving the soil, and that advice can be very helpful for the new gardener.

Soil tests do have their limitations. The sample you send to the lab is an average of soils collected throughout the garden. The smaller the garden, the more likely the sample is representative of the conditions there. Usually one test is all you need. Inexpensive home tests enable you to monitor soil pH, as well as nitrogen, phosphorus, and potassium levels routinely thereafter.

Desperately seeking structure

Soil structure is determined by the way the individual particles of sand, silt, and clay clump together. When a soil has good structure, it includes plenty of space for air and water. The earth under your feet is not as solid as your senses tell you. Healthy soil contains approximately 50 percent solids (mineral particles and organic matter), 25 percent water, and 25 percent air. Many physical forces (including root expansion in the soils, wet and dry cycles, freezing and thawing, and earthworm activity) push these solids together.

The glue that cements the lumps of soil together may be clay particles or chemical substances. One glue that you can easily add yourself is organic matter. Picture a bowl of dry popcorn and peanuts. Now imagine adding sticky syrup. If you pour the syrup over the top without stirring, a solid mass forms — a popcorn-peanut brick. But when you mix all the ingredients together, clumps form instead, and you end up with caramel corn. In much the same way, digging organic matter into light soils creates crumbs and openings *(pores)* that give plant roots, air, water, and nutrients easy access into and through the soil.

Organic matter is the cure to almost every soil problem you encounter. Adding it to sandy soil increases the soil's capacity to hold water and nutrients. Organic matter loosens clay and creates pockets for air and water. Organic matter also nurtures the populations of microorganisms, insects, and worms that make their home in the soil (see the section "Creatures of the Deep," later in this chapter). They, in turn, break the organic matter down into a form of nutrients that the plant roots can absorb.

Fertile soil contains a minimum of 5 percent decaying organic matter, but soil can hardly contain too much of this material if you compost and age the organic matter a while before you add it to the garden.

You damage soil structure by working the soil when it's wet or by compacting it (wet or dry) with machinery or foot traffic. To demonstrate compacted soil, take a shovel full of damp soil and fluff it up by turning it several times and breaking apart large clods. Now pile this soil onto a flat surface and step on it. It flattens considerably — you've just crushed out most of the pore spaces and compacted the soil.

Looking at layers

Soils occur in three separate layers, but only the top two layers, topsoil and subsoil, concern the gardener. You can easily observe the three layers in road cuts or excavation sites.

- ✔ **Topsoil:** The fertile band of soil on the surface, where organic matter accumulates and most of the soil organisms and plant roots reside, is called *topsoil.* This layer is usually 4 to 6 inches (10 to 15 cm) thick but is sometimes much deeper. Topsoil is deepest in prairies and meadows with moderate rainfall and is more shallow on slopes, in forests, and in areas with dry climates. In semiarid regions, topsoil is only one or two inches deep.

    When building a new residence, arrange for the contractor to save your topsoil and put it back when construction is complete. This valuable resource is worth the extra cost and work you put into preserving it.

- ✔ **Subsoil:** The layer under the topsoil, *subsoil* can be up to several feet (about a meter) deep. Subsoil stores water and nutrients that have rinsed through the topsoil from above. Usually low in organic matter and free of weed seeds, subsoil often has a finer texture because clay particles filter down and collect at this level. Subsoil is denser and more compacted than topsoil. The fill around a new house is often subsoil from the site's excavation.

- ✔ **Bottomsoil:** The bottom layer of soil is made up of decomposed bedrock. The only things you find growing in bottomsoil are tree roots.

Creatures of the Deep

A whole universe of microscopic organisms, insects, worms, and animals inhabit healthy topsoil.

- ✔ **Microorganisms:** The numbers of microorganisms are staggering — up to a few billion in one thimbleful of soil. Microorganisms in soil include bacteria, fungi, algae, actinomycetes, mycorrhizae, lichens, protozoa, and slime molds. Their busy communities consume wastes, have complex interactions with plant roots, and prey upon one another. Their populations are largest in soil that is warm, moist, and rich in organic matter.

- ✔ **Earthworms:** No other creature does more for soil health than the lowly, hardworking earthworm. These worms break up and turn over an enormous volume of soil. Large nightcrawlers can tunnel and bury deeply in the soil, improving even sterile subsoil. Wherever they go, worms leave behind wastes (called *casts*) that are rich in micro-organisms and fertilizers. You don't need to purchase earthworms. Add humus to your soil, and these opportunists appear as if by magic.

- ✔ **Larger animals:** Many insects, worms, and animals large enough to be seen without a microscope make their home underground. These rototillers of the animal world are mobile in the soil, excavating holes, burrows, and chambers; taking food, bedding, and droppings under-ground; and bringing huge quantities of soil to the surface. Moles, gophers, and other rodents don't usually inspire gratitude in the gardener, but they do much to improve soil fertility throughout the world.

Soil Chemistry Simplified

Soil *acidity* or *alkalinity* is expressed as pH on a scale of 1 to 14. The higher the pH, the greater the alkalinity; the lower the pH, the greater the acidity. A pH of 7.0 is neutral. For comparison purposes, the pH of grapefruit is 3.0 and the pH of milk of magnesia is 10. The optimum pH for most perennials is 6.5 to 7.5, though all but the most sensitive can tolerate a pH of 5.5 to 8.3 without developing problems. Some types of plants can grow at the edge of the 3.5 to 10 range, but only a limited number of plants can flourish where the soil pH is so extreme.

In pine and oak forests and in regions where rainfall exceeds 25 inches (60 cm) annually, soil tends to be acidic. Where rainfall is less than 25 inches annually, most soils are alkaline or close to neutral. But the only way to be certain is to test your soil. Kits that use litmus paper or a test tube are easy to use and inexpensive. They can be purchased at garden centers or hard-ware stores. Just follow the label instructions carefully.

Neutralizing very acidic soil

Where soil pH measures below 5.5, the selection of perennials that you can grow is severely restricted. Many perennials fail at this pH. Some essential nutrients become unavailable to the plant; others can rise to toxic levels. If your soil pH is below 5.5, you have two options:

- Choose perennials that are adapted to acidic soil (see Table 11-1 for a few perennials that don't mind acidic soil).
- Raise the pH by adding lime.

Lime is available as agricultural lime, ground limestone, calcium carbonate, or dolomite limestone. Check with your state's cooperative extension service for recommendations on which type is best for your local conditions, and follow their recommended application rates.

Don't attempt to raise the pH more than one point in a single season. Make it a gradual process for better results. Work the lime into the top 6 to 8 inches (15 to 20 cm) of the soil several months before planting, and don't add fertilizer within one month of adding lime. In cold weather, affecting a change can take as long as six months. In warm weather, three months is usually sufficient. Heavy, clay soils require more lime than light, sandy soils. Test the pH levels once or twice a season to monitor changes after adding lime.

Table 11-1	Perennials for Acidic Soil	
Common Name	*Botanical Name*	*Sun Requirements*
Butterfly flower	*Asclepias tuberosa*	Sun
Thousand-flowered aster	*Boltonia asteroides*	Partial shade/sun
Dutchman's breeches	*Dicentra cucullaria*	Shade/partial shade
Japanese iris	*Iris ensata*	Partial shade/sun
Lupine	*Lupinus* Russell Hybrids	Partial shade/sun
Himalayan blue poppy	*Meconopsis betonicifolia*	Partial shade/sun
Virginia bluebells	*Mertensia virginica*	Shade/partial shade
Allegheny monkey flower	*Mimulus ringens*	Partial shade
Cinnamon fern	*Osmunda cinnamomea*	Shade/sun
Primrose	*Primula auricula*	Partial shade

Coping with alkaline soils

Soils with a pH higher than 8.3 can limit the availability of phosphorus, iron, zinc, and magnesium. An irony with Colorado's soils is that, although their bright red color is caused by an abundance of iron in the soil, the iron is in a form that's unavailable to plants. Plants growing in this iron-rich soil often suffer from iron deficiency.

Acid-loving perennials are the least tolerant of high pH and become yellowed and stunted (a condition called *chlorosis*) due to nutrient shortages. Because these soils generally occur in arid and semiarid regions, they also tend to be low in organic matter and high in salts.

Lowering pH is more difficult than raising it, but you can do a few things to make alkaline soil more acidic. You can add peat moss, ground needles, or oak leaves and add acidifying minerals such as sulfur, ferrous sulfate, and ammonium sulfate. Follow the manufacturer's recommended amounts. Regular irrigation also eventually reduces pH unless the water is high in soluble salts.

Where pH is high and water isn't plentiful, prepare only one flower bed for your favorite perennials that demand altered soil. Then plan the rest of the garden around the wide selection of native and adapted flowers that accept the existing conditions. Keep in mind that perennials that originate in acidic soils may also be intolerant of the strong sunlight and the low humidity that are typical of climates where alkaline soils are common. In this case, locate the flower bed where it can enjoy the morning sun and afternoon shade.

Detecting Nutrient Deficiencies and Infertile Soils

Occasionally, folks tell me that nothing grows in their soil. Usually, the cause is improper gardening practices such as over- or under-watering. If a soil test indicates nutrient shortages, adding organic matter and a complete, balanced fertilizer quickly set things right. But sometimes, the problem is bigger than improper gardening practices or nutrient shortages.

Checking for chemicals

A thick, thriving stand of weeds doesn't make your yard the pride of the neighborhood, but it does indicate healthy soil. Figuring out what's happening in those places where even weeds won't grow takes some detective work.

Oil or other petroleum products dumped on your land or past applications of a persistent herbicide can prevent all plant growth. Standard soil tests don't check for these substances, and testing specifically for them can be prohibitively expensive.

A simple test that you can conduct is to plant radish seeds in suspect areas. Keep the soil moist and stand back! Radishes germinate rapidly. If they come up, chemicals aren't the problem. Amend the soil and try planting the flowers you want again. If the radishes don't come up or you detect the tell-tale odor of petrochemicals, remove the contaminated soil and replace it with new topsoil. Or you can be patient and wait for the toxins to wash out of the soil naturally. Depending on the chemical, this process may take a few years or a lifetime.

Coping with heavy clay soils

Heavy clay soil doesn't even come close to anyone's definition of an ideal soil. Most gardeners aim to create soil resembling chocolate cake crumbs — loose, rich, and crumbly. Damp clay, on the other hand, has the consistency and texture of fudge. It feels cold, slippery, and dense to the touch. When saturated with water, clay quickly becomes as structureless as quicksand (well, almost!). I have sunk in up to my knees many times after a rainstorm has drenched my clay soil. Dry clay is also formidable stuff. It deflects even the strongest hand. Attack bone-dry clay enthusiastically with a metal spade, and rather than plunging in, the spade clangs as resoundingly as if it had been slammed into a solid rock.

Clay soil is literally heavy — wet or dry. After hefting a few scoops, you start to imagine that you're shoveling cannonballs. Poor drainage is common in clay soils and may lead to a waterlogged site, a condition that few perennials tolerate without complaint. Conversely, clay can be amazingly good at resisting water. Some clays have pore spaces that are too small for water to penetrate easily, and water just runs off after moistening the surface.

This description sounds awfully grim, but clay soil also has some real advantages compared to lighter, sandier soil. It's loaded with nutrients and retains water well. Adding organic matter to clay remedies all of its unfavorable characteristics and results in a soil that requires less water and added fertilizer than a sandy soil. To create a soil favorable to a wide variety of perennials, add at least 4 inches (10 cm) of well-composted organic matter to the top 8 inches (20 cm) of the flower bed.

If you don't want to fight clay soil, plant your garden with a selection of perennials (see Table 11-2) that thrive in clay.

Table 11-2	Perennials for Heavy Clay Soil	
Common Name	*Botanical Name*	*Sun Requirement*
Lady's mantle	*Alchemilla mollis*	Partial shade/sun
Three-veined everlasting	*Anaphalis triplinervis*	Sun
Goat's beard	*Aruncus dioicus*	Partial shade/sun
False spirea	*Astilbe arendsii*	Partial shade/sun
Pigsqueak	*Bergenia cordifolia*	Partial shade
Purple coneflower	*Echinacea purpurea*	Sun
Daylily	*Hemerocallis* hybrids	Partial shade/sun
Plantain lily	*Hosta sieboldii*	Shade/partial shade
Bistort	*Persicaria bistorta*	Shade/partial shade
Self-heal	*Prunella webbiana*	Partial shade/sun
Buttercup	*Ranunculus aconitifolius* 'Pleniflorus'	Partial shade/sun
Lamb's ears	*Stachys byzantina*	Partial shade/sun

Sandy, gravely soils

Pure sand or gravel is essentially a sterile medium. It doesn't contain adequate nutrients to suit most perennials. Fertilizer and water filter on through. Trying to irrigate sand is about as productive and frustrating as catching water in a sieve. Your goal is to make this type of soil hold more water.

To do this, you need to dig in huge quantities of organic matter and other materials to soak up water and provide nutrients and trace elements. Mix in at least 1 foot (30 cm) of organic matter to the top foot of soil. Any soil amendment except more sand and crushed rock can improve the moisture-retaining capacity of sandy soils.

Peat moss acts like a super-sponge, absorbing up to 20 times its weight in water. It's worth the money you spend on it because it does such a great job of improving water retention. But because peat moss is also sterile, you need to use liberal amounts of compost and manure as well, to boost the nutrient content of the soil.

Amending sandy soils for flower beds is an on-going process. Whatever organic matter you add decomposes eventually and washes away, so you need to continually replenish it by top-dressing the flower bed with manure or compost once or twice a year and by covering the soil with a heavy layer of an organic mulch (see Chapter 13). Clean, unscented kitty litter and *turface,* a calcine clay, are absorbent, porous clay products that hold water efficiently and are durable — they don't readily break down. Or, if you have a source of heavy clay, you can dig in some of that, too. (Perhaps you can find a gardener who's struggling with clay soil and work out a trade!)

Table 11-3 lists a few of the perennials that prefer sandy soils.

Table 11-3	Perennials for Sandy Soil	
Common Name	*Botanical Name*	*Sun Requirement*
'Moonshine' yarrow	*Achillea* 'Moonshine'	Sun
Common thrift	*Armeria maritima*	Sun
Butterfly flower	*Asclepias tuberosa*	Sun
Bluebells	*Campanula rotundifolia*	Light shade/sun
Blue Cupid's dart	*Catananche caerulea*	Sun
Blanket flower	*Gaillardia aristata*	Sun
Sea lavender	*Limonium latifolium*	Sun
Catmint	*Nepeta faassenii*	Sun
Beardtongue	*Penstemon grandiflorus*	Sun
Showy goldenrod	*Solidago speciosa*	Light shade/sun

Breaking on through

Hardpan is a band of soil that water can't penetrate. When hardpan lies just beneath the surface, it can block plant roots and cause problems with irrigation and drainage. Hardpan in low spots can act as a dam; water doesn't drain away at all, and a pond forms after every rainstorm. You can either break up small areas of hardpan with a jack hammer or pick ax, or you can build raised beds to increase the soil depth (see Chapter 12 for more on raised beds).

In some geographic areas, compacted soil and hardpan occur naturally. But more often they are caused by the repeated use of heavy machinery. The cure is digging up and loosening the soil. If you're starting with a new landscape, you can hire a contractor to till the whole property with a tractor and at the same time add amendments to the top foot of soil. For a small area, you can correct compacted soils by hand in a process called *double-digging.* I can tell you from personal experience that double-digging greatly resembles grave digging (see Figure 11-2). My neighbors couldn't hide their

Figure 11-2:
Double-
digging is a
good way to
amend your
soil really
deeply.

curiosity when they saw me standing in a hole up to my knees shoveling away day after day. I think they were inventorying my family and pets to see whether any of them were missing.

To double-dig a garden bed, follow these steps:

1. **Dig out the top 10 inches (25 cm) of soil and put that soil aside.**

2. **Mix 2 to 3 inches (5 to 8 cm) of organic matter into the soil at the bottom of the hole.**

3. **Replace the top layer of soil, mixing 2 to 3 inches (5 to 8 cm) of organic matter into it, as well.**

Keep in mind that double-digging raises the soil height considerably.

Seizing the swamp

Continually wet soils can be caused by underground springs, which can pop up suddenly where you least expect them. Wet soils can also be caused by

- ✔ Natural bogs
- ✔ Swales (low-lying areas in heavy clay where water collects)
- ✔ Runoff from an adjoining property

You can direct the water away from the wet spot with drain tiles, perforated plastic tubing, or with surface drains. Or you can seize this opportunity to create a bog or wet meadow garden. This plan can backfire if the neighbor stops flooding your property, but the risk of that happening is probably not too great.

To test a soil's drainage, dig a hole 1 to 2 feet deep. Fill it with water and see how long the water takes to drain away. If no water is left in the hole after an hour or two, drainage is too quick: The soil dries out before the perennials have a chance to absorb the water. If the water is still in the hole 12 hours later, the soil holds water too well to grow perennials except those that thrive on wet conditions, such as the ones listed in Table 11-4.

Table 11-4	Perennials for Wet Places	
Common Name	*Botanical Name*	*Sun Requirement*
Sweet flag	*Acorus calamus*	Partial shade/sun
Camass	*Camassia*	Sun
Canna lily	*Canna* hybrids	Sun
Joe-pye weed	*Eupatorium maculatum* 'Gateway'	Light shade/sun
Daylily	*Hemerocallis* hybrids	Sun
Rose mallow	*Hibiscus moscheutos*	Sun
Japanese iris	*Iris ensata*	Partial shade/sun
Cardinal flower	*Lobelia cardinalis*	Light shade
Forget-me-not	*Myosotis palustris*	Partial shade/sun
Buttercup	*Ranunculus aconitifolius*	Partial shade/shade
Globe flower	*Trollius europaeus*	Partial shade/sun

Salty soils

Salt comes in many forms. Table salt is usually what comes to mind, but many other substances contain soil-damaging salt:

- ✔ Along the seaside or in regions where rainfall isn't heavy or frequent enough to rinse soils out, naturally occurring salts can accumulate to levels that are toxic to most perennials.

- ✔ Irrigating your garden with salty water is not good for your perennials. Never use *softened water* (water treated with sodium salt) on the garden. If your household water is softened, have a plumber rig the outside taps so that the water from those taps hasn't passed through your water softener.

- ✔ Another source of damaging salts is road salt, used to melt ice in the winter. You can't do much about what the road crews put down. But for your own sidewalks and driveway, use kitty litter or gravel instead of salt — or just use good old-fashioned shovel-power.

✔ Even fertilizers are salts, which explains why improperly applying fertilizers burns foliage (see Chapter 16).

To combat salty soil, you can flood the soil with several inches of water to wash the salts out. Improving soil drainage and structure by adding organic matter also helps the washing-out process. Raised beds are the best solution in places where water is scarce. A barrier, such as a weed fabric and several inches of gravel, must be placed between the salt-affected soil and the new topsoil to protect foraging roots (see Chapter 12 for more on raised beds).

Making the Bed

Prepare the soil several months before you anticipate planting if you can. This schedule gives a new bed time to settle down and microorganisms a chance to work on the soil amendments and sort out any imbalances. In cold climates, plan to do soil preparation in the fall in order to plant the following spring. Or reverse this schedule where summers are hot and winters are mild: Get the bed ready in spring or early summer for fall planting.

Mark the outlines of the flower bed according to your plan (see Chapter 3 for information on garden planning). Tie string between two stakes to mark straight lines and lay out flexible garden hose to define the curves. (Leave the hose out in the sun for a while if it is stiff or kinky. Rubber hoses are more flexible than plastic.) Play around with the dimensions and lines until you create a pleasing shape.

Clearing the site

Mow or use a power weed whacker to cut down any existing lawn or weeds. Be sure that you remove all the seedheads. For shrubs that need to be disposed of, cut off the tops and dig out the stumps and as many large roots as possible. Desirable shrubs can be carefully dug out and transplanted or left in place if your design calls for them. If left in the bed, leave as many roots undisturbed as practical. You can safely cut away those that are outside an imaginary circle on the ground that is as wide as the widest part of the top of the shrub.

Kill weeds or sod with one of the following methods:

✔ **Herbicides:** Use a product containing glyphosate according to the directions on the label. Persistent weeds may need multiple treatments.

✔ **Smothering with newspapers:** Spread a $^1/_4$-inch thickness of newspapers over the bed, overlapping the edges generously. Cover the newspapers with 6 inches of an organic mulch that decays rapidly. Straw or hay are good choices. Leave the newspaper in place for one growing season. If your soil is decent to begin with, you can plant right through the mulch and paper. If it isn't, dig the newspaper and mulch in together as a soil amendment.

✔ **Solarization:** *Solarization* is the process of sterilizing the soil with sunlight and the heat it generates. This process is especially useful where soil-borne diseases or pests are a problem. Animals simply leave, and most of the weeds and microorganisms (good and bad) are killed. After solarization, you need to reintroduce microorganisms by mixing compost or organic matter into the soil. (See the sidebar, "Solar power," for step-by-step instructions on solarizing your flower bed.)

To remove the dead sod, use a rented mechanical sod stripper or a spade. Better yet, till the sod right into the soil — sod is a great source of organic matter and nutrients. Left on the ground, the dead roots, leaves, and thatch create a well-amended layer 6 to 8 inches (15 to 21 cm) deep. Most important, you don't have to haul the heavy sod off to the compost pile to dispose of it.

Where the soil underneath is reasonably well-drained, you can save even more labor by planting right through the dead sod without rototilling. For each plant, cut out a circle of sod twice as large as the circumference of the plant container, or twice as wide as the root ball (if transplanting). Proceed by following the instructions for planting in Chapter 14.

TIP

Solar power

Because the process of solarization relies on the sun's heat, you must solarize in warm weather. To solarize your soil, follow these steps:

1. **Loosen soil with a rototiller or a shovel.**

2. **Water the area well.**

3. **Cover the bed with clear plastic sheeting.**

   Clear plastic sheeting is available in garden centers and hardware stores.

4. **Pin the plastic in place with landscape pins or pieces of wire and seal the edges with soil or boards.**

5. **Leave the plastic in place for several weeks or over the summer before proceeding.**

After solarizing your soil, be sure to import useful microorganisms back into the sterilized soil by digging in several inches of compost.

Amending your soil

When your site is clear of weeds, the next step is digging in the soil amendments.

If the soil is wet, postpone digging until it's only damp. To check the soil, grab a handful and squeeze. If water runs out or clay squishes between your fingers, wait until the soil is drier so that you don't damage the structure of the soil.

Amend the soil by following these steps:

1. **Choose the type of soil amendment you want and arrange for delivery.**

2. **Break up the soil, digging up a shovelful at a time.**

   Turn it over and use the blade of the shovel to chop up large clods. (Singing a chorus of "I want to break free!" helps pass the time!)

3. **Remove any large roots (over an inch [2 cm] or so in diameter), buried construction debris, and large rocks that you find.**

   If you hit bedrock just beneath the surface, you need to rethink the flower bed location or raise the bed.

4. **Next, spread 2 to 3 inches (5 to 8 cm) of soil amendment on the bed and dig it in thoroughly.**

   Now you can switch to a mechanical tiller or continue by hand. Add organic matter in stages, incorporating each layer into the soil well. Be careful not to till too much; the goal is to mix the materials into the bed but not pulverize the soil.

5. **Scatter commercial fertilizer or minerals on top of the last layer and mix them in.**

When you finish, your soil is light and fluffy. Make sure that you don't walk on it and compact it. Place boards or stepping stones where you need access to the bed. Let the area rest until time to plant or use a temporary cover crop to hold the bare soil in place.

Protecting the soil with a cover crop

A *cover crop* is any planting that comes up and fills in quickly. It prevents erosion, helps trap rainfall, and shades the ground (which deters remaining weed seeds from sprouting). Legumes such as alfalfa, clover, soybeans, and vetch are excellent choices, because all contribute significant amounts of nitrogen to the soil in which they grow. Buckwheat, grains, and grasses are also good choices.

To plant a cover crop:

1. **Rake the bed, broadcast the seeds, and rake the bed again to slightly bury the seeds.**

2. **Water to keep the bed moist until the seedlings are well up.**

   Don't let the cover crop go to seed, or it can become a reseeding pest in the flower bed.

3. **Mow off the tops and let the trimmings dry in place.**

4. **Till everything into the soil — roots and all — at least six weeks before you anticipate planting your flowers.**

Choosing a soil amendment

You can't add too much organic material to your soil — just be sure that you use material that is well-aged or composted. Use a minimum of one-third volume of organic material to one volume of soil to be amended. For example, dig at least 2 inches (5 cm) of organic matter into 6 inches (15 cm) of soil. Perfect soil, although rare, does exist occasionally. If you're one of the lucky ones and are starting out with a crumbly, rich loam, you have the option of skipping the whole process of soil amending if you want (although adding 2 to 3 inches (5 to 8 cm) of compost never hurts, especially if you plan to grow a large variety of perennials in close quarters). Where compaction is the only problem of an otherwise good soil, fluffing it up with a rototiller or hand digging may be all you need to do to restore good structure and prepare the bed for planting.

A valid alternative to soil preparation is choosing plants that are adapted to your existing soil. Very few soils are so poor that they can't support a satisfactory selection of flowers. But you must be content in this case to let the soil choose the flowers.

The following soil amendments are widely available. Your local garden center or hardware store may not carry all of them, but most of these stores offer a good selection to choose from:

- ✓ **Compost:** Whether your own or commercially developed, compost is the very best soil amendment. It contains beneficial microorganisms and important micronutrients and attracts earthworms that aid soil conditioning.

- **Cottonseed meal, alfalfa meal, blood meal:** These amendments are expensive but are good organic sources of nitrogen, which is needed for all plant growth, and organic matter.

- **Leaf mold:** Ground up, partially decomposed leaves make an excellent soil conditioner. Some communities compost leaves and return the leaf mold to residents.

- **Manure:** Manure can contain salts, so age it for one year and thoroughly compost it. You can use fresh manure if you don't plant the bed for several months after spreading. One drawback to manure is that it may contain weed seeds.

- **Peat moss:** Expensive, acidic peat moss is too fine to effectively break up heavy clay. Highly absorbent, peat moss is best used to improve the water-holding capacity of sand. Peat moss is sterile and free of weed seeds and diseases, but it contains no nutrients. Avoid using so-called "mountain peat," which can actually make your soil worse.

- **Perlite, vermiculite:** These are heat-treated mineral products. They are expensive and are best for seed starting and container-grown perennials.

- **Calcine:** Certain clay products, such as unscented, natural kitty litter and porous clay, improve the texture of sand or clay.

- **Pumice, crushed scoria:** These expensive materials can be used to loosen clay soils in small areas or added to soil mixes for container planting. They improves drainage and create pore spaces.

- **Polymers:** Manufactured polymers or starch crystals expand when hydrated and hold huge quantities of water. Research results are mixed, but some gardeners report real success with these products. Hydrate the products with hot water first and then mix them into soil with organic matter.

- **Composted sludge:** Composted sludge from municipal sewage treatment facilities is very much like manure and is a complete source of nutrients.

- **Superphosphate, bone meal:** Phosphorus doesn't move readily through the soil, so adding it during initial soil preparations ensures that it gets down into the root-growing area. Apply at the rate recommended by soil labs or follow the package instructions.

Chapter 12

Beyond Digging — Building Special Features for Your Flower Bed

Welcome to the sweat-making, blister-producing, muscle-building phase of gardening. During my own garden's construction stage, I was lucky to have the (mostly) enthusiastic help of a strong spouse and teenage sons. We spent the better part of five years hammering, sawing, hauling, and digging, and we killed a small station wagon by demanding that it double as a pick-up truck delivering lumber, brick, boulders, flagstone, manure, mulch, and gravel month after month.

We broke our large project into several stages and completed each stage before going on to the next. This arrangement allowed us to savor some sense of accomplishment while the garden was still a work in progress. Now that the building phase is finished, I truly miss it! Transforming a patch of weeds and dirt into a garden is a very rewarding experience.

For more specifics about building gardens, see *Gardening For Dummies,* by Michael MacCaskey (IDG Books Worldwide, Inc.), especially Chapters 1 through 4 and Chapter 13.

Getting professional help

None of the projects in this chapter is beyond the scope of the typical do-it-yourselfer. But the DIY-challenged can hire a landscape contractor to do the whole enchilada or any part of it. Building the structural details, amending the soil, mulching, and even buying the flowers and planting the garden are all tasks that you can delegate to a skilled worker, if you prefer.

To locate a good contractor, ask for referrals from friends and neighbors or check the phone book for a local or state landscape contractor's association.

Follow some simple tips when choosing a contractor:

✔ Get at least three estimates — prices can vary widely.

✔ Ask for references and then *call* the references to check whether other customers were satisfied and to make sure that the work was completed in a timely manner.

✔ Request a written proposal that clearly spells out the project, materials, and dates for beginning and ending the project.

Before You Build

Before you start working on any really ambitious garden plans (beyond flower beds), call your city's public works department (in the phone book under government listings) to see whether your city requires permits for any of the structural work you plan to do. Usually, permits are necessary only for walls over 3 feet tall (90 cm) or for concrete or electrical wiring installation.

Call your utility companies to find out the location of underground water, sewer, electrical, gas, phone, or cable lines on your property. If you damage these lines, you're responsible for the cost of repairs.

If you live in a covenant-controlled neighborhood, submit plans to the architectural control committee or the homeowner's association to ensure that you comply with its rules.

If you plan to build anything, even a small flower bed, along the property line, let the neighbors know what you have in mind. Keeping communications open with your neighbors can head off annoying grievances partway through your construction venture — and may even get your neighbors excited enough to pitch in and help.

When remodeling or starting from scratch, make sure that you don't paint yourself into a corner. The front yard may seem to be in more urgent need of cosmetic repair than the back. But don't block access to the rear so that you end up driving heavy equipment over your newly installed landscape to get to other parts of your yard.

You often save yourself a great deal of hauling labor if you have deliveries of heavy materials dropped off close to the work site. A rear alleyway or adjoining vacant lot provides convenient access. But be aware that vacant lots have a habit of sprouting up new houses when your back is turned, so keep a vigilant watch for grading equipment.

Be sure to kill any perennial weeds or grasses before starting construction. Some weeds are persistent enough to eventually work their way to the surface of the new soil and renew their enthusiastic terrorism of the flower beds. For the specifics on how to get rid of weeds, see Chapter 18, but keep in mind that hand pulling doesn't usually get rid of perennial weeds; it only makes them more resilient and determined. Every piece of root left in the ground can and usually does grow into a new weed.

The Magic of Raised Beds

Some soils and sites are so challenging for perennial gardening that your best option is to elevate the bed above ground level. When you're faced with a shallow soil over bedrock, put aside your crate of Acme dynamite and compromise by raising the bed.

A *raised bed* is any planting area in which soil is "raised" above the existing grade a few inches or more. Such beds may have sides of sloping soil, or they may be contained in planter boxes made of wooden frames or low stone walls. Figure 12-1 illustrates several types of raised beds that you can build.

Raising a flower bed enables you to deal with salt-affected soils without the time-consuming and often unsuccessful battle of getting the salts out of the soil. In addition, good drainage is absolutely assured in a raised bed, even over *hardpan* (see Chapter 11) or wet, soggy sites.

Controlling soil quality is simplified in a raised bed. You can choose exactly the right soil for the flowers you plan to grow. Use a good soil mix and fill the planter to within a few inches of the top to keep the soil from washing out. Fewer weed seeds find their way to an elevated surface, and those that do are conveniently within reach.

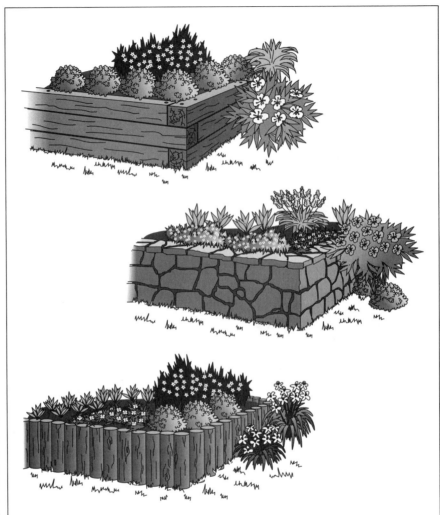

Figure 12-1:
Three
planter-box
types of
raised beds.

Raised beds offer many advantages beyond coping with bad soils:

✔ **Providing access for people with disabilities:** You can build raised beds to be just the right height to accommodate the needs of the wheelchair-bound or otherwise disabled gardener, as shown in Figure 12-2. Reaching the surface of the soil without having to bend or stoop is also a real help for anyone whose movements are restricted by back trouble. For even greater comfort, build benches right into the wall surrounding the raised bed so that you can garden from a seated position. Built-in benches also provide convenient extra seating for guests.

Figure 12-2:
Raised beds provide easy access to wheelchair-bound gardeners.

You can find inspiration from a host of gardens that have been specially designed for people with physical limitations. Some gardens, such as the Iselin Garden for the Blind in New Jersey, are specifically designed for people with sight impairments. Contact the Iselin Garden for the Blind at 1081 Green St., Iselin, NJ 08830; phone 201-283-1200, or online at `http://trine.com/GardenNet/GardensOnline/nj.htm#Iselin`. Visit GardenNet (`http://trine.com/GardenNet/GardensOnline`) for a list of nearly 50 gardens completely accessible by wheelchair, as well as fragrance gardens for people with sight impairments. Although not all of these gardens focus on perennials, they can certainly give you ideas for structuring your special-needs perennial bed.

✔ **Fixing property flaws:** You can use raised flower beds to break up uninteresting, flat pieces of property. Or terrace steep hillsides with a series of beds defined by short retaining walls and stairs to create more useful and eye-catching spaces.

✔ **Creating barriers:** Raised beds make effective barriers, directing traffic patterns around the bed and making it very clear that foot traffic is off limits there. Anywhere that a hedge seems an obvious choice, a raised bed provides a colorful, more solid alternative. Raised beds also add a decorative touch at the edge of walks, driveways, decks, and patios.

✔ **Extending the season:** Perennials benefit from raised beds even where soils aren't a problem. In climates with very short growing seasons, soil in a bed constructed from stone or brick thaws out and warms up faster in spring than soil at ground level. Stone and brick also collect and store heat during the day and slowly release it back into the bed when temperatures fall at night. Plants are thus protected from sudden cold snaps, and the growing season is extended. An extra few weeks can make all the difference in determining whether fall flowers have a long enough season to gather energy for their late show.

✔ **Protecting plants:** If you have small children or pets, putting the flowers in a raised planter keeps the flowers safe from casual assault. A single landscape timber is usually high enough to discourage drivers from running over and smashing flowers alongside a driveway, street, or alleyway. (If they do run over your flowers, you get satisfaction from knowing that the driver's tires probably took a pretty good beating in the process.) For a softening effect, plant flowers with a trailing habit at the edge of the bed so that they can spill out and flow down the sides.

Some gardens are completely overrun by gophers, moles, or other burrowing rodents. These furry gourmets enjoy nothing better than a meal of your perennials' roots. You can line the bottom of the planter box with wire mesh to prevent these pests from getting into the soil.

Boxes and berms

The simplest raised bed is a freestanding square or rectangular box, but you can build the bed in any shape at all. Design the bed to follow the contours of any feature in the landscape, or tuck a planter box against stairs or in front of an existing retaining wall to highlight or de-emphasize its structural character. For example, build a planter box at the foot of a tall, severe retaining wall to tone down that "Great Wall of China in the backyard" look. If you construct the planter box from the same materials as the retaining wall, the whole structure appears to be a single unit.

A *berm* is a mound of earth with sloping sides (see Figure 12-3). Berms are often less obtrusive than boxes are because they are completely free-form in shape and are the most flexible style of raised bed. Just be careful that the berm you build isn't too square, or it can look more like a bunker than a flower bed. Pattern berms after rolling hills — without obvious symmetry and sloped gently enough that gravity doesn't cause mini-landslides.

Berms must be stable so that they don't collapse when you stand on them to weed or care for the flowers. A few well-placed flat rocks give you a level surface to stand on and, at the same time, protect the soil from becoming compacted. Bury at least two-thirds of each rock into the hillside for stability and a more natural look.

Berms can be as simple as a dump truck load of topsoil or as complex as a formal rock garden. A foot of topsoil can also be layered over a core of tree trimmings, dead sod, or rock rubble. Whatever materials you use to construct a berm, allow for a great deal of shrinkage. Berms can settle as much as 50 percent the first couple of years.

Figure 12-3:
A berm is
just a
raised bed
without a
wall to
contain it.

Making the beds

Build a bed at least 12 to 18 inches (30 to 46 cm) high to create a deep space for plant roots to grow when your main objective is to raise the plants above bad soil or to improve inadequate drainage. A height of 6 inches (15 cm) is plenty when your only concern is deflecting foot or automobile traffic. If you plan to build benches into the garden wall, 14 to 18 inches (35 to 46 cm) is a comfortable height.

Make the bed no wider than you can easily reach across — 3 to 4 feet (90 cm to 1.2 m) when the bed is accessible from only one side, not much wider than 6 feet (1.8 m) when you can get to either side. In hot, dry climates, raised beds tend to dry out very rapidly. Wherever irrigation water is in short supply, keep the bed wide and low to slow evaporation and moisture loss.

Mortared brick, stone, or cinder blocks make elegant and durable planters. Stucco and patterned concrete are also strong, long-lasting materials. Drainage holes must be installed in any of these solid walls so that water can freely escape. Dry laid stone, recycled concrete chunks, and interlocking concrete modular systems are easy for the do-it-yourselfer with a strong back.

Stacking pressure-treated wood timbers, peeled logs, or railroad ties brings back memories of playing with Lincoln Logs, albeit very large ones. Cedar and redwood wear better than other wood products, but all wood deteriorates eventually from moisture, ultraviolet light, and attack from insects and microorganisms. In some climates, wood needs to be replaced frequently, perhaps in less than ten years. Wood may also attract termites. Where termites are a problem, don't build wooden beds close to the house or other structures.

To build a raised bed, follow these steps:

1. **Mark off the dimensions of the project according to the instructions in Chapter 3.**

2. **Kill any weeds by following the tips in Chapter 18.**

3. **Build the walls of the planter.**

   Of course, if you're building a berm, you can skip this step.

4. **If salty soils are the reason you're raising the bed, place several inches of gravel (available at most garden centers) in the bottom of the planter.**

   To counter salty soil, you must construct a barrier to keep the salt out of the new bed.

5. **Where the underlying soil is acceptable, use a spade or a shovel to loosen the top 6 inches (15 cm) of the soil.**

   Dig up one shovelful at a time, turning the soil and breaking up large clods with the shovel blade, to create a place for the plant roots to go deeper.

6. **Fill the planter with good soil.**

   If it's available, you can import good soil from other parts of your property. Otherwise, purchase soil from your local garden center.

Walks and Paths

Walks through the perennial garden serve a number of practical functions. They enable you to get up-close and personal with your garden. The viewer who can sit or stand inside the flower bed, surrounded by the flowers, feels less like a spectator than a person standing at the edge of a bed looking in to the flowers. Paths can also be used to divide large areas into several smaller and more easily managed sections, which creates the illusion of a larger space. The total area of the garden is expanded while reducing the size of the flower beds themselves — meaning more floral impact and less work for you.

Planning walks

Walks must always appear to have a logical destination. They can either pass completely through the garden, loop back on themselves, or lead to an objective. A bench, sundial, or piece of art placed at the end of a path gives a sensible reason for stopping at that place, whereas dead ends are unnerving. If you use curves, make them gentle and meandering, not twisting and turning. You can vary the width of the walk and create wide spots for standing or sitting to make the walk more interesting.

Paths are seldom wide enough to be practical or comfortable. Don't be skimpy. A 30-inch (75 cm) walk is adequate for a wheelbarrow or a lawnmower, but that width forces visitors to walk in single file. Two people strolling side by side need a minimum of 4 feet (1.2 m). Keep an eye on your paths; they have a tendency to shrink through the seasons. Flowers that are content to sit primly along the edges in spring have often thrown themselves out onto the path with careless abandon by mid-summer. They lie in wait to tangle and trip the unwary. After a rainstorm, every passerby is slapped and soaked by overhanging or path-encroaching wet foliage. Put a stop to this horticultural version of running the gauntlet with wider walks and timely pruning.

Choose both a material and a style that reflect the mood and nature of your garden as a whole. Straight lines and rigid brick or cut stone have a more formal air than curves and gravel. Consider coordinating with existing structural elements — for example, build a red flagstone walk to echo the rusty tones of a used brick house.

Working paths

Narrow paths do have their uses, especially as secondary trails that lead into the heart of the flower beds. Their purpose is to let you get close enough to weed and do other chores without stepping on and compacting the soil. Any bed wider than you can easily reach across needs working paths to prevent you from tumbling into the flowers as you try to get hold of a belligerent thistle just beyond your grasp. Make these working paths as unobtrusive as possible to discourage casual use by anyone but yourself — children and pets love these hidden passageways. Extra bricks or pieces of flagstone provide solid footing for you to hop from one to the next as you work.

Equally handy behind flower beds that border a fence or house wall are narrow catwalks. A 30-inch (75-cm) stretch of mulch gives you access for painting and other maintenance without smashing the soil or the plants.

Choosing materials

For safety and practicality, select materials for walks that are stable and fairly even. Nothing is more disconcerting than a surface that wobbles underfoot. Visitors should be free to enjoy the flowers, not subjected to an impromptu agility test. Avoid slippery or highly irregular textures that can cause tripping or injury. A level or only slightly sloping grade is best; anything steeper needs to be broken up with steps.

An almost infinite variety of materials is available for building walks:

✔ Choose brick or stone mortared onto a concrete base when permanence and ease of care are your first priorities. Utilitarian concrete also offers great durability and flexibility. Its stark commercial appearance can be disguised with textures, colors, stains, pebble aggregates, or a border of bricks. In fact, patterned concrete can be made to look like just about any material imaginable.

Laying bricks, stones, or pavers over a base of sand or gravel is within the scope of the do-it-yourself weekend project. For installation in a concrete base, you may want to hire a brick mason.

✔ Modular concrete and crushed stone bricks and pavers are being manufactured in a vast selection of sizes, colors, and shapes.

✔ Sod paths seem natural in flower gardens — the bright green carpet is a soft contrast to the rich texture of the flower bed — but remember that lawn demands regular care. If neglected for a couple of weeks, the flower bed doesn't change much, but lawn paths can't be left for more than a week without hiring someone to mow and edge them.

✔ I like the crunch of gravel underfoot. You may not. Placing gravel on top of finely crushed stone provides a firmer surface.

✔ A rustic path can be no more than a mulch of pine needles, wood chips, or shredded bark. These materials suit the character of the woodland garden especially well.

You can combine mulch or gravel with paving stones or cut rounds of wood. Underlay loose materials with plastic or weed barrier to prevent weed growth. Alternatively, plant the spaces between stepping stones with low, spreading perennials such as woolly thyme (*Thymus praecox* 'Pseudolanuginosus') or pussy toes *(Antennaria dioica)*. Just be aware that these low growers aren't very good at weed suppression.

Edging — Keeping the Garden Put

The key to easy maintenance in the flower garden is preventing different materials in the landscape from commingling. You've got to keep soil, mulch, and flowers in the bed, and keep the adjoining lawn out. Edging can solve this problem as well as provide a decorative finish to the flower bed, much like the piping on a birthday cake.

Edging types

Whether you prefer sharply or softly defined edges is mostly a question of personal taste. Give yourself the crayon test. Are you a stay-in-the-lines kind of person, or are you a scribbler? Do you feel more comfortable when everything has a place and stays in it, or does that kind of order make you nervous? If you're a neat freak, you probably can't imagine a garden without clearly marked boundaries. Luckily for all of us, many different types of edging are available.

After you identify your own tidiness preferences, you need to consider the practical side of edging. When a flower bed borders surfaces such as walks, patios, or driveways, the goal is to stop the contents of the garden from spilling out onto the pavement. By amending the soil, you have probably raised the elevation of the flower bed above the original level. So unless you're very fond of sweeping, you're going to have to install some kind of barrier.

You have two choices. You can go up or down:

- ✔ Edge the bed with a landscape timber, a row of small rocks, or any other barrier that is slightly taller than the bed itself to stop debris from traveling.

- ✔ Dig a trench 6 to 8 inches (15 to 20 cm) deep and 1 foot (30 cm) wide the whole length of the bed to trap falling mulch and soil.

For effective edging that doesn't obstruct regular lawn maintenance, bury a row of bricks at ground level around your flower bed. This type of ground-level edging gives your garden a border that you can mow right over, as shown in Figure 12-4.

Holding back an invading lawn

Ask any gardener — lawn grasses are among the worst weeds. The same quality that we ask for in grasses — the capability to spread and fill in gaps quickly — makes them bad neighbors for a flower bed. Lawn grasses can invade and smother flowers with lightning speed. They become so thoroughly entwined into the crown of plants that picking out the grass is often impossible without digging up the whole clump and physically separating them root by root. Even the products that are marketed to kill grass but not flowers sometimes damage the perennials, too.

Figure 12-4:
Bury a row of bricks at ground level to make light work of edging the lawn.

The only way to keep lawn and flower bed separate is to build a line and then stay vigilant. A trench works if you routinely clear grass out of it. Many inconspicuous metal and plastic barriers are also available. Because grass roots go down at least 6 to 8 inches (15 to 20 cm), choose the deepest barrier you can find.

Sharp edges can be dangerous to bare feet and pets' paws. You can buy plastic capping strips that are designed to cover the exposed edges on metal barriers. Some metal edging has a turned-down top for safety.

A hose pulled across a flower bed can chop the flowers out of the ground as effectively as a hoe. Garden catalogs carry a variety of decorative and utilitarian hose guides. When strategically placed at the corners of the flower bed, these devices catch the hose and prevent mutilation of the plants, as shown in Figure 12-5. As an inexpensive alternative, blocks of wood or turned posts perform the same function.

Figure 12-5:
Hose guides protect plants and make navigating with a hose simpler.

Heavy-duty edging

Keeping really invasive, spreading perennials or suckering trees out of the rich soil in the flower bed can be frustrating and time-consuming. A friend of mine who was weary of battling a neighbor's bullying goutweed *(Aegopodium podagraria)* developed an industrial-strength barrier. She welded together sheets of metal and then buried the sheet metal 3 feet deep (90 cm) at the fence line. A barrier like that can hold back any tree roots or the most invasive spreading perennial, but constructing it is a lot of work. Going to this extreme isn't usually necessary. A barrier of 8 to 10 inches (20 to 25 cm) is sufficient to stop most plant roots. After a barrier is in, it saves endless hours of cutting or pulling out the invading hordes.

Going Vertical

For the gardener who never seems to have enough room in the flower bed, a *trellis* — a framework of interwoven pieces of wood or sticks — is the shoe-horn that lets you squeeze in just one more plant. Beds along fences and walls can be trellised to within an inch of their lives with a continuous expanse of lattice-work, individual trellises spaced along the span, or unobtrusive wires stretched between hooks, screws, or other attachment devices. Then you can go wild planting non-aggressive vines to cover these structures.

Fanciful, free-standing supports of diverse materials and design are plentiful — find them in garden catalogs and nurseries. From rustic trellises of woven twigs and teepees of bamboo to elegant cast iron rose towers, anything that can support a vine is fair game. Use your imagination. Prop up an old, rusting garden gate or discarded chair to add a touch of whimsy. Search junkyards for interesting items and give them a new home. You can also encourage a few stems of each vine to escape the trellis and travel along the ground, weaving through and scrambling over taller flowers. Among the best choices for the small garden are the true annuals and a selection of relatively petite perennial vines.

Many tropical vines that can be used as annuals where they aren't hardy are also popular. These vines bloom the first year from seed. A few of them get too large to fit in a flower bed when grown in their native tropical or sub-tropical climates, but they can be cut back to the ground when necessary to keep them in bounds. Most of the better-known landscape vines are far too vigorous for the small garden bed. Many of these reach 50 feet (15 m) or more and can obscure entire buildings. Table 12-1 lists a few of the dozens of smaller vines that are compatible with the smaller-scale flower garden.

Table 12-1	Small Vines for Flower Beds	
Common Name	*Botanical Name*	*Exposure*
Chickbuddy	Asarina scandens	Sun
Pagoda flower	Clerodendrum speciosum	Partial shade
Glory bower	Clerodendrum thomsoniae	Partial shade
Violet trumpet vine	Clytostoma callistegioides	Partial shade
Cathedral bells	Cobaea scandens	Sun
Bonnet bellflower	Codonopsis clematidea	Partial shade
Dwarf morning glory	Convovulus tricolor	Sun
Yellow bleeding heart	Dicentra scandens	Partial shade
Annual bleeding heart	Dicentra torulosa	Sun
Morning glory	Ipomoea purpurea	Sun
Dusky coral pea	Kennedia rubicunda	Sun
Perennial sweet pea	Lathyrus latifolius	Sun
Sweet pea	Lathyrus odoratus	Sun
Annual passion vine	Passiflora gracilis	Partial shade/sun
Scarlet runner bean	Phaseolus coccineus	Sun
Cape plumbago	Plumbago auriculata	Partial shade/sun
Black-eyed Susan vine	Thunbergia alata	Sun
Nasturtium	Tropaeolum majus	Sun
Canary creeper	Tropaeolum peregrinum	Light shade
Flame flower	Tropaeolum speciosum	Roots in shade

Chapter 13

Mulching Around

● ●

In This Chapter
▶ Exploring the advantages of mulching
▶ Choosing the best mulch for your flower garden
▶ Avoiding mulch pitfalls
▶ Applying the mulch and keeping it in its place
▶ Comparing mulch options

● ●

*M*ulch is a layer of material spread over the surface of the soil between the plants in the garden. Almost any material works; shredded polyester leisure suits do just fine, if you've got a closet full of them that you can't get rid of at garage sales. In fact, vegetable gardeners are much more practical and less concerned about aesthetics than flower gardeners, and they use some pretty odd stuff for mulch — such as old carpet strips.

Nature provides a great model for mulching. Trees create their own mulch by dropping an accumulation of leaf litter on the forest floor. Even in dry regions, undisturbed soil is generally covered by broken rock or gravel.

What Mulch Can Do for You

You may balk at paying good money for a material that resembles a mix of twigs and sweepings from the workshop floor. But mulch pays for itself by reducing water bills and fertilizer needs, not to mention fostering an overall healthier garden.

Any mulch, regardless of what it's made of, acts as a protective covering to the soil and benefits your garden in a number of ways.

No bare earth

Some gardeners prefer to practice what, in Colorado, is called the "no-bare-earth" policy. Instead of using a mulch, they ignore spacing recommendations and place plants close together in order to shelter the ground. In effect, the plants and flowers act as their own mulch; their density prevents sunlight from striking the soil, and shades out weed seedlings.

The no-bare-earth approach works best in urban or woodland gardens where buildings or trees protect flower beds from drying winds and the full blast of the sun. By not using mulch, you avoid a few pitfalls (such as mulch migration, possible nitrogen depletion, and the bother of replenishing missing mulch), but you don't reap the many rewards, either.

Controlling weeds

No one likes to look at a weed patch, but weeds are more than just unsightly nuisances. They can readily outcompete their more civilized and polite companions for water and nutrients. Because bare earth is an invitation that no self-respecting weed can ignore for long, mulch is the garden's no-vacancy sign. The few weeds that manage to *germinate* (sprout and begin to grow) in organic mulch come up elongated and are easy to pull out (see the section "Choosing the Best Mulch for Your Garden," later in this chapter, to find out about organic mulch). Rock mulches aren't really as effective at discouraging weeds as the organics, so you must be more vigilant about weeding a flower bed with rock mulch in it.

Preventing soil erosion

Heavy drops of water from rainfall or sprinklers smash into the surface of unprotected soil and break a good soil's crumblike texture into very small particles. These tiny particles form a crust that facilitates runoff and soil erosion. You don't want the good garden soil that you worked so hard to build to wash away. Worse yet, water erosion can cut unsightly channels through your flower bed.

When water hits the nooks and crannies of a mulched surface, however, it gets trapped until it trickles down into the soil underneath — right where you want it to go.

Making your garden pretty

Spreading mulch between your flowers gives your garden a unified, finished appearance, especially if you use the same mulch throughout your landscape. Some types of mulch are really quite attractive in their own right. The edges of the flower beds act as a frame for your perennials, and mulch is the matting.

Mulch also stops soil from splashing onto foliage and adjoining walls and walks, where it leaves unsightly mud spots.

Slowing evaporation

Mulch helps the soil in your garden retain moisture by shading it from the full blast of the sun and wind, measurably reducing *evaporation* (losing moisture to the air). Using mulch nearly always results in lower water bills. Plus, you don't need to water as often — a real time-saver if you don't have an automatic irrigation system.

Preventing temperature swings

Mulch protects perennials from sudden changes in air temperature, allowing a more gradual warm-up as temperatures rise during the heat of the day, and a corresponding slower cool-down at night. In climates that experience wide seasonal swings of hot and cold, mulch creates an insulating blanket that gives the plants more time to adjust to the change of seasons.

Mulch also levels out the rise and fall of temperatures in the top few inches of the soil. This leveling can markedly improve a plant's performance, because extremes of hot or cold interrupt root growth.

- ✔ Mulched ground stays unfrozen longer in autumn, a time when roots grow rapidly if conditions are favorable.
- ✔ During the coldest months of winter, soil under the mulch stays more solidly frozen, and perennials are less likely to be subjected to *frost-heaving* (the alternating freezing and thawing of soil which can actually push a plant right out of the ground!).

Vegetable gardeners are eager to get the soil warmed up as soon as possible in spring for earlier planting, but flower gardens are better off if they aren't coaxed out of dormancy until the weather is more settled and reliably warm. Flowers that emerge too early in the false springs of late winter are at risk of frost damage that can kill the plant outright. Tender new growth is particularly vulnerable to a sudden drop of the thermometer, so keep your perennials safely tucked under a blanket of mulch.

REMEMBER

The effects of mulch on self-sowing seeds

Many types of organic mulches contain naturally-occurring chemicals that retard seed germination, which is the very reason that they are so effective for weed control. However, not many flower seeds germinate in these mulches either. This lack of germination can be a good thing for discouraging weeds, but if you're hoping for the serendipity of randomly self-sowing flower seedlings, you may be disappointed.

On the other hand, most seeds that land in gravel germinate readily. You may want to factor the extra maintenance of removing unwanted seedlings into the decision of whether or not to use a rock mulch.

Choosing the Best Mulch for Your Garden

Before deciding which kind of mulch is the best choice for your garden, you need to be aware of some very real differences among the various types of mulch. The three basic kinds of mulch are

- ✔ **Organics:** Derived from living plant residues, organic mulches are readily available in diverse forms as byproducts of the agriculture, timber, and horticulture industries.

- ✔ **Inorganics:** Various rock products, including gravel, stone chips, river rock, and lava rock *(scorea),* serve as inorganic mulch.

- ✔ **Weed control barriers:** Weed control barriers can be organic or inorganic, such as newspaper, or woven fabric. These barriers are best used along with a layer of an organic or inorganic mulch.

No one mulch is perfect for every situation. But keep in mind that choosing the wrong mulch is not a disaster — only a potential inconvenience. You can always take it off and try something else.

Going organic

One of the prime benefits of an organic mulch is that it gradually decomposes, and the resulting decayed matter works its way down into the soil. Teeming communities of insects and microorganisms thrive in the cool, moist shelter of a rotting mulch. As they digest the mulch, they release a steady, slow supply of nutrients. You get on-going passive soil amendment — without the back-wrenching digging. (For more on soil amendment, refer to Chapter 11.)

Pull back the leaf litter in a woodland, and you notice that the soil beneath resembles large crumbs. Decaying organic matter releases chemicals that cause small soil particles to clump together, helping to improve the soil's texture and health. This decaying process is especially important in perennial flower gardens, where you amend the soil only once and then leave it undisturbed for many years or perhaps a lifetime. No one-time soil amendment can be expected to last that long.

You need to replenish the top of the mulch as the bottom decays. How often you need to put down more mulch depends on where you live and the type of organic material you use. In wet climates, decomposition can be very quick. In drier areas, the same material may last several years. Small particles generally break down faster than large ones, and products containing a large percentage of wood decompose faster than bark. Water, heat, and fertilizer all accelerate the decaying process.

Here are some other factors to consider when choosing a mulch:

- **Flammability:** Recent social trends have created a new mulch hazard. When smokers go outside for breaks, dropped matches or cigarettes can ignite some organic mulches. Areas around public buildings are more at risk than areas around private residences, but be careful just the same, especially in fire-prone areas. Pine needles, recycled wood mulches, hay, and straw can all increase fire danger.

- **Nitrogen depletion:** *Nitrogen depletion* is the loss of nitrogen, an essential nutrient, from the soil. This problem is most likely to occur when you use finely chipped, woody mulches — sawdust is the classic example. Microorganisms that decompose the sawdust consume all the available nitrogen in the soil, depriving your perennials of the nitrogen they need. Plants that aren't getting enough nitrogen become stunted and *chlorotic,* or yellow-looking.

If a large percentage of plants in your garden show these symptoms, or if you want to prevent nitrogen depletion, add 2 pounds (1 kg) of complete fertilizer (look for at least 10-10-10) per 100 square feet (9 sq. m). Spread this fertilizer over the soil before putting down the mulch or scatter it on top of an existing mulch (see Chapter 16 for more on fertilizing).

- **Wet, low-lying areas:** Take care when using organic mulches in low, poorly drained areas where water collects. The decomposition that occurs in wet areas produces chemicals that are toxic to perennials. You don't want to make a wet spot even wetter, and mulch slows down the drying process.

Let's rock

Organic mulches help make the soil ideal for a wide variety of perennials, particularly perennials native to meadows and woodlands. But when growing *xeric* plants (plants from dry regions), the same conditions can actually damage plants, especially when you're trying to grow them in soggier climates. Plants from arid regions evolved in an environment that is radically different from what traditional perennials enjoy. Soils in these areas are high in mineral content, low in organic matter and microorganisms, and strewn with a covering of rock chips (if covered with anything at all).

Most dryland perennials can't cope with the large numbers of fungi and bacteria present in rich garden soils and can be very susceptible to damage caused by these organisms. Plants that don't succumb to disease sometimes grow themselves to death due to the abundant soil nutrients. They may become overly large and floppy or set seed and die quickly — essentially adopting the life cycle of an annual. Such plants are healthier and longer-lived when treated to a rock mulch that more closely resembles their natural conditions.

Several inches of gravel or rock chips hold the crown of the plant above the soil surface and improve up drainage while doing all those other things that a mulch does — holding moisture in the root zone and insulating the soil to maintain a more constant temperature.

Ultimately, the decision whether to choose an organic or a rock mulch usually comes down to what you like best. Most gardeners have strong preferences toward one or the other, and most plants adapt to either one.

Using weed barriers

Plastic films, landscaping fabric, newspaper, cardboard, old carpet, and roofing paper are all excellent materials for underlaying walks and placing between rows of a vegetable garden. These barriers are highly effective at preventing weed growth and can be used where low maintenance is a primary goal and a regimented look is acceptable.

Don't use clear or black plastic films or other nonporous materials on perennial gardens except during bed preparation (see Chapter 11). They block water and air exchange in the soil and can cause your perennials to rot.

To install weed barriers, follow these steps:

1. **Roll the weed barrier out over the prepared soil, overlapping the seams generously.**

2. **Fasten the material in place with landscape pins.**

   You can use pieces of wire or coat hangers, bent into a U-shape, in place of landscape pins.

3. **Cut holes (with scissors) for your perennials and then plant them through the openings.**

   Use care not to scatter soil on top of the fabric, because weeds will happily establish themselves there.

4. **Finally, spread a layer of an organic or rock mulch to a depth of 2 to 3 inches (5 to 8 cm) on top of the fabric.**

   This mulch layer protects the material from UV light, lends a more traditional appearance to the finished bed, and also holds the light-weight material in place.

Landscape fabrics have some drawbacks and cautions for use:

✔ Don't use weed barriers at the bottom of slopes, where soil can wash down from above.

✔ Avoid covering landscape fabrics with organic mulches composed of small particles that may decay quickly.

   Washed-down soil and decayed organic mulch both create excellent conditions for weeds to sprout. Weed seeds generally germinate from above, sending their roots downward through the fabric into the earth below. When weeds do take hold, their roots can become thoroughly enmeshed in the fabric's fibers. The weeds are almost impossible to pull out without tearing the fabric badly.

✔ A more critical problem with these types of barriers is that the soil is kept out of contact with the mulch, which means that you lose the benefit of passive soil amendment.

✔ A flower bed prepared in this manner is not very flexible. Every time you want to move or add a perennial, you must cut another hole, and more holes mean more opportunities for weeds to grow.

Rock or chunky mulches are the best mulches for suppressing weeds when used in combination with weed barriers.

A Compendium of Mulches

To find out what mulches are available in your area, visit local garden centers or check the telephone book for bulk mulch suppliers. Mulch products are generally less expensive in quantity than in small bags, although delivery costs can quickly eat up the savings if you only need a small amount.

Free sources of mulch may be available in your community. Some yard-care companies, utility companies, or municipalities offer recycled tree or shrub trimmings that you can pick up or have delivered for a small fee. (Denver, Colorado, collects discarded Christmas trees, grinds them up, and lets residents retrieve the resulting mulch at no cost.)

Organics

Out of concern for the environment, use locally manufactured organic mulch products whenever they are available. Most communities have by-products from tree-trimming operations or from agriculture industries sold as mulches. Choosing these mulches rather than alternatives trucked in from the far reaches of the continent not only saves energy but also ensures that these valuable local resources don't end up incinerated or disposed of in landfills as waste.

Don't buy organic mulch that smells like alcohol, vinegar, ammonia, or sulfur. These smells indicate the presence of chemicals that can badly burn plants. Note the decomposition rates in the following list. If soil amendment is your goal, choose an organic mulch that decays quickly. If durability is more important, choose a type that decays slowly.

Bark

- **Benefits:** Suppresses weed growth
- **Special Notes:** Shredded types are more stable for hillsides and slopes
- **Appearance:** Deep brown to reddish color; weathers to gray; replenish as needed to preserve color; more formal appearance; uniform, screened sizes are available
- **Drawbacks:** Large chunks are very slow to decompose; small chunks are prone to being blown by wind; floats easily
- **Application:** 2 to 3 inches (5 to 8 cm) thick
- **Cost:** Expensive

Compost

- **Benefits:** Improves soil fertility
- **Special Notes:** Many locally manufactured types are available; you can use your own compost before it fully decomposes
- **Appearance:** Fine, dark brown
- **Drawbacks:** May contain weed seeds
- **Application:** 1 to 2 inches (2 to 5 cm) thick
- **Cost:** Free, if you make it yourself

Grass clippings

✔ **Benefits:** Decays rapidly; amends soil; excellent source of nitrogen

✔ **Special Notes:** Best when left in place on lawn but can be collected from unenlightened neighbors

✔ **Appearance:** Not attractive

✔ **Drawbacks:** Don't use clippings if the lawn they're from is treated with weed-and-feed products (lawn fertilizers containing weed killers) or other herbicides

✔ **Application:** 2 to 3 inches (5 to 8 cm) thick; spread in shallow layers; allow each layer to dry before adding more to prevent a slimy mass

✔ **Cost:** Free

Hay and straw

✔ **Benefits:** Decays rapidly

✔ **Special Notes:** Buy hay or straw at agricultural feed stores

✔ **Appearance:** Casual-looking

✔ **Drawbacks:** Flammable; may contain weed seeds

✔ **Application:** 2 to 3 inches (5 to 8 cm) thick or 5 to 6 inches (13 to 15 cm) thick as a temporary winter mulch

✔ **Cost:** Inexpensive

Leaves and leaf mold

✔ **Benefits:** Decomposes quickly; amends soil

✔ **Special Notes:** Best when ground up with a leaf shredder or a lawn-mower (run the mower back and forth over shallow piles until the leaves are ground up); especially appropriate for shade and woodland gardens

✔ **Appearance:** Natural-looking

✔ **Drawbacks:** Must be renewed annually

✔ **Application:** 2 to 3 inches (5 to 8 cm) thick

✔ **Cost:** Free (collect the neighbors')

Manure

✔ **Benefits:** Decays quickly; amends soil

✔ **Special Notes:** Better used as soil amendment (see Chapter 11) or fertilizer (see Chapter 16)

✔ **Appearance:** Not attractive

- **Drawbacks:** Odor may be offensive; fresh manure can damage plants; best if aged or composted; often contains weed seeds
- **Application:** 1 to 2 inches (2 to 5 cm) thick
- **Cost:** Free or inexpensive

Peat moss

- **Benefits:** Not an effective mulch (use as soil amendment; see Chapter 11)
- **Special Notes:** Use only sphagnum moss; don't use peat moss harvested from alpine regions
- **Appearance:** Attractive, uniform brown
- **Drawbacks:** Lightweight; doesn't stay where you put it
- **Application:** 1 to 2 inches (2 to 5 cm) thick
- **Cost:** Expensive

Pine needles

- **Benefits:** Light and airy; won't mat down
- **Special Notes:** Pine cones can be left in the mulch for added texture
- **Appearance:** Casual-looking
- **Drawbacks:** Flammable; slow to decay
- **Application:** 3 to 4 inches (8 to 10 cm) thick
- **Cost:** Free when you can find a source

Sawdust

- **Benefits:** Cheap or free material; recycles lumber industry waste
- **Special Notes:** Must be kept moist to prevent loss due to wind
- **Appearance:** Casual-looking
- **Drawbacks:** If not aged, may cause nitrogen depletion (amend soil with nitrogen before applying)
- **Application:** 1 to 2 inches (2 to 5 cm) thick
- **Cost:** Inexpensive

Wood chips, pole peelings, and recycled wood products

- **Benefits:** Recycles tree trimmings and construction waste; durable
- **Special Notes:** Best choice for weed suppression; amend soil with nitrogen before applying to prevent deficiency; best if composted or aged; don't use if it smells unpleasant or sour

✔ **Appearance:** Untidy appearance when first applied; weathers to uniform gray

✔ **Drawbacks:** May contain trash or debris; if improperly stored, it can become toxic to plants; prone to developing interesting but harmless fungal growths

✔ **Application:** 2 to 3 inches (5 to 8 cm) thick

✔ **Cost:** Free or inexpensive

Other regionally available products

These products include buckwheat, cocoa bean or peanut hulls, ground corncobs, cranberry clippings, spent hops, mushroom compost, seaweed, and tobacco stems.

✔ **Benefits:** Recycles waste products

✔ **Special Notes:** Most are not commercially available outside a small geographic area

✔ **Appearance:** Most are attractive; uniform in appearance

✔ **Drawbacks:** If not aged, some may cause nitrogen depletion

✔ **Application:** Fine materials: 1 to 2 inches (2 to 5 cm) thick; coarse materials: 2 to 3 inches (5 to 8 cm) thick

✔ **Cost:** Free or inexpensive

Inorganics

Most garden centers and hardware stores sell landscape fabric, and some also carry rock and gravel. Check your local yellow pages for rock and gravel companies. Be sure to compare prices — rock mulch can be very expensive.

Gravel and rocks

✔ **Benefits:** Prevents fungal growths and diseases

✔ **Special Notes:** Marble chips can raise soil pH (see Chapter 11)

✔ **Appearance:** Decorative; available in many sizes and colors

✔ **Drawbacks:** No soil amendment action; weeds germinate readily but are easily removed

✔ **Application:** 2 inches (5 cm) thick

✔ **Cost:** Expensive

Weed barrier fabrics

✔ **Benefits:** Allows passage of air, water, and nutrients; good weed suppression

✔ **Special Notes:** Use with second mulch on top

✔ **Appearance:** Unattractive if not completely covered by another mulch

✔ **Drawbacks:** Inflexible; not the best choice for flower beds

✔ **Application:** Follow instructions earlier in this chapter

✔ **Cost:** Expensive

It's Mulching Time

Timing is critical when laying down mulch. Weed seeds germinate readily in a newly prepared flower bed, so you need to apply mulch as soon as possible after planting. The optimal depth of the mulch varies, depending on which type of mulch you use and the character of your soil. As a general rule, use only enough mulch to completely cover the surface of the soil. Use more on sandy soils and less on clay. Guidelines for depth and coverage are

✔ 1 to 2 inches (2.5 to 5 cm) of very fine materials (for example, compost or buckwheat hulls)

✔ 2 to 3 inches (5 to 8 cm) of coarser materials (for example, shredded wood or bark)

✔ 3 to 4 inches (8 to 10 cm) of loose materials (for example, hay, straw, or pine needles)

One cubic yard covers a 10 x 12-foot (120 sq. ft.) area to a depth of 1 to 2 inches. (One cubic meter covers a 3 x 4-meter or 12 sq. meter area to a depth of 2 to 5 cm.) See the Quick Reference Card in the front of this book for additional coverage rates.

The following are step-by-step instructions for applying mulch:

1. **Spread the mulch between the plants to an even depth.**

   A three-pronged tiller is handy for smoothing the mulch out.

2. **Keep organics away from the crown of each perennial.**

3. **Leave a shallow crater around each perennial (see Figure 13-1).**

4. **After applying the mulch, water thoroughly.**

   Wet the mulch so that it doesn't pull moisture from the soil or blow away.

Figure 13-1:
When
spreading
mulch,
always
leave a
crater
around
each
perennial.

Avoiding the Mulch Uglies

Sometimes, you learn the hard way. I built a path on the side of the house and mulched it heavily with several inches of small bark chunks. Within a month, a single, strong storm blew all that expensive bark away, presumably to Oz. Chagrined, I swept up what little was left and replaced it with heavy river cobble, hoping that it was heavy enough to withstand the next strong wind. I'm happy to report that the river cobble has stayed put!

Keeping mulch in its place

The greatest difficulty with lightweight organic mulches is keeping them in place. Mulch tends to suffer from wanderlust. What doesn't blow away often floats off instead. Every time we have a real gully-washer, all the chunk bark in the entire neighborhood washes away into the storm drains. Hillsides present an even worse problem, because gravity causes many materials to tumble down the slope. Solutions that use chicken wire, plastic mesh, or inverted wire U's are not very conducive to flower gardening. Shredded or fibrous organic mulches mat down and stay in place better than fine compost or bark nuggets. Gravel and rock chips work better yet. Larger rock, such as 4- to 6-inch (10- to 15-cm) river stones, withstand almost any force of nature.

Mulch scattered onto sidewalks, patios, driveways, and lawns is a real nuisance. You can corral the mulch by digging the level of the flower bed several inches lower than surrounding areas. Or dig a trench approximately one foot wide and several inches deep alongside the edge of the flower beds to trap mulch that falls, like the one shown in Figure 13-2. As the trench fills with mulch, simply toss it back onto the flower bed as part of routine maintenance.

Figure 13-2:
Dig a trench
alongside
pavement
to catch
falling
mulch.

Keeping out the debris

When tree leaves, twigs, and other garden litter fall into an organic mulch, they can be left to be absorbed into the mulch. With a rock mulch, anything that lands on it immediately looks messy. (I watched in utter amazement as one of the major thoroughfares near my home was shut down for a week one summer so that work crews could wash the cobble mulch in the center median with high power hoses!) Never use rock mulch at the bottom of a hillside, where soil or organic mulch from above can easily wash down onto it. A power leaf blower does a respectable job of cleaning rock mulch, but take care to use the blower when the flower bed is dormant in order to prevent plant injury.

Don't mix mulches

Another common problem with mulches is using two incompatible types where they can intermingle. Organics and rocks don't combine attractively, and few people have the patience to separate the two. Choose one or the other for the whole bed. You can safely use different mulches in non-adjoining flower beds to accommodate more than one plant community's needs — but use a barrier in between. The wider the barrier, the more effective it is. For example, an expanse of lawn or a brick walk always works better than a strip of metal edging.

Layering different types of organic materials on top of one another is fine, because they all eventually weather to a uniform brownish gray. For economy, place a free or inexpensive mulch underneath a thin layer of a more costly product, such as shredded cedar or redwood. Add more of the attractive mulch whenever necessary to keep the color looking fresh. Different rock types don't blend well, but for a more natural look, you can mix several sizes of the same type of rock.

Always check out the neighbor's landscape before putting a flower bed on the property line. Coordinate with any mulch on the other side for ease of maintenance. If the existing mulch is too weird for you (you don't like white marble chips, for example), you may want to rethink the placement of your flower bed. If anything is worse than white marble chips, it's white marble chips decorated with your cedar bark!

Creatures in the Mulch

A wide range of critters — some beneficial, others not so welcome — make their home in the cool, moist shelter of an organic mulch. When you spread organic mulch, expect to see increases in the numbers of wood-eating and wood-inhabiting insects as well as pillbugs, earwigs, millipedes, and centipedes. Most mulch inhabitants are harmless to living plants, and some of them prey upon one another, helping to keep things under control.

Molds and fungi

With the increased use of recycled wood products, some really interesting organisms are becoming more prevalent.

- ✔ One mulch invader that always gets a reaction is *slime mold* — a yellow, frothy growth that looks very much as though the dog's been sick in the garden. But don't be alarmed — these curiosities are completely harmless to plants, pets, and humans. They just eat the mulch.

- ✔ Another oddity that you may run into is *bird's nest fungus*. This growth usually appears in organic mulches that have been down for two or three years. This harmless fungus consists of tiny, cup-shaped bodies that are filled with egg-shaped, spore-filled sacs.

- ✔ *Artillery fungus* can be a serious annoyance to the fastidious. It shoots spores up to twenty feet and targets light-colored surfaces. When these spore masses stick to house walls, as they often do, the black dots look like fly specks and are almost impossible to scrub off.

Although you can ignore all these growths (or use them as conversation starters), prevention strategies do exist. Because most of these growths develop in cool, damp weather, raking or cultivating the mulch during periods of such weather interrupts their spread. Or you can switch to (or top-dress with) a layer of cedar or redwood products. Both contain natural fungal inhibitors. If all else fails, eliminate their food source by removing the mulch.

Perennial pests

Insect pests and diseases that attack the same perennials year after year can take up residence and spend the winter in the organic mulch underneath the plant. Because most problems are *host-specific* (meaning that they attack only one species or family of plants), you can break the cycle by thoroughly cleaning out the mulch from around any plant that's under siege. Compost the old mulch or move it to another section of the garden (most pests can't easily make their way back). Then replenish the mulch with fresh, new material that's free of pests and their eggs. (If insects or diseases are a problem in your flower bed, turn — without delay — to Chapter 18.)

Chapter 14

The Good Part: Buying and Planting Flowers

. . . .

In This Chapter

▶ Ordering from nursery catalogs

▶ Shopping the local nurseries

▶ Finding and choosing the healthiest perennials

▶ Deciding when to plant

▶ The how-to's of planting

▶ Caring for the newly planted garden

. . . .

*A*fter you develop a garden plan (Chapter 3) and finish building the flower bed (Chapter 12), the really fun part begins. Now you get to flip through catalogs and visit nurseries, choose from a dazzling array of flowers, and experience the amazing sense of accomplishment that comes from transforming a patch of bare dirt into a sensational flower garden.

Sending Away for Mail-Order Miracles

When my brothers and I were growing up, we eagerly anticipated the arrival of the Sears catalog each fall. We spent endless hours poring through this wish book, searching for that one perfect toy to make our lives complete.

As an adult, garden catalogs bring back much of that same thrill for me. Their mailings are cleverly timed to tempt gardeners at their most vulnerable — during the winter doldrums. For the gardener socked in by inclement weather, looking at garden catalogs is the equivalent of grocery shopping on an empty stomach — it may be unwise but, boy, does everything look good. My garden is never more perfect than the virtual reality of my midwinter musings.

Finding catalogs

You may already receive several garden catalogs in the mail each winter and spring. Hundreds are available — from spartan typed lists with minimal descriptions and no illustrations to works of art filled with glamorous photographs that put glossy fashion magazines to shame. Some catalogs specialize in only one type of perennial; others present a vast array for every climate. The best ones are packed with information describing each plant, detailed cultural information, and design advice.

No nursery has the space to stock even a fraction of the thousands of perennials in cultivation. Mail-order sources are often the only way to locate the rare, the unusual, and the avant-garde of gardening.

Nearly every garden magazine advertises dozens of mail-order nurseries. Most mail-order nurseries require a small fee to send you their catalogs, but they usually refund the amount after you make your first purchase. Publishers and catalog companies share your name with competitors, so after you subscribe to a single garden magazine or send for the first catalog, more catalogs and magazine offers arrive as well. (Check out the appendix for a list of mail-order catalogs.)

Placing an order

You must exercise some prudence and caution when deciding which plants to order from a catalog. A few catalogs make exaggerated claims of performance, desirability, or hardiness. A little research often saves great disappointment later. Find out whether each perennial you have fallen in love with works in your climate. Losing your heart and your common sense to a pretty picture is all too easy.

My method for catalog ordering involves making a series of lists:

- ✔ The first list is a free-for-all of unfettered greed as I check off every remotely interesting and desirable plant in the catalog.

- ✔ After the first round, in which I usually circle or underline most of the catalog, I begin the process of weeding out. "No," I concede, "I probably won't get around to digging a bog this year, so those plants can go." "No, those eastern woodlanders probably won't adjust to my hot, arid region, and all those subtropical selections are probably pushing it a bit in my cold-climate garden." And so on.

- ✔ Then I subject the pared-down list to the calculator test. The shock of realization sets in when the total still exceeds the GNP of many small nations. The last list, the one that passes the reality check, is the one I actually send off.

Most mail-order nurseries have minimum shipping fees. Some have a flat fee per order; many have minimum order amounts. You can almost always save money on shipping costs when you get together with a group of friends and combine several orders. One clever bulb company, Dutch Gardens, encourages this practice by sending out several order blanks with each catalog.

Shipping considerations

Shipping plants has some inherent problems. The cost is high, and most nurseries try to keep the weight down by sending their plants either *bare root* or in small containers filled with lightweight, soil-less mix.

Bare-root plants are just that — plants whose roots have been unearthed and are completely, unabashedly exposed. Mailed with their roots packed in moistened moss or wood shavings and wrapped in newspaper or plastic, these plants are very fragile and perishable. They must not be allowed to dry out, but leaving them in their damp shipping material for very long encourages rotting.

The time of year that your plants are shipped and the shape they're in when you get them depend on what type of plants you order.

- ✔ Bare-root plants arrive in a dormant or semi-dormant state, usually in late winter or early spring.

- ✔ Bulbs and fleshy-rooted perennials are also shipped in summer and hardly seem to notice that they're out of the ground. Peonies, bearded iris, daylilies, hostas, and liatris don't object to this treatment in the least. (See Chapter 10 for more about bulbs.)

- ✔ In some cases, your perennials can arrive quite unhappy and indignant (no matter what time of year they're sent) and may require pampering for a full year to recover their former health and vigor.

Arrange for your plants to be shipped by the quickest option, especially during hot months when the poor plants can easily cook or dry out in transit. Ask that your order be sent at the proper planting time for your area and at a time when you can be at home to receive the package. Even plants that survive the initial journey don't last long if you leave them unattended on a hot porch.

When the plants arrive

On that great day when your plants finally arrive, unpack the box immediately in a cool, shaded location. Check off on the invoice each plant you unpack to make sure that your order is complete. Keep each label with its plant — green and brown lumps tend to look alike at this stage.

You can store plants shipped in pots for several days in a shady spot with plenty of indirect light. Be sure to water the pots whenever they dry out, but don't overwater them. If their bed isn't ready, you must find a temporary home for them. A vegetable garden is an ideal holding area for new perennials.

Many garden guides recommend *heeling in* bare-root plants. This process involves digging a trench, laying plants in it at a 30-degree angle, and covering the roots with soil. Heeling in works fine for shrubs but isn't a good practice for perennials. Flowers prefer you to plant them properly in their interim location and then transplant them later, after they establish strong new growth.

Most mail-order nurseries send instructions with your order. File away these instructions away for future reference along with your receipt and invoice. Many companies guarantee their plants, and you need the paperwork to request a refund or replacement if the original plant fails. I always keep the catalogs, too, as a source of information and to cut up to make garden records (see Chapter 3). Notify the nursery right away of any problems. (Once, instead of the plant I ordered, I received a very healthy, carefully wrapped dandelion!)

Taking the Nursery Safari

Shopping for plants at a nursery is much like shopping for plants from a catalog, but with fewer restraints. In nurseries, the plants are harder to deny — they're right in front of you, most of them presumably perfectly compatible to your local climate and conditions. Self-control (and the limit on your credit card) can be sorely tested. Before you know it, you've filled one shopping cart to bulging and are seriously contemplating a second (and these are usually large carts!).

Whenever you have a choice between buying a plant by mail or from a local nursery, always go with the nursery. A plant purchased locally is almost always cheaper than one ordered by mail because you aren't paying those high shipping costs. The nursery plant is also usually healthier because it hasn't been subjected to the trauma of traveling — at least not recently.

Most nurseries bring in some of their stock bare root in the winter and grow it in containers before offering it up for sale. This way, the nursery takes the risk, and you buy only those plants that survived and prospered. Also, at a nursery, you can actually see the plant you buy and can pick out the best of the batch.

Save catalogs for the perennials that you can't find locally — you'll discover plenty of those. A few perennials, such as daylilies, irises, hostas, and peonies, have hundreds of named varieties. A wider selection of these varieties is available by mail order, compared with only a few at each nursery.

Locating nurseries

Large nurseries and garden centers advertise in the Yellow Pages of the telephone book and in the garden section of the local newspaper. Small specialty growers can be harder to track down. Ask a gardener or call a regional plant society to find, for example, a daylily grower in your area.

Choose a nursery where the plants look healthy and the staff is knowledgeable and helpful. Many good nurseries offer gardening classes and employ a master gardener to answer your questions. They may also group plants by their cultural needs to help you decide what goes where. Shade plants are generally protected under some sort of structure.

When you purchase plants, ask about a guarantee and save your receipts. Many reputable nurseries don't warranty the plants, however, because what you do to the plant after you leave the store is out of their control.

Buying from discounters

With the burgeoning popularity of perennial gardening, many home improvement centers, supermarkets, and discount stores carry a wide variety of perennials. Sometimes, these discounters offer perennials as *loss leaders,* heavily discounted products sold as a marketing strategy to get you into the store.

Some real bargains are possible at non-nursery stores, but you're usually more or less on your own to determine which plants are the healthiest or what cultural conditions they require. Although some stores try to find informed help, others don't even seem to understand that plants need water to survive. Plants may be selected for a national market and can be entirely inappropriate for the regions where they end up. I cringe every time I see hapless subtropicals going home to a certain death and a disappointed gardener in hardly-subtropical Colorado.

On the other hand, I can't resist a bargain, and I suspect that you can't either. But do some homework first to make sure that the plants you buy have a ghost of a chance in your garden. Also, buy them as soon as they've been unloaded from the truck — hopefully before they've been mishandled or mistreated.

You can also find some great deals on nursery plants by watching for end-of-season clearance sales. Some of the plants are looking shop-worn by this time, but I figure that only the really strong-willed can survive several months on the sales bench. So these last plants, the rejected and over-looked, are usually worth the risk.

Getting the pick of the litter

When purchasing a perennial, look for one with a compact form and proportioned-to-the-pot size. Pass on any plants that are tall and leggy or flopping over to one side.

You want lean and mean, not overly lush. Check the foliage for any signs of disease. Don't buy plants that are wilted, yellowed, or mottled. Avoid plants that have orange, brown, or black spots or that have distorted or curled leaves. Flip a few leaves over to see whether tiny mites, aphids, or white-flies reside there (see Chapter 18 for more on these critters). Look along the stems for scale insects. Don't be put off by a few holes made by chewing insects — these culprits are either long gone or large enough to remove easily.

Perennials come in many pot sizes. Occasionally, first-year seedlings are available in six-packs, the standard container for bedding annuals. These packages can be real money-savers when they contain varieties that mature quickly and bloom the first year from seed. Otherwise, you may have to wait a year or two to see the flowers. Perennials are more customarily sold in 2$^1/_4$-, 4-, and 6-inch containers. The larger plants are more expensive because they cost more to produce. Most nurseries start their perennials in small pots and move them up to larger ones as they outgrow each size. Some perennials have large, fleshy roots and are only available in 6-inch pots because they just don't fit in anything else.

Small plants are much easier to transplant — they require smaller holes, after all. But the trade-off is that the little ones need more care initially. They dry out faster and may need watering as often as twice a day until they're established and growing strongly.

Healthy roots mean healthy perennials

Healthy roots are just as important as the above-ground parts of the plant, but they're more difficult to assess. Judging roots involves a bit of detective work. A top-quality container plant has a vigorous root system that fills but doesn't outgrow its pot. Ideally, the volume of roots and soil is about 50/50.

You can get some idea of what condition a potted plant's roots are in by checking the surface of the soil. If you can see roots circling or trying to climb out, ask the clerk to remove the pot so that you can get a better look. Nurseries routinely turn their pots upside down to monitor root status, so this request won't seem odd to the clerk, although it may seem strange to you.

Excess roots can displace most of the soil in a container, making the plant *root-bound,* a condition that causes a couple of problems. First, without enough soil to retain water or fertilizer, the plants quickly start to suffer from drought stress. More importantly, the roots don't have anywhere to go, so they start to circle and grow into a tight ball.

Too few roots is just as bad a sign as too many. Reputable nurseries don't routinely sell perennials that are too recently transplanted, but occasionally a few slip through quality control. Roots should expand out at least to the edges of the container. If they don't, you're paying for a small plant and some very expensive potting soil. Carefully tip the pot over and look at the bottom. A few small roots should be visible at the drainage holes.

Reviewing the Planting Basics

In theory, you can plant container-grown perennials at any time of the year when the ground isn't frozen. But in reality, survival rates improve when you take your climate into consideration and schedule your planting accordingly. Newly transplanted perennials need a period of intensive care while they settle in and adjust to their new home. Strong sunshine, drying winds, and intense heat can stress any plant. These conditions are especially damaging to plants that have been recently disturbed and are busy repairing torn roots and coping with the inevitable trauma that transplanting causes.

Timing is critical

By planting at a time of year when you can count on the weather to be mild for a while, you give the garden a head start. In cold-winter regions, planting in early spring gives perennials a couple of months to get used to the climate before hot weather sets in. Only bulbs, bearded iris, peonies, and oriental poppies are safe to plant during the fall in the coldest winter regions. But in areas where winter temperatures don't fall below –20° F (–29° C), early fall is another excellent time to plant the flower bed. Even though the days are shorter and cooler, root growth continues unimpeded after frost has blackened the top of the plant, not stopping until the ground freezes solidly.

Gardeners in mild coastal climates can plant their flower beds at any time of the year, whenever planting is convenient. In hot, humid, mild-winter regions, fall planting is preferable. Planting in fall enables perennials to grow strong root systems before they're subjected to the heat of summer.

Whatever time of year you decide to plant your flower bed, make sure that you can give it your full attention for several weeks afterward. A new garden needs vigilance — it's as needy as a new puppy. Check the flowers for wilting or other signs of distress at least twice a day until they start to put on new growth. Right after planting isn't a good time to leave for an extended vacation.

Hardening off

Hardening off is similar to the tanning routine that people had to put themselves through each spring before the invention of sunscreens. You probably remember lying out in the sun for a few minutes each day and gradually lengthening the exposure time until you could withstand several hours of sunshine without blistering. Your plants may need a similar routine to get accustomed to sunshine.

Plants that have been growing outside at the nursery can go right into the ground without a period of hardening off. But greenhouse-grown plants are lush and soft and have never known a single day of sunshine in their lifetimes. They must be introduced slowly to the harsh, real world.

Leave the plants in their containers and put them in a shaded area with some indirect light for a few days. A north-facing covered porch is ideal. Whenever a freeze is predicted, bring the plants inside overnight. If these are shade plants, you can leave them in this protected site for a few more days and then put them in the garden. For sunny-spot plants, give them a few days in the shaded area and then place the plants in a sunny location for an hour one day. Give them a couple of hours of sun the next day, and so on, increasing their exposure each day. At the end of a week, the plants are thoroughly accustomed to sunlight and wind and are ready to go into their new home.

If you don't have time for all this hardening-off nonsense, simply buy plants that the nursery has had growing outside for at least a while (ask if you have any doubts about which ones have been outside or for how long).

Picking the perfect day to plant

To get your plants off to a vigorous start, you need to choose your planting day carefully. In some parts of the country, the perfect day is such a rarity that calling in sick to take advantage of it is justifiable. In other regions, every day is a good day.

You're looking for a cool, overcast day, preferably the first of many with no record-breaking heat predicted for the near future. An imminent threat of a rainstorm is better yet, if you can get your bed finished before the storm strikes. If cooperative weather is not in the forecast, plant early in the morning or in the evening.

Digging In — It's Showtime!

After you choose a spot for your garden, prepare your soil, purchase your plants, and harden them off (if necessary), the big day finally arrives. Put on some old clothes, get out a pair of gardening gloves and a shovel (and maybe a bottle of champagne), and prepare to get dirty!

If your flower bed is wider than you can easily reach across, lay some old boards or some stepping stones throughout the area. Standing on these additions keeps you off the fluffy soil.

Distribute container plants, following your plan — if you've made one. (If you haven't yet made a plan but want to, see Chapter 3.) Mark spots for bulbs and bare-root perennials with empty pots or stakes. Make certain that you've allowed adequate spacing for each plant to spread to its mature size; the nursery tag often has this information. Take note of where you need to add annuals for temporary fill until the perennials actually use their allotted space (see Chapter 10 for a list of annuals).

Planting potted perennials

Planting a potted perennial is easy with a little practice. Make a copy of these instructions to take into the garden with you (or write them on the back of your hand). Keep the instructions with you until you have the knack. Plant the largest pots first; the smaller ones are easier to tuck in afterwards. Finish planting each perennial before going on to the next.

1. **Dig a hole for the plant using a shovel or a spade.**

   Make the hole at least double the diameter of the pot. (See Figure 14-1.)

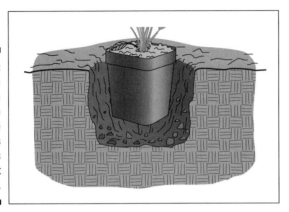

Figure 14-1:
Dig a hole
large
enough to
fit in the
plant's
roots
without
crowding.

2. **Remove the plant from the pot.**

   This step isn't always as simple as it sounds. When things are going well, you cradle the top of the plant between the fingers of one hand, tip the pot upside down, and slip the plant out to rest snugly against the palm of the opposite hand. (See Figure 14-2.)

Figure 14-2:
Getting a
plant out of
its pot.

However, often the plant refuses to budge. If this happens, try rapping the bottom of the pot smartly with your unoccupied hand. If that attempt fails, lay the plastic pot on its side on the ground and gently step on and compress the pot just a little. Next, give the pot a quarter turn and step on it again. Whatever you do, don't try to pull the plant out by its top. The top usually breaks off in your hand — instead of liberating the plant, you kill it.

Small pots can usually be coaxed into releasing their contents by pinching and poking through the bottom of the pot. You can also tear off a small pot. When these other options fail, cut the pot off with heavy-duty shears — which is not as easy as it sounds and should always be the last resort.

3. **Place the plant gently into the hole.**

   You want the crown of the plant — where the top of the plant meets the roots — at ground level, as shown in Figure 14-3, so you need to adjust the soil level until the root ball sits at about the right height. Don't bury the crown or lower leaves. Break off any layer of moss or crud on the surface of the soil surrounding the plant. (You can drop whatever you break off into the hole for extra soil nutrients.)

   Check for and remove weeds (see Chapter 18). Also look for slug eggs — masses of tiny clear balls — and dispose of them. (See Chapter 18 for more on slug solutions.) Tease a few roots away from the root ball. Try to straighten out any large, fibrous roots. If the hole isn't large enough for a relaxed fit for the roots, remove the plant, enlarge the hole, and try again.

Breaking up root balls

Occasionally, you bring home a root-bound plant despite your best efforts to avoid them. Maybe it's the only one of that particular plant in the whole city or it may be an end-of-season bargain. If you plant the root ball intact, you may find it in the same shape and size when you dig up the carcass two years later. You can succeed with root-bound plants, but you need to treat them very roughly before you plant them.

Break apart the root ball as much as you can, untangling the largest roots as you go. Sometimes the only way to do so is to *butterfly* the root ball. Lay it on the ground and cut the root ball in two, approximately two-thirds of the way toward the crown. Spread the two sides apart and plant with the roots in this position.

Figure 14-3:
Plant the
perennial at
the same
depth
as in its
container.

4. **Fill the hole back up with dirt.**

   Fan out the plant's roots in the hole. Hold the plant with the crown at
   the proper height with one hand and start refilling the hole with the
   other hand. Add a handful of dirt at a time, breaking up large chunks as
   you go. You don't want to leave huge holes underground because the
   roots need to be in direct contact with the soil.

   Pat the soil around the plant carefully. No stamping of feet is allowed,
   especially on clay soils. Remember that you want 25 percent of the soil
   to be air pockets when you're finished (see Chapter 11 for details).
   Check to make sure that all the roots are underground and all the
   leaves are above the surface.

5. **Water the plant.**

   With a watering can or a hose turned on very low, saturate the newly
   planted area with water. Some of the soil always collapses inward at
   this point, so add more as necessary. If the whole plant sinks, carefully
   pull it back up again and push some more soil underneath the root ball.

6. **Label the plant.**

   Use the plastic nursery label or make a homemade label. Push the label
   about two-thirds of the way into the soil near the crown of each plant,
   so that you can find it when necessary but it isn't particularly visible
   otherwise.

7. Feed the plant.

Pour a weak solution of manure tea or liquid fertilizer (see Chapter 16) mixed at one-fourth the usual strength recommended on the label. Use just enough of the solution to reach the soil at the base of the plant. This first feeding helps improve the perennial's chances of survival.

8. Move on to the next plant, repeating Steps 1 through 7.

9. Spread the mulch last, after you have watered, labeled, and fed all the perennials.

If you plan to use a mulch (as described in Chapter 13), apply it immediately after planting so that weeds don't get a running start in the bare soil.

10. Get yourself a piece of cheesecake (or open up that bottle of champagne).

You've earned a reward!

Planting "exceptional" perennials

A few varieties of perennials require special planting techniques. They may have special kinds of roots or prefer to be planted with their crowns deeper than ground level. Here are some specifics on a few common perennials that need a little special treatment:

 Bearded iris: Iris plants have a swollen, fleshy root called a *rhizome.* Green leaves, called a *fan,* protrude from the bottom. To plant an iris, dig a large shallow hole and build up a center cone of soil. Place the rhizome against the cone with the fan facing outward and the roots spread out and downward. If you're planting several rhizomes of the same iris, place the fans in a circle around the soil cone.

ECO-SMART

What to do with all those pots

After you finish planting your garden, you may wonder what to do with all those plastic pots.

Most nurseries happily take back their pots and trays for reuse. They usually don't want the empty four-packs or six-packs, but you can use those for starting seeds. Or you can find gardening friends or neighbors who grow most of their own flowers or vegetables from seed. They're usually delighted to recycle your discards.

Press soil over the roots and the rhizomes to keep the fans from falling down. Barely cover the rhizome with soil in cold climates. Leave the rhizomes partially exposed in warm, wet regions to improve the drainage.

✔ **Peonies:** Herbaceous peonies are an exception to the general rule of planting the crown of a perennial at soil level. Peonies prefer to be planted with their *eyes,* the buds emerging from the crown, 1 to 2 inches (2.5 to 3 cm) below the surface of the soil. If you plant them any deeper, peonies often fail to bloom.

✔ **Oriental poppies:** Oriental poppies like to be planted deeply with their crown buried 3 inches (8 cm) deep (measured from the top of the crown to the surface of the soil).

Planting bare-root perennials

The first time you unwrap a package of bare-root perennials, you're probably in for a bit of a shock. Often, the whole shipment appears to be dead. Both the roots and the tops are brown when the plants are in a dormant state, and sometimes you can hardly tell what side goes up. You may find swollen buds or remnants of dead leaves at the crown of the plant, or fleshy roots may look more alive than the top. If you really can't tell the top from the bottom, call the nursery that you ordered from for advice.

To plant bare-root perennials, follow these steps:

1. **Carefully unwrap and remove the packing material.**

2. **Soak the roots in a bucket of water for a few hours or overnight.**

   Don't cover the whole plant, just the roots.

3. **Dig a roomy hole.**

   Build a cone of soil in the center of the hole.

4. **Spread the roots over the cone.**

5. **Refill the hole.**

   Hold the crown of the plant at the soil level and form the soil around the roots with your fingers.

6. **Water the plant evenly and fill any sinkholes with additional garden soil.**

Protecting New Transplants

Sometimes, the weather forecaster turns out to be wrong, and the promised cloud cover burns off. Your new garden is now faced with full sun and rapidly rising temperatures, and you must create temporary shelter quickly.

Placing evergreen boughs in a tent around the plant, stems poked into the ground and tips facing inward, does an effective job of protecting individual plants. You can overlap boughs to cover a whole flower bed if the plants aren't tall enough to be smashed down by the boughs. My favorite material is one of the new lightweight, spun-bonded landscape fabrics. Simply spread this fabric over the flower bed and anchor down the corners with stones or other heavy objects. These materials are porous, so you can leave them in place for as long as you need — water and air pass through readily.

No matter how careful you are, you may very well lose a few of your newly planted perennials. The reason why is usually a mystery. You may have two identical plants placed only inches apart — one lives, the other dies. Some plants just don't seem to have a strong will to live.

What kills most newly planted perennials is *transplant shock*. Its symptoms are leafs and flowers that drop and wilt — even when the soil is damp.

Don't water a plant exhibiting signs of transplant shock without first checking the root ball to see whether it is dry. Overwatering usually hastens the demise of a plant in this situation. Shelter the plant for a few days, cross your fingers, and hope for the best. Burning candles at the altar or repeating a mantra may not hurt, either. Most plants recover — even plants that appear dead can come back the following spring from live roots. Don't be too hasty to give a perennial the 10-count.

Part V
Care, Feeding, and Propagation

The 5th Wave — By Rich Tennant

"Remember—this is just until the jonquils come in."

In this part . . .

Just like a new puppy, perennials need a bit of extra attention and TLC when you first plant them. In time, however, you can establish a fairly simple routine that meets all your garden's needs and is actually fun for you, rather than a chore. Knowing when and how to water, fertilize, and tend to your perennials can mean the difference between a thriving, low-maintenance garden and a sickly, burdensome eyesore. Best of all, if you care for your perennials properly, they reward you by making baby perennials of their own.

Chapter 15

Grab Your Watering Can

. . . .

In This Chapter

▶ Figuring out how much to water

▶ Choosing a watering device

▶ Deciding when to water

▶ Avoiding problems from over- and underwatering

▶ Getting water to the roots

▶ Conserving water

. . . .

*F*iguring out how to water effectively and efficiently is the trickiest part of the whole gardening maintenance routine. It's the old "Goldilocks and the Three Bears" conundrum. Overwatering drowns your perennials; underwatering causes them to dry up and get crispy. Determining how much water is "just right" is the challenge.

Most homeowners judge how long and how often to run the sprinkler based solely on what *feels* right, leaving the plants to fend for themselves. The plants getting too little or too much water die, and the survivors end up labeled "easy-care."

Determining a Plant's Water Needs

How much water each perennial requires to stay fit and healthy depends on a number of factors:

▶ **Climate:** In climates where rainfall is regular and reliable, watering isn't a pressing need, except during occasional prolonged dry spells or drought. (Every climate undergoes a dry spell periodically. I was quite surprised to experience two hosepipe bans, during which watering the garden was forbidden, due to drought during the four years I lived in generally drizzly England.)

In arid regions, irrigation is often an all-consuming activity. Watering becomes the garden's artificial life-support system. Ironically, the same perennial that insists on frequent irrigation to survive in a hot, dry environment may rot in a wet climate.

✔ **Weather:** *Climate* is determined by average prevailing weather conditions; *weather* is what's happening outside as you read this. Out-of-the-ordinary weather can wreak havoc on your plants. Windstorms and high temperatures can dry out a garden very quickly. My carefully tended fern garden in Southern California was burned to the ground, in a manner of speaking, in one afternoon of hot desert winds.

✔ **Soil types:** Different soil types also affect how often the garden needs water. Sand holds moisture about as efficiently as a sieve. Water penetrates sandy soil readily and deeply but tends to filter right on through. Heavy clay is the exact opposite. Its dense soil particles crust over and deflect water drops. Water applied slowly and in stages soaks in; water applied quickly just runs off. But after clay is saturated, it holds water very well — sometimes so well that the plants rot.

Add organic matter to cure both sandy and clayey conditions. Sandy soil that has been amended retains water better; organic matter breaks up clay and improves its drainage. (See Chapter 11 for more information on soil types and amending soils with organic matter.)

✔ **Location, location, location:** In general, shaded gardens need less water than gardens in the full blast of the midday sun. However, in places where trees are responsible for casting the shadow, their roots may greedily grab water, outcompeting the flowers. In this example, sometimes no amount of water is ever enough to satisfy both the trees and the flowers.

✔ **Genetic disposition:** Some plants are splendidly adaptable, enduring swamp or desert with equal aplomb. But most plants prefer some approximation of their natural habitat. Plants from wet places generally need more water than plants from dry places. This rule may seem quite obvious, but many gardening disasters result from a failure to follow it. (See the nearby sidebar, "Grouping plants according to their needs.")

Getting Water to the Garden

Watering cans are a good short-term measure for new transplants, and standing in the garden with your thumb over the end of a hose may be relaxing and give you a sense of accomplishment. But neither method is satisfactory for providing the thorough soaking an established garden needs.

The three primary methods for irrrigating flower beds are the following:

✔ **The portable system:** You probably already know the old hose-and-sprinkler routine all too well. The advantage is the low cost — one hose and one sprinkler at the bare minimum. The drawbacks, however, are legion — rolling out the hose and moving the sprinkler from place to place is always a chore, and water coverage is generally poor. Tall plants block the water spray either to their own roots or to their bed mates behind (see Figure 15-1).

Sprinklers work best when every flower is the same height. Most sprinklers spray in uneven patterns, so don't place them in the same spot each time.

Sprinklers wet the foliage, which may spread diseases in the flower bed, making them a bad choice in hot, humid climates. But in hot, dry climates, wetting the foliage rinses dust off the leaves and helps prevent spider mite infestations.

Figure 15-1:
Taller growth sometimes blocks spray from a sprinkler, causing dry spots in the back of the flower bed.

✔ **Drip irrigation:** Two main types of drip irrigation are available: leaky hoses and individual emitters. Leaky hoses are either porous tubes manufactured from old tires, or flat tapes with slits cut at intervals. You can lay either kind directly on top of the soil under the mulch (as shown in Figure 15-2), or bury them a few inches deep. I prefer the first method so that I can easily get to the hose to repair the inevitable geysers. Leaky-hose products I've used have been uneven in water distribution, especially on hillsides, but they're still my favorite method for irrigating flower beds.

In another type of drip irrigation system, you wind rigid plastic tubing through the flower bed. You place the individual emitters that are attached to the line directly on the root ball of each perennial. This system is highly efficient at delivering water. Keep in mind, though, that every new plant needs its own emitter.

✔ **The automated system:** Automatic systems can be real time-savers and can give you freedom to safely take a vacation in the middle of summer (with only an overseer — possibly the kid next door — to ensure that the system is actually working while you're away). You can even purchase built-in timers or moisture sensors so that the system comes on when needed, rather than on a fixed schedule. Both sprinklers or drip irrigation can be fully automated.

Figure 15-2:
Snake leaky hoses back and forth between the plants in the flower bed.

Grouping plants according to their needs

In Colorado, landscapers love the look of pines and aspen trees growing together. The problem is that aspens like constant moisture and pines need to be relatively dry. Eventually, one or the other always dies because their cultural needs are just too incompatible. A neighborhood near me replaces a dozen expensive 10-foot pines every single year because the trees die from too much water.

The one most important factor in creating a successful garden is grouping plants that have the same cultural needs so that you can tend to them as a group, rather than individually. Build separate flower beds for flowers with dissimilar needs, and each bed can have its own personalized schedule for watering and other maintenance tasks.

Deciding When to Water

Most perennials require water only after the top few inches of soil dry out, but before the plant starts to show symptoms of drought stress. Perennials from arid habitats benefit when the dry interval between waterings is longer. Plants from wet places prefer to never completely dry out.

Problems occur when the soil is either too wet or too dry for too long. But, just to complicate matters, overwatered and underwatered perennials exhibit nearly identical symptoms. Both conditions cause plants to wilt and droop miserably, to develop yellowed leaves with brown edges, and to experience stunted growth. Flowers and leaves start to drop off, and eventually the pitiful thing just dies. You can't tell by looking whether too much or too little water is the culprit. Your first inclination may be to just grab a hose or watering can. But you must actually feel the soil to be certain whether the soil is too wet or too dry.

Don't simply feel the surface of the soil to check for over- or underwatering. The top few inches can be deceptively different from the soil underneath. When your perennials first start to show signs of stress, dig a small hole several inches deep and feel the soil. If the soil's wet, you know that you need to cut back on water. If the soil is dry, water more frequently. Clay is more difficult to judge than sand. The tiny clay particles can grab hold of moisture so tightly that the soil can feel cool and somewhat moist, and yet the plants can't get the water. Amending clay soil with plenty of organic matter alleviates this problem (see Chapter 11 for more on amending soils).

You can buy an electronic moisture monitor to help you decide when to water. Or you can use a long screwdriver as a low-tech soil probe. If you can easily push the screwdriver deeply into the soil, your garden probably has enough moisture.

Accounting for seasonal variations

After one season of careful monitoring, you start to get a sense of how often your garden wants water. At this point, you can safely begin to use an automatic timer for the sake of convenience. But don't set the timer in the spring and leave it unchanged for the whole growing season. A plant's water demands change with the seasons.

Adequate and even moisture is essential for most perennials during their spring growth spurt. But many regions have special watering needs:

- ✔ Mediterranean flowers and others from coastal regions often require a summer dormancy period and must be kept fairly dry during their nap. During the summer, give them only an infrequent deep soaking when the soil is completely dry.

- ✔ In regions with cold winters, always start lengthening the intervals between waterings in late summer to toughen your plants for winter (a process that gardeners call *hardening off*). You don't want your perennials to face the first frost with lush, easily damaged new growth.

- ✔ Where winters are cold *and* dry, the garden benefits from a drink once a month, whenever it hasn't rained or snowed for a few weeks. Water your garden on a day when temperatures are above freezing and the surface of the soil is thawed so that the water doesn't simply run off.

Considering the time of day

An old adage warns never to water during the middle of a sunny day, lest the water droplets burn the foliage like a magnifying glass. I have doubts about this warning (although salt residue left from rapid evaporation may burn the leaves). The real reason you shouldn't water in the hottest part of the day is efficiency. Much of the water from a midday watering evaporates before it has a chance to soak in. The same goes for watering when a wind is blowing. Watering in the evening or early morning is preferable wherever you live, but keep in mind the following tips:

- ✔ Water whenever the soil is dry and plants are wilting or showing signs of imminent death. Most perennials wilt on a hot day, regardless of whether or not they need water. Water only when the soil is dry and the plants don't recover from their "faint" overnight.

- ✔ You're usually better off watering in the morning than in the evening. Mornings aren't as windy as evenings, so less water gets blown away. Also, the moisture from a morning watering recharges your plants for the day.

✔ In tropical regions, wet foliage may help spread some diseases. If you live in a steamy, damp climate, it's especially important to water early in the morning so that leaves dry off quickly as the day heats up.

✔ If you live in a dry region, watering in the evening gives plants ample time to absorb the water overnight.

Taking care of new transplants

Newly transplanted perennials are especially vulnerable in the first few weeks. Extra pampering gets them off to a good, strong start. Little root balls can dry out very quickly. During really hot spells, you may need to water more than once a day. Water new transplants every time their roots dry out, whether the surrounding soil is still damp or not. The only way you can tell whether the root ball is dry is to push your fingers into the soil at the base of each plant and feel for yourself.

A process called *wicking* can cause a newly planted root ball to remain absolutely dry, even while standing in a puddle of mud. Wicking can occur whenever two different types of soil meet. The soil in the prepared flower bed is almost always heavier and denser than the potting mix surrounding the root ball. Moisture is pulled out of the light soil, leaving the new plant high and dry. After a few weeks, the roots travel out into the new soil, and the problem is solved. But in the meantime, you must make certain that the root ball is actually getting wet.

Here's a good, low-tech, temporary, and free method you can use to water new transplants. This process creates an all-day, automatic drip system.

1. **Rinse out a 1-gallon (2-liter) plastic bottle or jug.**

2. **Using a needle, poke a small hole in the bottom near a corner.**

   You want a very slow drip, so that it takes several days for all the water to drain out of the container.

3. **Fill the container with water.**

4. **Set the container next to a newly transplanted perennial.**

5. **Refill the container as needed.**

   Leave the container in place until the plant puts on several inches of new growth.

Watering cans are another easy way to take care of your transplants' watering needs. Choose a can with a soft spray attachment. A hard splash can wash away soil and expose the tender roots.

Knowing How Much to Water

Perennials generally spread most of their roots in the top 12 inches (30 cm) of the soil, although roots may grow deeper in sandy, fast-draining soils and more shallowly in clay. Watering a few inches deeper than this root zone encourages roots to dive deeper, where they're protected from fluctuating surface temperatures. Roots grow best at constant, cool temperatures, and shallow-rooted perennials dry out too quickly and must be watered more frequently.

You can't tell how deeply the water is penetrating by looking at the surface of the soil. The only way to tell whether the water is soaking down deeper than the roots is to dig a few test holes and check. The best method for determining how long to water your garden is to follow these steps:

1. **Wait until your soil is fairly dry at least 6 inches (15 cm) deep.**

2. **Set up whatever system you plan to use (whether sprinkler or soaker hose) and water the flower bed for a set period of time — say 30 minutes.**

3. **Some time the next day, dig a hole to check how deep the soil is wet.**

   Use a narrow-bladed trowel to dig a small hole only 2 to 3 inches (5 to 7 cm) wide. Make the hole 1 foot (30 cm) away from the base of a plant. Don't worry if you cut into the roots — they grow back.

4. **If 30 minutes wasn't long enough to wet the soil 10 to 12 inches (26 to 30 cm) deep, let the soil dry out for a few days and water again — longer this time, say 45 minutes — and dig another hole.**

5. **Repeat this exercise until you discover just how long you need to run the water to get the soil wet to a depth of 1 foot (30 cm).**

   Different irrigation systems deliver water at varying rates, so retest whenever you change to a new sprinkler, hose, or system.

Watering too shallowly is wasteful because most of the water evaporates quickly, before the plants get a chance to quench their thirst. Watering too deeply is also wasteful because roots can only go so far down.

Cutting Down on Water Waste

Water shortages are a reality in any climate and region, and bans on watering are not uncommon. The following list outlines a few things that you can do when water is scarce or limited, when you want to reduce your water bill, or when you just want to conserve the precious resource of fresh water.

- ✔ **Turn off the water.** This piece of advice may seem obvious, but it's easy to leave a sprinkler running and then get busy and forget to turn it off. Set an egg timer to remind you or buy a faucet timer that automatically shuts off the water.

- ✔ **Choose a drip-irrigation method.** Sprinklers waste a great deal of water, throwing much of it into the air where it either evaporates or is blown away.

- ✔ **Collect rainwater.** A barrel like the one in Figure 15-3 collects rainwater from the gutters and holds it until you need it.

Figure 15-3: To catch rainwater, place a barrel at the end of a rain spout.

✔ **Divert rainwater.** Divert the rainwater from downspouts to flower beds by using French drains and pits filled with gravel. A *French drain* is simply an underground plastic pipe, sometimes with holes along the sides, that directs the water flow from the drainspout to the garden.

✔ **Mulch the garden.** Mulch helps hold water in the soil (see Chapter 13 for more details).

✔ **Irrigate deeply.** If you water too shallowly, most of the moisture evaporates before the plants can get it (see "Knowing How Much to Water," earlier in this chapter).

✔ **Measure rainfall.** Use a rain gauge to keep track of rainfall. If you have a fixed watering schedule, skip a watering whenever you record $1/2$ inch (1 cm) or more of rain.

✔ **Plant a water-conserving garden.** Choose flowers that can get by on the average rainfall in your area. Then you can skip the chore of watering entirely, except while getting the perennials adjusted to their new flower bed and during occasional dry periods. (See Chapter 4 for details on this type of gardening, called *xeriscaping*.)

Chapter 16

Fertilizer: Food for Your Flowers

· ·

In This Chapter

▶ The mysteries of fertilizer unraveled

▶ All those essential elements

▶ The effects of shortages

▶ Forms that fertilizer comes in

▶ When and how to apply fertilizer

· ·

*J*ust like people, plants need vitamins and minerals in the right amounts to maintain good health. Unfortunately, choosing the right fertilizer is much like shopping for vitamins. The store shelves are lined with a dazzling array of products, and you don't know which one to choose.

You don't need a degree in chemistry to pick the right fertilizer for your perennials. You just need to know a few basics to make sense of all the muddle surrounding fertilizers. This chapter can help you make an intelligent purchase.

Vitamins for Your Garden

Research has identified 17 essential elements that plants must have for proper growth. Plants automatically get adequate supplies of carbon, hydrogen, and oxygen from water and air, so you don't have to worry about those three. Sunlight provides free fuel for *photosynthesis* — the process plants use to feed themselves. Everything else comes from the soil. When the soil is deficient in any of the remaining elements, you must replenish them or your flowers suffer.

Fertilizing your garden is the way you remedy the problem of malnourished soil. A *fertilizer* is any natural or manufactured material that you add to the soil in order to supply plant nutrients.

All perennials use up relatively large amounts of three *primary nutrients:* nitrogen, phosphorus, and potassium. In fact, many fertilizers contain only these three elements. Products containing all three are called *complete,* even if they are missing any or all of the remaining 11 elements.

Perennials need *secondary nutrients* (calcium, magnesium, and sulfur) in smaller amounts, and *micronutrients* (iron, manganese, copper, zinc, boron, molybdenum, chlorine, and cobalt) in still smaller quantities. Like the primary nutrients, these elements are essential for robust plant growth, but they are less likely than the primary nutrients to be deficient in your soil. Some commercial formulas add a selection of these other elements for extra insurance. The label often says "with iron" or "with micronutrients" to indicate their presence in the mixture.

You don't have to have a degree in chemistry to garden, but you *do* need to know that all plant nutrients are forms of salt. Just as too much salt in your diet isn't good for you, too much fertilizer is harmful to your plants. The salt concentration in the soil pulls water from the plant's roots, mimicking the effects of too little water. Consequently, the plants appear scorched even when the surrounding soil is wet.

Coping with nutrient shortages

A shortage of *any* nutrient eventually leads to problems. Plants exhibit a variety of symptoms, but the most common symptoms are slowed and stunted growth and pale, yellowish, or otherwise discolored foliage.

Fortunately, if you amended your soil with plenty of organic matter (following the guidelines in Chapter 11), it probably contains all the micronutrients your flowers will ever need. But the primary nutrient nitrogen is the one your garden depletes most quickly. Plants and microorganisms consume relatively large quantities of nitrogen, and it washes out of the soil more quickly than other nutrients. You generally need to add nitrogen to your perennial garden every year.

Shortages of elements vary by region. Also, different elements may be inadequate or unavailable to your perennials where the pH is either high or low (see Chapter 11 for more on pH). Here's where a soil test proves its worth. It tells you exactly which elements your soil already carries in sufficient amounts and which are lacking. Use a home test kit (available at most garden centers) or a professional soil testing lab (call the nearest agricultural university for a list of labs). Directions that come with the soil test results tell you precisely what fertilizers to add and in what amount, freeing you completely from guesswork. My soil, for example, is high in potassium, so I don't add more. Too much fertilizer throws things out of whack just as badly as too little. The goal is to create a balance.

Reading the label

In order to decide which fertilizer to buy, you must first figure out how to decipher those intimidating labels. Some standardization of information exists, but every company chooses to present the information in its own way. Somewhere on every package are the manufacturer's name, address, the product's name, the guaranteed analysis of the contents, a list of ingredients, and the weight. Most packages also include directions and suggestions for using the product — such as how much to apply, when, and how. To get an idea of what a fertilizer label looks like, see Figure 16-1.

The three prominently displayed numbers separated by dashes and the section labeled *guaranteed analysis* below them tell you the percentages of nitrogen, phosphorus, and potassium the package contains by weight and volume. Nitrogen is always the first number, phosphorus the second, and potassium the third. (If any of these three elements is not in the formula, its spot contains a 0.) So, for example, a 100-pound bag of fertilizer marked 10-10-10 has 10 pounds (or 10 percent) of actual nitrogen.

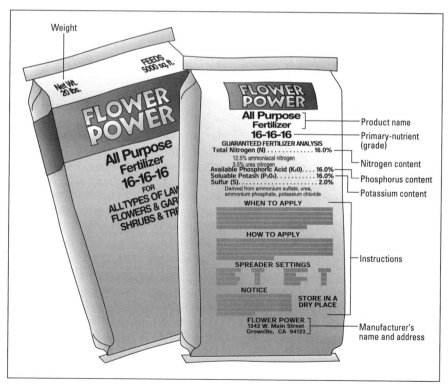

Figure 16-1:
A fertilizer label.

A 10-10-10 fertilizer is called *complete* because it contains all three primary nutrients in sufficient quantities to be of value as nutrients. The numbers 10-10-10 refer to the guaranteed analysis, or *grade*.

If you're the thrifty type, you're probably wondering why you would buy a 100-pound bag of fertilizer if it only contains 30 pounds of nutrients. Good question. The answer can get complicated, but from a gardener's point of view, convenience is a major factor. More concentrated fertilizers are more difficult to apply because a little too much here or there can do more harm than good. Also, the other 70 pounds in the example above usually isn't totally useless. It sometimes includes other nutrients that benefit soils and plants.

Fertilizers are sometimes marketed especially for certain flowers. For example, you can find rose or rhododendron food. Generally, these specialty products are more expensive than all-purpose fertilizers — and, honestly, the rose doesn't know the difference. Compare products with and without the extras, and the cost of buying micronutrients separately. Then buy whatever is cheapest and still meets your needs.

In some regions, fertilizers are marketed to meet local conditions. These products can be helpful if your garden suffers from the targeted defects. In Colorado, for example, many brands add iron because iron tends to be deficient in this area's soils.

Forms of Fertilizer

Commercial fertilizer products are available in many diverse forms. You may need to try out several different kinds until you find the one you like to use.

- ✔ **Granular:** You can purchase both *synthetics* (man-made) and *organics* (natural materials) in granular form. Granular is usually the least expensive type of fertilizer. It's also moderately fast-acting and the most widely available form of fertilizer.

- ✔ **Pellets:** The pelleted forms of fertilizer look like colored BBs. Many brands are coated with resin or polymer so that they dissolve gradually and are available to the plants for a longer period of time. Most pellet fertilizers need to be applied only once a season. Because they release their nutrients slowly, less fertilizer is wasted and washed away before your perennials can grab what they need. These products are more costly when compared to granular forms.

✔ **Solid tablets and spikes:** Tablets and spikes are made of compressed fertilizer. Pushed into the soil at intervals, the nutrients they contain tend to stay in concentrations high enough to burn and kill plant roots. Your goal is to spread the fertilizer as evenly as possible throughout the garden — which is impossible with these products.

✔ **Liquids and soluble powders:** Synthetic fertilizers and organics such as manure teas, seaweed extracts, and fish emulsions are available premixed and ready to apply. They also come in liquid or soluble powdered concentrations that you mix with water. All can be sprayed directly onto the foliage, where they are quickly absorbed. Liquid fertilizers are the fastest treatment for a nutrient deficiency, but they're short-acting and may need to be applied several times during the growing season. You can also spray them onto the ground. These fertilizers are fairly expensive.

✔ **Chelated minerals:** The word *chelated* on a fertilizer label means that this mineral has been specially processed so that plants can absorb it more efficiently. Chelated products are expensive, but they're worth the extra cost because they last longer.

✔ **Bulk organics:** Organic fertilizers come from diverse sources such as animal manure, sewage sludge, plant and animal residues, and mined minerals. Most contain nutrients in much lower concentrations than the synthetics, but they have some real benefits. Organics improve soil texture, hold water in the soil, and support communities of earthworms and microorganisms.

You can buy most organics either bagged or in bulk. Generally, you apply organic fertilizer as a *top-dressing* — one to two inches (3 to 5 cm) spread, once in the spring and once in the fall, directly over the mulch or soil, where the materials can filter down into the soil.

✔ **Designer fertilizers:** Chunks of manure shaped into decorative forms are all the rage as gifts for the gardener who has everything. These sculptures are cute but expensive methods of applying fertilizer. The preceding information on "bulk organics" applies to these products, as well.

✔ **Weed-and-feed products:** Be careful not to accidentally use weed-and-feed products on your perennial garden. These products are formulated for lawn care and kill most garden flowers just as they kill weeds. I know — once, under the influence of the flu, I picked up a bag of weed-and-feed by mistake and scattered it all over my flower beds. Plants started dying left and right before I realized what I'd done. If you ever make this mistake, the remedy is flooding the garden with large quantities of water to rinse out the herbicide.

When to Fertilize

Some gardeners fertilize every couple of weeks throughout the growing season, no matter what. Such compulsive behavior usually isn't necessary and can actually be harmful. Flowers getting excessive nitrogen, for example, may stop blooming altogether and just put on new foliage instead. Overdoing organic fertilizer is more difficult, because it isn't as concentrated as synthetics.

If your soil test indicates a shortage, add the missing nutrient at least once a year, in spring, using either a synthetic or an organic fertilizer. Watch your flowers for clues that all is not well. If they don't seem to be actively growing or if they become pale or discolored, give them a shot of liquid fertilizer, and they should perk up.

If you don't want to mess around with a soil test, simply apply a complete, balanced product formulated for general garden use (or for flower beds) once a year, in early spring. To make sure that your garden has enough micronutrients, also top-dress it twice a year with compost or well-aged manure (at least one year old or not too strong-smelling — if it burns your eyes, it will burn your plants!).

How to Fertilize

Always read the entire label and follow the directions carefully. Treat all fertilizers with care. Many can irritate your lungs if you breath in the dust or burn your skin or eyes upon contact. Wear gloves, eye protection, and a dust mask when handling any fertilizer. Store all fertilizers out of reach of children and pets — just as you do all other household chemical products.

Fertilizers that contain iron sulfate stain concrete walks and driveways, so sweep up any spilled granules or pellets. Dilute spilled liquids with water.

All fertilizers are salts and can burn plants if used improperly. The best time to apply most fertilizers is on an overcast, cool day or in the morning or late afternoon. Some fertilizers — especially ones that are water soluble or that contain a high percentage of nutrients — are more likely to burn plants on hot days than on cool days. Don't apply more fertilizer than the manufacturer recommends.

A sample fertilizing routine

When, how, and how much you fertilize depends on your particular flower bed, but the general procedure is about the same for all gardeners. My fertilizer routine is typical.

My soil was originally low in nitrogen and phosphorus. When I amended each bed (as described in Chapter 11), I added phosphorus. This mineral is quite stable in the soil, so I won't need to add it in large amounts again soon. Nitrogen is the mineral my garden uses up quickly. I buy a high-nitrogen product in a slow-release pelleted form and spread it throughout my flower beds once a year in the spring. To provide micronutrients, I also top-dress with manure or compost once in the spring and once in the fall.

My soil's pH is extremely high, so occasionally a few flowers start to look sickly yellow. When this occurs, I spray a soil acidifier on the foliage for a quick fix. (I really should eliminate the problem by digging out the finicky flowers, but I don't have the heart!) I test my soil every couple of years just to make sure that everything's going well.

Using liquid and soluble powders

The goal when using liquid fertilizers is to wet the entire plant and the soil beneath. These products are absorbed quickly through the leaves and then more gradually through the roots.

To apply to small areas, mix the appropriate amount in a watering can. Hose-end sprayers (see Figure 16-2) are real time-savers when fertilizing large gardens. Some packages include a sprayer with the fertilizer. You can purchase refills later as you need them.

Figure 16-2:
Apply liquid fertilizer to individual flowers with a watering can or spray the whole flower using a hose-end sprayer.

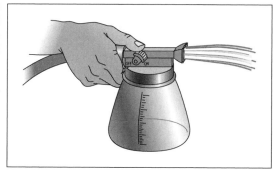

Applying granules and pellets

Because the nutrients from fertilizer granules and pellets are absorbed by the roots, they are more effective when you scratch them into the soil around the base of the plant. You can mix the fertilizer into the soil before planting your perennials or, after your flower bed is growing, follow these steps:

- ✔ For small gardens, spread the granules or pellets around the base of each plant and then scratch them into the top 1 to 2 inches (2 to 5 cm) of the soil, using a three-prong cultivator tool or a trowel.

- ✔ For large gardens, you *can* toss the fertilizer out of a bucket by hand (wearing gloves). But using a hand-held crank-type spreader (called a *broadcaster*), as shown in Figure 16-3, is easier, faster, and gives a more even application. You can buy a hand-held spreader at any garden center or hardware store.

Figure 16-3:
Broadcasting fertilizer pellets with a mechanical spreader.

Spread the fertilizer right on top of the soil or mulch. Then water well to wash off any pellets that landed on leaves and so that the roots of the plants can absorb the fertilizer.

Chapter 17

Keeping Your Flowers in Tip-Top Shape

· ·

· ·

S ome maintenance tasks require devotion to a regular routine during the blooming season to keep your flowers looking good. Other chores — such as getting the flower bed ready for winter — are seasonal. If you've ever had the burden of caring for a lawn, you'll be pleasantly surprised to find that flowers require much less attention than grass. Flower-garden maintenance can almost always wait until you have time for it.

Getting the Tools You Need

My garage is filled with gardening tools, but I find myself grabbing the same ones every time I head out the door. Start out with a few essentials, and you can always add to your supply later. (You don't actually *need* more tools than these essentials, but some folks are absolute tool nuts and can't resist collecting every new garden gadget on the market.)

Here's a list of the basic tools you need in order to work in your flower garden:

✔ **Buckets:** Buy several buckets. You need something to carry your small tools in as you work. A bucket is also perfect for mixing small amounts of soil and for carrying plants, trash, or weeds.

✔ **Hand trowel:** A *hand trowel* looks like a very small shovel. It's the tool you use the most in gardening, so buy a good one. A high-quality hand trowel costs as much as a shovel, but don't skimp. You use it to transplant small flowers and bulbs, to enlarge holes you've dug with a shovel, and to weed. You may want to buy two sizes — one with a wide blade for digging and one with a narrow blade for weeding. If you only buy one, get the wider size.

✔ **Pruning shears:** Dozens of types of pruning shears are available, but the two main classes are *anvil* and *bypass.* Get the bypass shears, because they make cleaner cuts. These shears look and work much like snub-nosed scissors. They fit into tight spaces and cut cleanly.

Try out shears before you buy them to get a comfortable fit. Some stores keep twigs in their pruning-shear displays for just this purpose. When you hold the handles open in your hand, they shouldn't extend past the reach of your fingertips. Good pruning shears are very expensive, but they stay sharp longer than a cheap pair and have parts that are replaceable if they wear out.

✔ **Scissors:** A pair of lightweight aluminum household scissors are really slick for cutting foliage and lightweight stems (much larger handfuls than you can manage with pruning shears) and for all-around snipping. Scissors are also handy for cutting twine and opening bags (I can never get those stringed tops to unravel the way the directions say they do!).

✔ **Shovel or spade:** You need a shovel or spade for digging holes and for mixing amendments into the soil. I prefer a round-nose shovel, but many other gardeners swear by a short-handled, flat-bladed spade. Find a gardening friend who has both so that you can try them out before making your choice.

✔ **Stiff-tined rake:** A stiff-tined rake is helpful for smoothing out the surface of the soil and for spreading mulch. Use it with the tines up for spreading fine materials, tines down for coarse materials.

✔ **Watering can:** Use a watering can for spot-watering transplants and for mixing small batches of liquid fertilizer.

✔ **Wheelbarrow or garden cart:** Use a wheelbarrow or a garden cart (similar to a wheelbarrow but with two wheels) for carrying soil amendments, mulch, tools, and plants from the car to the flower bed. A wheelbarrow or garden cart is a real time- and back-saver. Buy one that you can handle easily.

Buying the right tools

Always buy the best quality tools you can afford. Cheap tools break too readily to be a true bargain. I've had countless trowels bend in half the first time they struck soil. Now I wouldn't accept a cheap trowel as a gift.

Don't order tools through the mail without first trying them out. One size doesn't fit all. You actually need to heft a tool to see whether you can use it comfortably. A bad fit guarantees backaches and blisters. After you know which tools suit your grip, go ahead and order them from a catalog, especially if you can save some money by doing so.

Small tools have a way of getting lost in the nooks and crannies of a flower bed. Two minutes after I set a trowel down, it vanishes. I swear they bury themselves. To make your tools easy to locate, paint a band of bright color or wrap a strip of colored tape on the part of the handle that you don't grab hold of. Some tools have a hole at one end so that you can hang them on a nail; tie a piece of brightly colored yarn through the hole to make your tool stand out against the garden's neutral backdrop. In this case, garish is good.

Good tools last a lifetime if you take care of them. Don't ever leave them outside where they can rust. Always quit gardening for the day while you still have enough energy and daylight to clean your tools and put them away.

Renting the really big puppies

Large, gasoline-powered machines are a real help with large projects, but they're expensive to buy and take up a great deal of storage space. Renting or borrowing these machines when you need them is more practical. Look in the Yellow Pages of your phone book for rental agencies. Usually, these machines are rented out by the hour or the day. Unless you have a hitch on your vehicle and a small trailer, expect to pay a delivery charge as well. Rental costs vary but are usually about the same as a moderately priced dinner. The two most useful large machines are power tillers and chipper-shredders:

✔ A *power tiller* is a mechanical soil mixer. It can make really light work of soil preparation, but after you dig your garden, you don't need to use a tiller again. Rather than buy your own, rent this big boy when needed.

✔ *Chipper-shredders* grind up twigs, branches, and other garden waste and can reduce a huge pile of such stuff to a small pile of chips and shreds. These little pieces rot much more quickly than unchopped material in the compost bin. Many communities no longer accept garden waste in the garbage pick-up, so you need to do something with it. You can either rent a chipper-shredder machine once a year, when you do a big cleanup, or hire a garden maintenance company to come in and grind the prunings for you.

Getting into a Maintenance Routine

Garden chores have several missions. Some are necessary mostly for the sake of tidiness. Others help preserve good garden health. Most gardeners fuss in their gardens much more than is necessary, just because playing in the garden is such an enjoyable and relaxing thing to do. A 100- to 200-square-foot (9- to 18-square-meter) flower garden shouldn't take more than a few minutes a week of tending, with a couple of hours of major cleanup several times a year. This section covers the housekeeping aspects of gardening, such as trimming, staking, and preparing your flower bed for winter. Watering (Chapter 15) and fertilizing (Chapter 16) are such important topics that they warrant their own chapters.

Deadheading

No, *deadheading* is not some kind of homage to Jerry Garcia. Flowers in a vase eventually start to wither and die, and so do flowers in the garden as they age. Removing these crumpled corpses serves several purposes:

✔ Dead flowers aren't very pretty. Cutting them off improves the look of the garden.

✔ Most dead flowers form seeds — which can be a good or a bad thing. Some plants replace flowers with really attractive seedheads. But others scatter their seeds all over the garden, much like a dandelion does. You often wind up with dozens of baby flowers that you have to pull out to avoid ending up with a hundred daisies in one square foot of garden soil. Cutting off flowers before they form seeds prevents this maintenance headache.

✔ Many perennials stop blooming after they form seeds, so removing the fading flowers before they can complete the process encourages the plant to continue blooming. Some perennials have their biggest burst of bloom in the spring but will rebloom in the fall if you cut off the first flush of flowers after they start to turn brown.

To deadhead, simply cut the dead flower off — using scissors for lightweight stems or pruning shears for heavy and thick ones. Cut the stem below the flower at the first leaves or flower bud you come to.

Disbudding

If you like your flowers really big, you may want to indulge in the practice of *disbudding.* Before the buds start to open, remove all but one or two flower buds on each stem. The plant then directs all its energy to the remaining buds, resulting in large flowers.

Gardeners commonly disbud dahlias, chrysanthemums, peonies, and carnations.

If you want more flowers rather than larger flowers, don't disbud. Every bud you remove is a flower you don't get to enjoy later.

The kindest cuts

Here are more things you can do with your pruning shears and scissors:

✔ **Pinching:** To keep perennials denser and shorter, you may want to pinch or shear them, as shown in Figure 17-1, a couple of times early in the season. This process is called *pinching* because you can actually pinch off the top of each stem between your thumb and forefinger — but using scissors or pruning shears is quicker and easier.

Figure 17-1:
To keep late-flowering perennials more compact, shear or pinch a couple of times early in the season.

Simply snip (or pinch) off the top few inches (8 cm or so) of the plant when it grows to a foot tall (30 cm) in spring and again in the middle of summer. Every stem you cut grows several new stems. The result is stocky sprays of more, but smaller, flowers.

Chrysanthemums and asters are two perennials that are routinely pinched. Otherwise, they tend to get floppy.

✔ **Shearing:** For a quicker alternative to pinching, use scissors or pruning shears to cut the top 6 inches (15 cm) off your plants a couple of times before midsummer.

✔ **Cutting back hard:** When the directions for a plant tell you to *cut it back hard,* this means to reduce the height of the plant by approximately one-third to one-half. Use either scissors or pruning shears to cut the stems. Sometimes, this hard pruning is recommended solely to improve the appearance of the plant, but it may also be necessary to renew a plant's vigor.

Staking perennials with bad posture

Some perennials slouch and sprawl as badly as a group of teenage boys in the neighborhood park. If slumping perennials were simply a problem of aesthetics, you could just ignore them, depending on your inclination toward discipline in the garden. But when a large perennial leans over on top of smaller, weaker companions, the bully may steal all the sunlight or actually crush the little ones. During fall cleanup, you often find that plants subjected to this treatment didn't survive the season.

Fortunately, you have many ways to prop up unruly (or just plain lazy) plants. Here are a few popular methods and devices for staking perennials, as illustrated in Figure 17-2:

✔ **Bamboo stakes:** Bamboo makes good support for flowers with tall, single spikes — such as delphiniums and lilies. Wait until the stems are several feet tall and starting to form flower buds. Pound the stake several inches into the ground at the base of the plant and tie the stem loosely to the stake. Use breadbag twist-ties, twine, or whatever you have on hand.

You can also encircle wide multistemmed perennials with bamboo-type stakes and run twine around the circumference and back and forth across the center a few times to make sort of a net — this way, the stems can grow through the twine and be supported.

✔ **Branches:** When you prune shrubs, save any trimmings that are 2 to 3 feet (60 cm to 1 m) and long and brushy at one end, resembling brooms. When a perennial reaches about a foot tall, poke several of

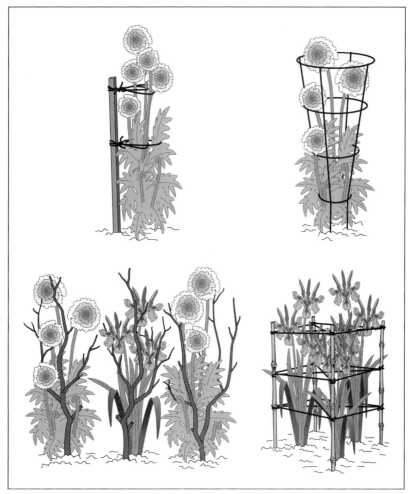

Figure 17-2:
A few popular devices for preventing tall, floppy flowers from falling on their faces.

these branches — bushy side up and leaning slightly inward — into the ground around the plant. The stems grow up through this circle of branches, while the supporting mechanism is hidden by the foliage of the perennial.

Branches are also the best form of remedial support after your poor perennial has fallen flat on its face. Have someone gather up the sprawling stems while you shove a branch underneath, bushy side up, to hold the stems up. Using branches in this way isn't a perfect solution, but it's better than nothing.

✔ **Commercial supports:** You can buy artistic metal supports from garden centers and nursery catalogs. The wire cages I use for my tomato and peony plants are at the low end of the market. Also available are wrought-iron stakes and collapsible frame types.

A born-again staker

I used to be anti-staking. Many garden writers suggest planting your perennials tightly together so that they hold one another upright. This advice appears to be sensible and less work — and I always opt for less work. But this strategy hasn't worked for me. My perennials are packed together as densely as carpet pile, but several still manage to flop over and do a great deal of damage, in spite of their crowded conditions.

Staking after the flop is much harder than staking beforehand, so, every year, the list of perennials I stake grows longer. I use commercial tomato and peony cages — contraptions made of wire rings and legs. They're inexpensive and easy to install. You just push them into the soil so that they surround the perennial as it emerges in the spring. In the fall, the cages go back into the garage for storage.

Curing overpopulation woes

Overplanting initially is easy. Everyone does it. Envisioning the space that a full-grown peony needs is difficult even for the most cautious among us. Besides, the perennials don't read descriptions of themselves, and they don't always stop growing when they reach the allotted width. Many continue to widen indefinitely, until they hit a physical barrier that stops them. During the first few years, you're certain your garden is never going to fill in. But by the third or fourth year, you have more flowers than you know what to do with.

Many perennials also spread by seed. Even if you deadhead scrupulously, a few flowers inevitably form a few seeds, which then germinate. You may be greeted one spring by dozens of Shasta daisies where you had planted three the previous year. To restore some order, you need to occasionally intervene. Otherwise, after several years the pushiest perennials are the only ones left in the flower bed. Weaker flowers have been overrun by the advancing hordes.

Spring and fall are good times to look things over with a critical eye. Yank out seedlings as they come up in crowded areas. If you decide to leave a few seedlings to fill a bare spot, thin them to at least one foot (30 cm) apart. Put a stick next to the ones you plan to keep and pull out all the others. (You can replant seedlings in other parts of the garden, give them away to friends and neighbors, or compost them.)

When clumps of flowers outgrow their space, dig up the whole bunch and *divide* them. For instructions on how to divide, see Chapter 19.

A Schedule of Chores

The easiest way to see that necessary chores get done in a somewhat timely fashion is to set up some sort of schedule. Don't fret if you're out of town for a couple of weeks; the flower garden can wait until you get back without getting too impatient.

Weekly work

Take a few minutes each day to walk outside and have a look at your flower bed — just for the sheer heck of it. At least once a week, take along a bucket with a hand trowel, scissors, and pruning shears and spend a few minutes tidying up. These are some of the things you should do:

- Cut off dead or dying flowers or leaves.

- Pull any weeds you find.

- Toss straying mulch back into the flower bed (for more about mulch, see Chapter 13).

- Squash any bad bugs you can catch (to recognize the good, the bad, and the ugly bugs, turn to Chapter 18).

- Stake any flowers that look as though they may topple over.

- Treat plagues of bugs or diseases that have appeared during the past week (see Chapter 18).

- Water as necessary. (See Chapter 15 to help you decide when *necessary* is.)

Monthly maintenance

In addition to your weekly gardening chores, other jobs need attention about once a month. You can work these tasks into your weekly routine, allowing yourself a little extra time once a month.

- Adjust your watering as the weather changes. Give your flower bed more water during hot weather, less during cool weather (see Chapter 15).

- As each perennial stops blooming, cut it back by about a third. Or, if you want, you can cut the old stalks to the ground *after* new leaves start to sprout from the base of the plant, for the sake of appearance. It's your call.

- Make notes in your diary of both artistic and practical successes and failures — "The daisy and the ornamental grasses are pretty together" or "The neighbor's cat ate the catmint," and so on.

Springtime strategy

Spring is the busiest time in the garden in most regions. As the weather starts to warm up, funnel some of your spring-fever energy into garden chores:

- ✔ In cold-winter and cool-summer climates, spring is the best time to plant perennials in your flower bed (see Chapter 14).

- ✔ Renew your mulch by adding a few inches of fresh material, if the old material is getting thin (see Chapter 13).

- ✔ Plant summer bulbs (see Chapter 10).

- ✔ In cold-winter climates, plant annuals (see Chapter 10).

- ✔ Fertilize the flower bed (see Chapter 16).

Autumn action

Fall is the second busiest season in the garden. After a long summer of sipping lemonade and admiring your garden handiwork, you need to devote a short burst of activity to your garden before winter sets in:

- ✔ In hot-summer, warm-winter climates, plant perennials in the fall (see Chapter 14).

- ✔ Plant spring bulbs (see Chapter 10).

- ✔ Prepare flower beds for planting the following spring (see Chapter 11).

- ✔ You may want to build other structures — such as trellises, walls, paths, and so on — in the fall, while the weather is cool (see Chapter 12).

- ✔ In warm-winter climates, plant annuals (see Chapter 14).

Putting the garden to bed for winter

If you live in a warm-winter climate, you can skip this section. All you need to do is clean up year-round, whenever your flowers show signs of wear — cutting off dead flowers, leaves, and stems as they materialize.

However, if frosts and snows are an annual feature of your backyard, the onset of winter is the time to do a few things to protect your plants:

✔ Water less frequently. For example, if you've been watering twice a week, switch to once a week. Cutting down on water helps signal to the plants that they need to toughen up and hunker down for winter.

✔ Dig and store tender bulbs (see Chapter 10) after the first frost has blackened the foliage.

✔ Replace mulch from under any perennials that were besieged by insects during the growing season. Getting rid of the mulch also gets rid of any eggs.

You can safely compost the old mulch.

✔ Place a 4- to 6-inch (10-to 15-cm) layer of organic mulch around perennials that you planted in late summer and fall, if you haven't done so already (see Chapter 13). You can also let leaves that fall into the flower bed stay where they land to add to the mulch layer.

✔ Cut back the stems on perennials (at least the ones that don't have pretty seedheads) to within 8 to 10 inches (20 to 26 cm) of the ground. (Turn to Part III for help in deciding which perennials may have attractive seedheads or dried flowers.) In really severe winter climates — where the temperature is often below 0° F (–18° C), don't cut back your perennials until late winter or early spring. The debris helps protect them from the cold.

✔ After the ground freezes (or in midwinter if the ground doesn't freeze), cover your whole flower bed with a loose mulch of hay, straw, or evergreen boughs. This extra layer protects your fragile perennials from severe cold. Leave this mulch in place until early spring and then remove it *gradually* as the weather starts to warm up.

✔ In dry-winter climates, water the flower bed once a month whenever snow or rain hasn't fallen in recent memory. Water on a warm, sunny day so that the water can soak into the ground (see Chapter 15).

Whenever an unseasonable frost is forecast, you can save your flowers by covering them with old sheets or special frost blankets, as shown in Figure 17-3. (Don't cover your flowers with plastic; it conducts cold too readily.) Leave the sheets or frost blankets in place until the cold snap is over. Cold-weather gardeners always need a few lengths of frost blanket, which is available from garden centers. This magical material is fairly expensive, but it lasts many years if dried between uses and stored out of direct sunlight.

If you live in a cold-winter climate, don't fertilize your plants after midsummer. Fertilizer encourages plants to put on soft new growth, which is really vulnerable to frost damage.

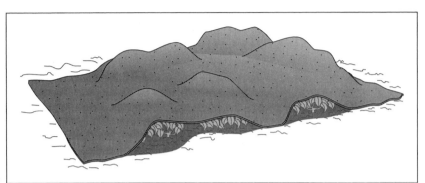

Chapter 18

Trouble in Paradise

- -

In This Chapter

▶ Forming a realistic pest policy

▶ Distinguishing between pest damage and environmental damage

▶ Beating back the insect hoards

▶ Dealing with bigger critters

▶ Preventing a weed invasion

- -

1 am going to let you in on one of gardening's dirty little secrets: You can *ignore* most of the bugs that visit your garden.

Folks that make and sell bug-killing products may try to convince you otherwise, but don't believe them. Doing nothing at all about bugs is often the best policy. Ninety-five percent of the bugs that visit your garden are either beneficial or neutral — neither good nor bad. But ignoring even the genuine pests gives nature's own controls the time they need to kick in. In most cases, nature's way is a much better remedy than anything you can buy.

True, some folks feel compelled to grab a can of insecticide every time they see a bug in the pantry. But applying the same standards of pest control in your garden as you do in your house is pretty unrealistic. The outdoors is always crawling with critters. When you plant flowers, you're inviting more. Pests view a flower garden as a giant smorgasbord. All gardeners are delighted to find that their flowers attract butterflies, hummingbirds, and other wildlife that score a high cuteness quotient. But most folks aren't so happy to discover that creepy critters such as snakes, bats, and rodents also intend to move in and make themselves at home.

A Plan of Action

You can make your garden as sterile as ground zero of a nuclear blast site if you use enough poison. But doing so isn't a very practical goal, and sterile conditions don't make for very satisfying gardens, either. If you enjoy butterflies, you must be prepared to put up with their caterpillars eating the leaves of your flowers. No caterpillars, no butterflies! Similarly, songbirds don't stick around long if your garden has no bugs for them to eat.

The key is to strike a balance — tolerating some damage to accommodate the needs of wildlife that you want to attract, but acting quickly when outbreaks of harmful insects or disease threaten to get out of control.

An ounce of prevention

Preventing a problem is easier than treating its results. Here are some things you can do to head off disasters before they strike:

- **Keep your flowers healthy and strong.** Just as you are more susceptible to the flu when you're run down, opportunistic bugs and diseases move in for the kill when flowers are weakened by improper growing conditions. Placing flowers where their sun, soil, water, and fertilizer requirements are met helps them fend off these attacks.

- **Practice good housekeeping habits in your garden.** Remove dead and diseased leaves and stems promptly to get diseases out of the garden before they spread. Keep the flower bed clear of weeds, which may play host to diseases or insects. Clean and disinfect pruning shears and scissors (dip them in a solution of household bleach and water) after cutting diseased plants. If you smoke, wash your hands before gardening — tobacco can contain viruses that infect flowers.

- **Shower your flowers.** If you use drip-type irrigation, occasionally wash the dust and small insects off your flowers by using a spray attachment on the end of a hose. Get up underneath the leaves to knock off bugs that are clinging there.

    Spray your garden in the morning so that the foliage dries quickly, especially in hot, humid weather. Continually wet leaves promote some diseases. (See Chapter 15 for more watering tips.)

- **Provide good air circulation.** If you have disease problems, give the plants more space. Diseases spread more quickly when plants touch.

✔ **Don't bring bugs or diseases into your garden.** When you buy new plants, check them over carefully to make sure that insects or their eggs aren't lurking on the undersides of the leaves. Don't buy plants with mottled, discolored, or spotted foliage. Look for pearly clumps of snail or slug eggs when you remove your flower from its pot, and destroy any that you find. Pull off any weeds that are hitchhiking with your flower before you plant it in your garden.

✔ **Encourage natural helpers.** Learn to ignore the good guys (even the creepy ones), and they'll do much of your work for you. Snakes eat slugs and mice. Bats, spiders, toads, and lizards all eat huge quantities of bugs, if you let them.

✔ **Get rid of problem plants.** Be hard-hearted and replace any flower that's a perennial problem. Too many healthy choices are available for you to put up with disease and bug magnets.

Playing detective

Spotting damage on the perennials that you're working so hard to grow can be frustrating, but don't overreact. Perennials are a tough bunch. A few holes in their leaves doesn't damage their vigor and probably aren't noticeable at ten paces, anyway.

If you're using insecticide to control bug damage, you may actually be aggravating the problem. For example, spraying insecticides indiscriminately can kill the insects that normally eat spider mites, resulting in a population explosion of the mites. (Some insecticides don't kill the mites because mites aren't true insects.)

Before you get involved in chemical warfare, find out exactly what's causing the problem. Environmental damage often creates symptoms that look very much like disease or insect mischief. Ask yourself whether any of the following conditions may be responsible for your flowers' ill health.

✔ **Air pollution:** Some flowers are sensitive to smog. Their leaves may appear bleached or distorted. If air pollution is your problem, select resistant perennials. If you live in an area where smog is a problem, ask a local nursery person to recommend resistant varieties.

✔ **Chemical damage:** A *herbicide* is anything that kills plants, although it's usually intended to kill only weeds. Use herbicides on cool, still days to prevent spray from accidentally drifting or descending as a vapor cloud onto your flower beds. Swimming pool chemicals can also damage plants. Mix all chemicals away from the flower bed and immediately put the lid back on the container to limit vapors from escaping. Symptoms of chemical damage include distorted and twisted stems and foliage, browning in an even pattern over the whole plant, or irregularly-shaped brown spots.

✔ **Drought:** Too little water causes plants to become warped-looking, stop growing, and develop brown tips or yellowing leaves. (See Chapter 15 for advice on watering.)

✔ **Fertilizer burn:** Applying fertilizer improperly can scorch plant leaves. Too much can actually kill the plant. (See Chapter 16 for tips on fertilizing.)

✔ **Fertilizer deficiency:** Shortages of any of the essential plant nutrients can cause stunting and leaf discoloration. *The Ortho Home Gardener's Problem Solver* has color photographs of plants afflicted with many types of nutrient deficiencies, if you need to see what these problems look like. (See Chapter 16 for fertilizer information.)

✔ **Freeze damage:** Frost can either blacken the most exposed parts of the plant or kill the plant to the ground. Hardy perennials usually grow back after freeze damage, but, just to be safe, protect plants from unseasonable cold spells by temporarily covering them with old sheets or blankets. Don't use plastic — frost goes right through plastic.

✔ **Inadequate sunlight:** When a flower isn't getting enough light, it turns sickly pale and its stems become long and spindly. If you plant in a shady area, choose shade-tolerant flowers. (See Chapter 8 for a list of shade-tolerant perennials.)

✔ **Poor drainage:** Flowers that are too wet become yellowish or brown, wilt, and eventually die. Plant flowers that are tolerant of wet conditions or improve the drainage in your flower bed. (See Chapter 11 for a list of plants that enjoy wet conditions.)

✔ **Salts:** Salt can either occur naturally in the soil (see Chapter 11) or get carried to your garden on salt-ridden breezes, if you live near the ocean. Cars can also splash salt onto your garden when roads are salted in the winter. When salt concentrations build up, your flowers can become stunted and brown. The cure is to rinse the soil with plenty of fresh water.

✔ **Sunscald:** When shade-loving flowers are getting too much sunshine, they first become pale all over and then may develop papery patches or dark, irregular burns. Move the plant to a shadier location.

✔ **Transplant shock:** A recently moved flower can go into a real sulk and wilt badly. Provide temporary shelter from the sun and wind until the plant recovers and has settled into its new home. (See Chapter 14 for guidance on protecting new plantings.)

If you're certain that a pest is responsible for your flower damage, you need to clearly identify which insect is the guilty party. Don't jump to conclusions. Consider a damaged plant covered with both aphids and ladybugs. Without your glasses, you may not be able to see the tiny aphids, so you may assume that the ladybugs are eating your flowers. Actually, the ladybugs are dining on the aphids, who are the real culprits! Use a magnifying glass to look for wee pests.

A marauder's row of insects

If you think that insects are eating your flowers, the first thing you need to do is identify the suspects. Then you can decide how to best rid your garden of them. Don't panic when you look over the following list. Most insect infestations are localized — you aren't likely to ever get to know *all* these pests, unless you move around quite a bit. Insects also have good and bad seasons. You may be thoroughly plagued by leafhoppers one year but not find a single one the next.

The following list describes the most common insect pests of perennial gardens and how to get rid of them. If you can't identify the bugs in your garden, take one on a field trip to a local nursery or see whether your local library has a book with photos of garden pests. If you can't find anyone locally who knows what the invading bug is, send a sample of your bug to the nearest university that has an entomology department.

- ✔ **Aphids:** Often the first indication of aphid infestation is an odd twisting and distortion of the foliage. A close-up look reveals crowds of pear-shaped little bugs, which suck plant sap with their needlelike noses (see Figure 18-1). Some aphids are wingless; others have wings. Aphids come in a rainbow of colors. Wash them off with a spray of water or use insecticidal soap. You can buy this liquid soap, which you mix with water at specified concentrations, at any garden center.

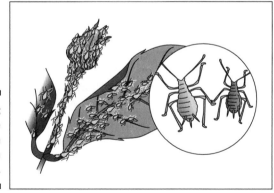

Figure 18-1:
Aphids are a common garden pest.

- ✔ **Beetles:** Many types of beetles eat perennials; many other types eat bugs. If you catch them in the act, you can tell the difference. Other-wise, capture one and take it into a nursery or your local cooperative extension office to find out whether yours is a good beetle or a bad beetle. My policy is to ignore the odd beetle and only take notice if hordes of them appear. Knock slow-moving beetles into a bucket of water, hand-pick and smash them, or spray them with *neem, rotenone, or sabadilla* (these are relatively safe plant-derived insecticides that you can buy at any garden center). Figure 18-2 shows an up-close-and-personal view of a Japanese beetle.

Figure 18-2:
The Japanese beetle is a common pest in many regions.

✔ **Caterpillars:** Caterpillars are the larvae of moths and butterflies. Usually, butterfly caterpillars are big, brightly colored, and travel alone. You may decide to look the other way when one of these critters inches by. Other types run in packs and do a great deal of damage munching on leaves and flower buds. Still another type of caterpiller, called *borers,* tunnel destructively through stems or roots.

Cutworms (pictured in Figure 18-3) are soil-dwelling caterpillars who cut off whole young plants at ground level. Hand-pick and cut these invaders in half with scissors. Alternatively, you may spray them with *Bt* (*Bacillus thuringiensis*, the fancy name for a bacterial disease that infects caterpillars). Be aware, though, that Bt dispatches the butterfly caterpillars just as efficiently as the caterpillers you don't want.

Figure 18-3:
Cutworms are a common pest of young plants.

✔ **Leafhoppers:** Little wedge-shaped leafhoppers suck plant juices but don't do much damage themselves. However, these insect Typhoid Marys carry a disease called *aster yellows,* which does particularly nasty things to flowers. When the leafhoppers appear in swarms, spray them with neem or rotenone.

✔ **Leaf miners:** Leaf miners are tiny fly maggots that tunnel in leaves, resulting in tell-tale trails (see Figure 18-4). Remove infected leaves and dispose of them — bugs and all. Or spray the whole plant with neem or a summer horticultural spray oil.

Figure 18-4:
You can spot leaf miners by the trails they leave.

✔ **Mealybugs:** Furry little white oval-shaped critters, mealybugs would be cute if they didn't do so much damage and multiply so rapidly. Spray them with insecticidal soap, neem, or summer horticultural spray oil. (See mealybugs in Figure 18-5.)

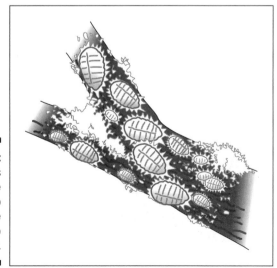

Figure 18-5:
Mealybugs don't move much, so they're easy to spot.

✔ **Spider mites:** As their name implies, spider mites are actually tiny arachnids, not true insects. Usually, the first hint of a spider mite invasion is a mottled bronze tint to the foliage. A closer look reveals minute, traveling dots about the size of the period at the end of this sentence (see Figure 18-6). Wash the spiders off with a strong spray of water or spray them with insecticidal soap, sulfur, or summer horticultural spray oil (available at your local garden center).

Figure 18-6:
Individual spider mites are tiny, but the damage caused by hundreds is easy to spot.

✔ **Thrips:** If your flowers turn brown and are distorted and streaked with silver, tiny thrips are the culprit. Cut off and dispose of the infested buds. Knock the bugs off with a strong spray of water or spray them with an insecticidal soap, summer horticultural spray oil, or neem.

✔ **Weevils:** Beetles with long snouts are called *weevils*. They often drill holes in flower buds so the flowers don't open properly, if at all. Hand-pick and destroy them or spray with neem.

✔ **Whiteflies:** Small, snow-white whiteflies suck plant juices and reproduce at lightning speed. Symptoms of whitefly attack are mottled and yellowed leaves. Spray infested leaves with insecticidal soap, summer horticultural spray oil, or neem. Figure 18-7 shows a leaf infested with whiteflies.

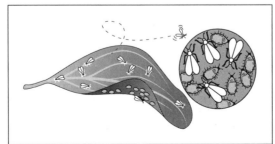

Figure 18-7:
Whiteflies are sometimes called "plant dandruff."

Using insecticides

Before you purchase an insecticide, be sure to accurately identify the pest. Most insecticides don't kill all insects. Some bugs are resistant or immune to certain insecticides, so you need to be sure that the product you buy kills the bug you're hunting.

Applying a product that doesn't kill the beasts that are eating your flowers is a waste of time and money and can be harmful to the environment. Read the label to make sure that your target bug is listed.

To use insecticides wisely and safely, follow these precautions:

✔ **Use insecticides as a last resort.** You can control many outbreaks of small insects by simply washing them off the flowers with a strong spray from a hose.

✔ **Use the least poisonous product that does the job.** All the recommendations in this chapter are relatively safe products that don't leave dangerous chemical residues in your garden, but you must be careful with *any* insecticide.

✔ **Read the label carefully and thoroughly.** Don't guess at how much insecticide to use or when or how to apply the product. Every insecticide has a unique set of instructions. The label tells you exactly how to use the product correctly and safely.

✔ **Wear protective clothing.** Cover up bare skin — wear long-sleeved clothing, rubber gloves, a nose/mouth mask, and goggles.

✔ **Spray the undersides of leaves.** Most insects and their eggs hide underneath leaves. Aim for a direct hit for better results.

Playing Doctor with Plant Diseases

You may be surprised to learn that plants can get sick by their own versions of the same organisms that attack you and me — fungi, bacteria, viruses, and microplasma. Although flowers can't go to the doctor when they get sick or get vaccinations to prevent disease, you can do plenty to limit the spread of diseases in your flower bed.

Plants are much more susceptible to disease when they're tired. Keep your flowers growing strong and, most important, don't overwater. Plant diseases are primarily water-borne. Letting the soil dry out between waterings is the simplest way to slow down their spread.

✔ **Aster yellows:** Aster yellows would be thoroughly entertaining if it didn't do so much damage. Plants infected with this disease become bizarrely deformed and distorted — the flowers may start to grow strange protrusions and the leaves curl and twist. Aster yellows is spread only by leafhoppers (an insect described in the preceding section). Pull and dispose of diseased plants.

✔ **Gray molds:** Ever-present fungi grow on dead plant tissue, but when conditions are to their liking, molds sometimes invade healthy plants. Fuzzy brown or gray mold forms on leaves and flowers, and stems may become soft and rotten. Cool temperatures and humidity encourage their growth. Where this disease is a problem, water in the morning so that plants dry quickly. Remove damaged leaves and flowers and destroy badly affected plants. To prevent mold, space flowers in the garden widely enough that they don't touch and clean up dead plant debris promptly.

✔ **Leafspots:** Brown or black irregular blotches or circular spots can be caused by both viral and bacterial infections. Remove leaves with these symptoms; simply removing the infected leaves may be enough to stop the spread of the infection. Destroy badly infected plants. Water early in the day so that foliage can dry out.

✔ **Nematodes:** Nematodes are actually microscopic worms that can damage plant roots or foliage. Root nematodes live in moist, sandy soils. Adding large quantities of organic matter seems to be of some value in stopping their spread.

✔ **Powdery mildew:** Plants infected with powdery mildew look as though they've been dusted with talcum powder. This disease requires heat and a brief period of high humidity to form; the attack often occurs after the flowers have finished blooming. Some perennials are highly susceptible to powdery mildew, so plant resistant varieties. If it strikes, cut the stems down to within a few inches of the ground and discard the trimmings. See Figure 18-8.

Figure 18-8:
Powdery
mildew
causes
leaves to
curl and
shrivel.

✔ **Rust:** This disease is so named because it resembles rust on metal. Yellow, orange, or brown bumps that appear on stems or leaves may be caused by rust fungi. Keep plant foliage dry and pick out infected leaves. See Figure 18-9.

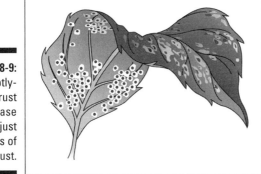

Figure 18-9:
Aptly-named rust disease looks just like spots of iron rust.

✔ **Viruses:** Leaves infected by viruses may be mottled in irregular or sometimes circular patterns or may be yellowed overall. Plant viruses are transmitted by insects. Destroy infected plants and practice good sanitation (wash hands and tools thoroughly).

✔ **Wilts:** When the whole plant wilts and dies, sometimes overnight, fungal or bacterial root rots may be responsible. Nematodes (described earlier in this list) or gophers can cause the same symptoms. If root rots are the cause, continually wet soil encourages their growth. Improve the drainage and don't replant the same flower in affected soil. If wilt-resistant or wilt-tolerant varieties of your favorite plants are available, plant those instead.

Other Garden Nuisances

Bugs and diseases are not the only pests interested in eating your flowers. King-sized pests can damage more than a few leaves. One time, a neighbor's goat got loose and ate my whole garden to the ground in a single afternoon. Let's hope you don't ever find a goat (or cow or other large herbivore) in your garden, but you'll probably encounter some of the following troublesome creatures.

Snails and slugs

If large patches of foliage disappear overnight, suspect snails and slugs. These heavy feeders come out at night, so it isn't always obvious who's causing the mischief. Look for telltale silvery slime trails or go outside with a flashlight after dark. You can often find the guilty parties in action.

I get a great deal of satisfaction from taking a pair of scissors into the garden with me at first light and chopping up every slug I can find. The more squeamish among you may prefer to trap the slugs. Moisten a newspaper and roll it loosely into a cylinder. Slugs and snails will seek shelter in it during the daylight hours. You can pick up the paper and dispose of it, sleeping guests and all. Or place a board in the garden — the slugs and snails will seek refuge underneath, and you can easily pick them off. Another technique people often use to combat snails and slugs is to set saucers of beer up to their rims in the ground. The marauding mollusks fall in and can't get out. On the upside, the slugs die happy; on the downside, you use up all your good beer.

Wildlife vandals

Deer are undoubtedly the number-one nuisance for suburban gardeners. But the little vole, rabbit, squirrel, or gopher can be just as aggravating. You may need to employ multiple, thoughtful strategies to outwit these garden pests. Traps and barriers are probably more effective than repellents or frightening techniques. Sometimes, the animals seem to gleefully accept the challenge of getting past bad smells, loud noises, or lights.

Several options are available for declaring your flowers off-limits to the local wildlife:

- ✔ **Physical barriers:** Electric fences discourage deer. Buried *hardware cloth* — a type of heavy-duty metal mesh sold at building supply stores — prevents burrowing animals from entering the garden underground. Where all else fails, build raised beds and line them with hardware cloth (see Chapter 12 for more on raised beds).

- ✔ **Repellents:** Repellents are supposed to offend the animal's taste or smell enough to drive it away. The effectiveness of repellents varies. Some animals actually seem to develop a fondness for noxious substances. If you want to give repellents a try, you can buy them at garden centers.

- ✔ **Scare tactics:** If you've ever seen crows sitting on the scarecrow, you already have some idea of how well scare tactics work. The effect is usually temporary. A hungry animal can get used to loud noises and flashing lights. Most garden-invading creatures aren't particularly nervous by nature, anyway.

- ✔ **Trapping:** Live traps are available to capture small animals. After you catch the little critters, you can release them in an unpopulated area. Be sure to check the trap daily so that the little fellers don't have to go without water for very long.

WARNING!

Protecting yourself

Gardens are full of critters. Unfortunately, rather than appreciating your hard work in their Eden, most of these little fellows view you as a threat to their well-being. I've been dive-bombed by nesting birds, had a close call with a skunk, been bitten by ants, and stung by bees — all while going about my own business.

Whenever you work in the garden, dress defensively. Wear shoes, long sleeves, and long pants to cover your skin. If ants are a problem, pull your socks over the bottoms of your pant legs to keep the little armies from biting your exposed ankles. Gloves protect your hands from slivers and thorns. And don't forget to put on sunscreen and a hat to prevent a painful sunburn. You can easily lose track of time while you're working in the garden.

If animal pests are more than just passing problems, you have two options: Learn to live with them (perhaps by gradually switching over to plants that the pests don't like to eat), or enclose your garden. Enclosing the garden may mean building a fence around it, but draping netting over plants is often effective enough.

Human damage

Suburban gardens attract kids, who have a universal fascination for anything out of the ordinary. Kids sometimes inflict real havoc accidentally, pursuing fleeing beasts such as snakes or toads. Or, occasionally, they give in to the sheer pleasure of mischief-making. I recently caught a group of little boys in the act of joyously tossing my entire cactus collection over the fence. The easiest way to prevent such raids is a fence and a padlock on the gate.

One immutable fact that you — like all gardeners — must face is that when you put flowers within reach of pedestrians, you have to expect a few flowers to "walk away." No child can resist picking the occasional daisy. When adults yield to temptation, they sometimes dig up the whole plant. Here are some tips to cut your losses:

- ✔ The best defense is to plant rugged and heavy-blooming perennials so that you don't miss the flowers that grow legs.

- ✔ Save your most expensive treasures for less public flower beds.

- ✔ One perennial gardener I know leaves bunches of cut flowers in her front yard with a note that says *Free*. This tactic has stopped her problem of people picking her flowers and has helped her meet many of her neighbors.

Weed Whacking

Contemporary writers struggle over the definition of *weed*. In the flower garden, no such philosophical introspection is necessary — a weed is simply any plant growing where you don't want it to be. This name applies regardless of whether you're referring to an errant plant that's globally accepted as a pest (such as a dandelion) or a Shasta daisy baby boom. If you want three Shasta daisies, the fourth one is a weed — plain and simple.

Besides being misplaced or unattractive, weeds are also bothersome because they're usually much more vigorous plants than your average garden perennial, so they steal water and nutrients from your flowers. Like rude guests who shove their way to be first at the buffet table, the weeds gobble up an unfair share of the water and fertilizer. Weeds may also carry diseases and attract harmful insects.

Soil contains millions of weed seeds. These seeds are just waiting patiently for something to disturb the soil and bring them to the surface, where sunlight wakes them up. A constant supply of weed seeds also blows in on every passing breeze. More are carried to your garden by birds, on the fur of your pets, or even in the mud on the soles of your shoes. The only way to restrain this weed invasion is to cover exposed soil so the seeds can't get enough light to germinate. Several inches of organic mulch is the surest way to prevent sunlight from reaching the soil surface (see Chapter 13).

Weeds come in two main groups — annuals and perennials, just like flowers:

- The annuals form staggering quantities of seed; some produce up to 500,000 per plant. Each of these seeds has the potential to grow into a new weed. The way to stop annuals is to pull them out of your garden before they form seed.

- Perennial weeds are harder to control. They seem to live forever and expand by sending out roots or running stems for several feet in every direction. These weeds want to conquer the world. Pulling and digging at them appears to make them mad; they seem to spread even faster in response. Bindweed is one of the most notorious.

 Perennial weeds also form seeds, so don't ever let them get to this stage. Unfortunately, mulch doesn't stop their roots or runners. If you pull out every sprout, you can eventually starve the roots and kill the plant. But if you forget even once, the weed is off and running with renewed enthusiasm.

The most effective way to dispatch perennial weeds is with an herbicide. The safest products are those containing *glyphosate*. Use the herbicide to kill off all weeds before preparing the soil. Really finishing off persistent types may take several applications. Follow the instructions *carefully* and remember that these products kill any vegetation, including shrubs and trees. Be certain to confine the spray to the weeds.

Killing perennial weeds in the crowded flower bed

When perennial weeds pop up in an established flower border, getting the herbicide on the weed but not the flowers is difficult. I use a plastic bag to isolate the weed. Here's how:

1. **Cut a hole in the bottom of a plastic bag.**

   The hole needs to be large enough that you can fit the weed through the hole.

2. **Pull the weed through the hole in the bottom of the bag, making sure to pull all of the weed into the bag.**

3. **Place a stone in the bottom of the bag to hold it in place.**

4. *Carefully* **spray herbicide into the top of the bag.**

   If you accidentally spray or spill some herbicide on adjoining flowers, immediately rinse them off with water.

5. **Seal the top of the bag with a twist-tie and leave the bag in place until the weed is dead.**

Some perennial flowers are quite weedlike themselves, producing huge amounts of viable seed and scattering it throughout the flower bed. Where you had a trio of flowers a couple of years ago, you now have a large marching band. To prevent this spread, deadhead your flowers (see Chapter 17). Pull all the seedling plants just as you pull any other weeds.

Pulling weeds

If your soil is loose and crumbly, a light tug is probably all you need to yank out the most stubborn weed. But in dense soil, what usually happens is that you tug at the weed and the top comes off neatly in your hand. The roots happily grow a new top, and the next time you look, the weed is back, looking refreshed and smug!

To kill most weeds, you must get the root. Here's the simplest technique to do so:

1. **Slip the blade of your hand trowel into the ground straight down, next to the main root of the weed.**

2. **Push the trowel blade firmly against the root to loosen it.**

3. **Grab hold of the base of the leaves and pull.**

   Most of the time, this action gets you the whole weed — roots and all.

Postmortem for a Dead Perennial

New gardeners view the death of each plant as a real tragedy, but experienced gardeners kill many flowers and develop a fairly callous attitude about doing so. Sometimes, the death is their fault and they know it. The gardener who has been through the entire palette of safe and easy plants becomes tempted by the forbidden fruit of other climates. When you challenge the boundaries of common sense, you occasionally make new discoveries. After all, no one would ever know whether a particular plant is hardy beyond its natural range if someone didn't try it out in a different place. But for every one that works, hundreds die.

New gardeners who are still conducting memorial services for their dead flowers find it hard to be grateful when space opens up for something new and different, but owners of mature gardens spend more time attempting to find room for a new perennial than planting it. You may not believe it now, but you will eventually come to view the death of each plant as an opportunity to try something new.

What killed my plant?

Sometimes, the cause of death is splendidly obvious — you did the deed and you know exactly what you did. You stepped smack in the middle of a plant and hoped it didn't notice. Or you ignored the frost warning and decided to put the petunias out anyway. You know that some actions are a bad idea even as you start them, but you're in a hurry or you figure that just once won't hurt. Those are the easy lessons. You hit yourself in the forehead, buy new plants, and vow never to do it again.

But, frustrating as it may be, in some cases you never, ever discover what killed a particular plant. Unless the problem is really widespread or severe, save yourself the expense of calling in an expert. (Save this action for really important stuff like sick shade trees.) Flowers are mercifully inexpensive and easy to replace. In five minutes, you can yank out the corpse and pop in a replacement in full bloom and effect an instant cure.

Make certain your plant is dead

Before you pull out a plant, make sure that it's really dead.

The first time you grow a bleeding heart or an oriental poppy can be unnerving. The plant does magnificently until summer, and then it suddenly flops over like an actor in a spectacular Shakespearean death scene. Both of these flowers go dormant after blooming. *Dormant,* in this case, translates to "looks dead." (The nursery label probably didn't mention this habit because "looks dead in July" doesn't sell very many plants.) Many perennials that are evergreen in mild climates go dormant where winters are frigid.

Late-sleeping plants may also lead you to a greatly exaggerated diagnosis of death (to paraphrase Mark Twain). Late emergers are the adolescents of the plant world — they sleep until noon. Butterfly flowers and balloon flowers don't venture even a peek out of the ground until early summer, which may prompt you to plant another perennial on top of them. Mark these late emergers so that you know where they are and don't inadvertently chop them up.

Chapter 19

Growing Your Garden from Scratch

• •

In This Chapter

▶ Dividing your way to free perennials

▶ Cultivating cuttings

▶ Sprouting seeds

• •

*I*f you're limited by a tight budget but have plenty of time and patience, you can cut costs by growing your own new perennials. But thrift isn't the only motivation for bringing new perennials into the world. After you fill your own garden to capacity, you can experience the satisfaction that comes from sharing your bounty with friends and neighbors. Most perennials multiply as rapidly and as easily as field mice. Where you plant one happy Shasta daisy, you may be surprised to find a dozen the next season.

The easiest way to generate more perennials is simply to pull apart clumps of flowers that have reproduced by themselves. Perennials that don't have the right anatomy for the simple pull-apart method reproduce from cuttings or from seed.

Multiplying Perennials by Division

A young perennial starts out with only one tuft of leaves and one set of roots. Many perennials reproduce themselves by sending out a length of root or stem from which a whole new plant grows. Eventually, a cluster of loosely connected but separate plants forms.

Like the brooms carrying buckets of water in Disney's *Sorcerer's Apprentice*, perennials keep expanding indefinitely. The process of pulling clumps of perennials apart to create new ones is called *dividing*. Each piece then grows into a new clump that you can divide, and so on.

Reasons to divide

Producing more plants is the main reason to divide your perennials, but it's not the only reason. Some types of perennials reproduce themselves so quickly that they can overrun the whole flower bed if you don't intervene. Whenever you feel the need to restore order, dig up these miscreants and put a piece of them back where you originally planted them. Give the remaining pieces away. Other types of perennials (such as peonies, baby's breath, and hostas) enlarge slowly and gradually, so you never need to divide them to keep them in their place.

A few perennials die out in the center of their clumps as they spread, creating a noticeable bald spot. Instead of contemplating some sort of a floral toupee, you can easily correct the problem by digging up the whole plant and dividing it.

Perennials that don't tolerate division

Division works best on perennials that grow into *colonies* — groups where each new plant develops its own set of roots and leaves. Similarly, most bulbs reproduce by forming clusters of new bulbs, which you can divide in exactly the same way you divide colony-forming perennials. Perennials with a single, large taproot and those with multiple stems arising from a single crown don't divide well.

The following perennials don't tolerate division well. Try to divide these and, instead of getting more plants, you're likely to end up with one dead plant.

- ❀ Monkshood *(Aconitum napellus)*
- ❀ Butterfly flower *(Asclepias tuberosa)*
- ❀ Basket-of-gold *(Aurinia saxatilis)*
- ❀ Blue wild indigo *(Baptisia australis)*
- ❀ Pinks *(Dianthus)*
- ❀ Bleeding heart *(Dicentra spectabilis)*
- ❀ Gas plant *(Dictamnus albus)*
- ❀ Globe thistle *(Echinops exaltatus)*
- ❀ Baby's breath *(Gypsophila paniculata)*
- ❀ Candytuft *(Iberis sempervirens)*
- ❀ Sea lavender *(Limonium latifolium)*

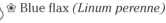

❀ Blue flax *(Linum perenne)*

❀ Lupine *(Lupinus)*

❀ Oriental poppy *(Papaver orientale)*

❀ Balloon flower *(Platycodon grandiflorus)*

❀ False lupine *(Thermopsis carolinian)*

A lesson in division

You can divide perennials whenever the ground isn't frozen, but the best time of year for division is a couple of months before severely cold or hot weather sets in. You want to give newly planted sections a chance to settle in and get a strong start before they have to cope with weather extremes.

If you live in a cold climate, divide your perennials either in spring, when the newly emerging foliage is up several inches, or in late summer, six to eight weeks before temperatures are expected to drop below freezing. In warm-winter regions, divide your perennials in the fall.

To divide perennials, follow these steps:

1. **If the soil is hard and dry, soak the ground a few days before you plan to work.**

   Ideally, the soil should be soft enough that you can dig into it easily with a shovel or spading fork, but not so muddy that it sticks to you or your tools.

2. **Cut all the stems down to 4 to 6 inches (10 to 15 cm) from the ground.**

3. **Use a shovel or spading fork to dig up the whole clump.**

   Cut a circle a few inches outside the edge of the clump you're planning to divide. Don't worry if you cut roots — they grow back.

4. **Place the whole clump on a tarp or an old sheet and look it over.**

   Some plants come apart as easily as pull-apart cinnamon rolls. Others are impossibly dense and tangled. Tug at the crowns (the points where the plant rises from the ground) and see what happens. If the plant doesn't come apart easily, you have two options:

   • Soak the whole plant in a large bucket for a few hours to soften the soil and then rinse it off with a hose. Now, you can untangle the exposed roots by using your fingers to separate the individual crowns (see Figure 19-1).

   • Use a shovel or a sharp knife to slice the root mass into as many chunks as you need (as shown in Figure 19-2). For really tough roots, you may need to use an ax.

Figure 19-1:
Pulling
apart
rooted
divisions
by hand.

Figure 19-2:
Cutting a
plant into
multiple
rooted
sections
with a
shovel.

5. **Pull off and discard all the dead stuff and any tough, woody parts.**

   Make certain that each plant has both roots and leaves. Keep the biggest, healthiest chunks and compost the rest.

6. **Replant according to the instructions in Chapter 14.**

Growing Perennials from Cuttings

Growing perennials from cuttings involves creating a new plant from a stem that starts out with no roots at all. If you've ever stuck a stem of ivy in a glass of water and watched it grow roots, you already have some idea how this technique works. Not all perennials can grow from cuttings. Use the cutting method for perennials that don't form multiple crowns. (See "Perennials that don't tolerate division" earlier in this chapter.)

Follow these steps to coax your cuttings into growing roots:

1. **Punch a few pencil-sized holes in the side and bottom of any clean, flat, shallow container to provide drainage for excess water.**

   For a large number of cuttings, a plastic kitty litter tray is a good size. A plastic container of any sort works well if you're rooting only a few cuttings (recycled food containers are perfect).

2. **Fill the container with a moist, not soggy wet, mixture of 50 percent fine peat and 50 percent washed coarse sand.**

   Alternatively, you can use vermiculite or any potting medium labeled for starting cuttings. All these materials are available at your local garden center.

3. **Using a clean, sharp knife or scissors, cut the top 4 to 6 inches (10 to 15 cm) of the stem, just below a leaf or cluster of leaves.**

   Take your cuttings when the plant is growing vigorously but not blooming.

4. **With a knife or scissors, remove all the leaves from the bottom 2 inches (5 cm) of the stem.**

5. **Use a pencil or screwdriver to make a hole (2 inches [5 cm] deep and a little wider than the stem) in the sand or potting mix.**

   Make additional holes several inches apart if you're starting more than one cutting.

6. **Use a rooting hormone (available in powder or liquid) to stimulate root growth on the cutting.**

   You can purchase rooting hormone at a local nursery or most garden centers. Be sure to follow the instructions on the product you buy.

7. **Stick the stem into the hole and gently press the potting mixture against the stem so that no air holes remain.**

8. **Cover the container with plastic wrap or a clear plastic bag to prevent moisture loss.**

9. **Place the container in a brightly lit location (out of direct sunlight) or under a grow light.**

10. **Water with a misting spray bottle as necessary.**

   Keep the potting mixture moist, but not soaking wet, at all times.

When the stems start to grow new leaves, they're ready for transplanting. Most cuttings are well-rooted in about a month. Transplant the cuttings following the directions in Chapter 14.

Sprouting Perennials from Seed

Starting perennials from seed gives you the chance to grow literally hundreds of plants from one package of seeds. The problem is that you probably don't want hundreds of identical plants. Even more frustrating is the fact that, unlike most vegetables and annuals grown from seed, most perennials you grow from seed take several years to bloom for the first time. Some types are also extremely fussy and require very exacting conditions to germinate.

But sometimes, the only way to get your hands on a certain perennial is to grow it yourself. You can also grow extra plants to give to appreciative friends and neighbors. Best of all, you get a very real sense of parental pride from homegrown perennials that the store-bought variety just can't provide.

Just like when you bring home a new stereo, the first thing you need to do with a packet of seeds is carefully read the directions and suggestions. In fact, even if you're the type of person who tosses out instructions without giving them a glance, you should still read the seed packets; after all, we're talking about the creation of life here!

Seeds of most annuals germinate just fine when you plant them directly in the garden. But most perennial seeds don't germinate very successfully planted outside. By growing your seeds indoors, you can create an artificial environment to meet their needs.

You can grow perennials indoors any time of the year. But if you start them in late winter or early spring, the seedlings are usually large enough to go into the garden by early summer. For best results, plant seeds outside at the time of year recommended on the seed packet. Some seeds need cool weather to sprout, and some need hot.

Here's a list of items you need to start seeds inside:

- ✔ **A light stand:** You can buy a stand like the one in Figure 19-3, or you can construct one yourself by using grow lamps or fluorescent shop lights. Rig the lamps so that you can adjust their height up and down. You can also place seed trays on window sills, although you'll have a more difficult time regulating temperature and light.

Figure 19-3:
You don't have to own a greenhouse to grow hundreds of flowers indoors. Rig up or buy a rack to fit even the smallest space.

- ✔ **A sterile potting mix labeled for seed-starting:** Don't buy regular potting mix or use outdoor soil, because neither is sterile (free of disease organisms). You can buy sterile potting mix at any garden center.

- ✔ **Suitable containers:** "Suitable" translates into anything that potting soil and seed can fit into. You can buy commercial seed trays, but my favorite container is a plastic margarine tub with a snap-on lid.

  Run your containers through the dishwasher or wash them in a weak solution of household chlorine bleach. Use a paring knife to poke holes in the bottom and sides so that excess water can drain away.

✔ **A misting spray bottle filled with water:** Pick up a plastic, glass, or metal spray bottle at any nursery or discount store.

Don't use a bottle that has previously held chemicals. The chemical residue may burn your seedlings.

✔ **Liquid or powder fertilizer:** Many types of fertilizer are available in any garden center.

✔ **Plastic trays to hold several containers:** I use cookie sheets, but they rust; plastic is a better choice.

Use the following instructions to start your seeds the first time. As you gain experience, you can customize the process and find your own shortcuts. (Okay, I know this is a book about perennials. But just so you know, the following directions work equally well for starting annuals or vegetables from seed, too.)

1. **Put the potting mix in a pan or bucket and gradually add warm water, stirring the mix by hand or with a large spoon, until it's evenly moist but not sopping wet.**

   The mixture is wet enough if you can form a handful of it into a ball, but too wet if it drips. If you get the mixture too wet, add more potting mix or let the mixture dry out overnight.

2. **Fill your containers with potting mix to within ¹/₂ inch (1 cm) of the top; pat the mix down lightly to press out air pockets.**

3. **Using your forefinger and thumb, sprinkle the seeds over the surface of the potting mix.**

   As a general rule, use twice the number of seeds as the number of plants you hope to grow. (Not all your seeds will germinate, but they all have the potential to, so don't dump in the whole package unless you're prepared to grow that many plants.)

4. **Cover the seeds with dry potting mix according to the packet instructions.**

   Some tiny seeds — those smaller than grains of table salt — don't really need to be covered — you can just lightly press these seeds into the soil, using your fingertips.

5. **Label the container.**

   Write the name of the plant, the date you planted it, and any other information you think may be useful.

6. **Cover the container with a lid, plastic wrap, or glass.**

   If the instructions tell you to exclude light, cover the container with aluminum foil instead of plastic wrap or glass.

7. **Place the seed containers on trays and set them on the stand under grow lights.**

   For those seeds that require heat, you can buy special heating cables to keep the trays warm if your location isn't warm enough.

8. **Open the container and check the seeds every day.**

   If the potting soil starts to dry out, wet it with a couple of squirts from your misting spray bottle.

9. **The moment you see little green specks emerging from the soil, remove the lid (to keep the tiny plants from rotting) and lower the grow light until it's positioned a couple of inches above the seedlings.**

   Raise the light as your plants grow taller.

10. **Continue to water with the misting spray bottle until your seedlings start to form real leaves; then water from the bottom by placing the container in a sink filled with a couple of inches of lukewarm water, which the potting mix absorbs like a sponge.**

    The first pair of leaves that appear are *seed leaves,* not true leaves. Seed leaves feed the young plant until it can grow the real thing.

    When your seedlings grow four true leaves, it's time to transplant them to larger individual containers.

11. **When the time comes to transplant your seedlings, fill the new pots with damp potting mix and use a pencil to make a hole in the potting mix in each pot.**

    Recycled 2¼-inch (6 cm) and 4-inch (10 cm) nursery pots are handy for this purpose. If you prefer, you can use Styrofoam cups, but be sure to punch a few holes in the bottom of the cups for drainage.

12. **Dump the seedling container gently onto your fingertips and then place the seeding clump upright on a tray.**

13. **Pull a seedling away from the clump, holding it by a leaf, and use a pencil to guide the roots into the hole you made in the potting soil.**

    Press the potting mix gently around the roots so that the stem is at the same level it was in the seedling pot.

14. **Use a weak solution of liquid fertilizer (mixed at about a tenth of the normal label recommendation for perennials) to water the plant.**

    I use a kitchen measuring cup and pour the solution around the base of the plant.

15. **Water from the bottom until the seedlings double in size; then use a watering can.**

16. Fertilize once a week, gradually increasing the strength to the rate on the label for seedlings.

Grow newly transplanted seedlings under grow lights or in a brightly lit location out of direct sunlight. When the plants are several inches tall, harden them off and plant them in the garden according to instructions in Chapter 14.

You can also grow perennials outside by following the preceding steps. But instead of placing your pots on a light stand, put the pots outside where they can remain undisturbed until they germinate. You can build a frame or a low box to house the pots. Some perennials may take years to germinate, so don't give up on them too hastily.

Part VI
The Part of Tens

The 5th Wave   By Rich Tennant

©RICHTENNANT

"The seeds fell out of Walt's pocket six years ago and since then every August we just sit somewhere else."

In this part . . .

Ready for some quick gardening wisdom in neat packets of ten? This part debunks ten myths about perennials, suggests ten terrific perennial combos, offers ten ways to dress up your flower bed, and (because no one can choose just ten perennials to highlight) lists ten *sets of ten* perennials for a variety of conditions and occasions.

Chapter 20

Ten Myths about Perennials

*T*his chapter reveals a few rumors and misconceptions for you to be wary of. Disregard these bits of wisdom, no matter who you hear them from. Some get your expectations up too high; others make you do unnecessary work.

Perennial Flowers Live Forever

A few perennials, such as peonies, do live a very long time. Others — blue flax, for example — are as fleeting as annuals. Most perennial flowers manage to hang around for three to seven years. Giving each perennial appropriate cultural conditions and care, of course, has much to do with extending its longevity. Perennials are living plants, after all, and they can be killed by all manner of mistakes.

Perennials Are Less Work Than Annuals

The assumption that perennials are easier to manage than annuals arises from the fact that, unlike annuals, perennials grow back year after year. However, each year, some perennials die and have to be replaced. No garden is labor-free, not even a garden of perennials, so grow perennials because you like to work in the garden, not because you're trying to impress your mother-in-law or your neighbors.

A few households in my neighborhood have switched to silk flowers in an attempt to create a flower garden without the sweat and toil. I suspect that those flowers still need the occasional bath, and I think that seeing poinsettias blooming in summertime and petunias poking through the snow is unnerving. If you really want a garden without the work, join a local botanical garden and visit it regularly.

A Perfect Garden Climate Exists Somewhere

If this myth were true, all the serious gardeners would have discovered this paradise and moved there long ago. Human nature being what it is, they wouldn't be able to keep the climate's location a secret, because they would boast about it. Garden magazine articles and books would talk about this place, and you'd know where it is, too. *All* gardeners, no matter where they live, have to cope with bad weather, pests (large and small), and the frustrations of not being able to grow some plant that they have their hearts set on.

Native Perennials Are Easier to Grow

This one occasionally pops up in books and articles about native plants. The idea is based on the fact that flowers from the field or the roadside care for themselves. After all, no one is tending them in the wild. This theory is true in some cases but not all, depending entirely on which flower you're trying to tame.

One of the most widespread families of wildflowers in the western U.S. — the paintbrushes *(Castilleja)* — are nearly impossible to grow in a garden. Some folks manage to keep a few alive, but I've never seen the masses that are so common in nature duplicated in anyone's garden. Wildflowers can be very fussy and exacting in their requirements. Garden flowers, on the other hand, have often been subjected to decades of selective breeding that eliminated the persnickety among them ages ago.

Growing Flowers in the Shade Is Impossible

Growing *sun-loving* flowers in the shaded garden *is* impossible. The trick to successful shade gardening is to select flowers that prefer shade. Fortunately, you have dozens of shade-lovers to choose from, so you have no excuse not to have just as successful a flower garden in the shadows as in the sun. Check out Chapters 6 and 8 for lists of shade-lovers and tips to keep your shady characters happy.

Nature Always Arranges Flowers in Groups

Where wildflowers can spread out casually into colonies, they often do so. But nature isn't that predictable. Fields of wildflowers are sometimes a real mixture, with placement as random as a tossed salad. If you prefer your flowers in groups, by all means arrange them that way. If you like them all mixed up, that's okay, too.

Purple Coneflowers Are Drought Tolerant

Purple coneflowers have developed a reputation for drought tolerance because they can survive a dry season several months long when they're grown in damp climates. But many people mistakenly apply this fact to drier regions. Now purple coneflowers show up on every xeriscape (dry-climate gardening) list.

Drought tolerance is a relative term. Purple coneflowers are not happy campers in arid and semiarid regions. They can endure rainless spells, but the rest of the year they want water — *a lot* of water. I don't mean to pick on purple coneflowers; I just want to warn you to exercise healthy skepticism whenever you come across gardening advice that doesn't measure up with your own experiences or the experiences of other gardeners in your region.

You Have to Cut Iris Fans After They Bloom

Your grandmother may insist that you cut iris leaves into triangular configurations after the flowers fade, but this activity just creates busy work for you — and it isn't very good for the iris, either. Plants feed themselves through their leaves. When you cut down the amount of surface space they have to catch sunlight, you put your iris on a diet. Just cut the dead flower stalks so that the plant doesn't waste energy forming seed and then pull off browned foliage — all year round — to keep your irises clean and healthy.

Always Clean Up the Flower Bed in the Fall

You can clean up the flower bed if you want, but if you're really busy in the fall, you can also wait until spring to do the major housekeeping. Do make time in the fall to remove diseased leaves and replace the mulch under any of your plants that were plagued by insects during the growing season to prevent eggs and larvae from spending the winter there, all tucked up and cozy in the mulch. But leave the rest of the debris in place to create a natural winter mulch to protect the crown of the plants during winter's coldest weather.

Orange and Pink Clash

Mothers and garden designers perpetuate this myth, but clashing colors aren't covered in natural laws. You know what you like, so don't be intimidated into limiting yourself to other people's color tastes. Orange and pink flowers sometimes look stunning together. Everyone's favorite, purple coneflower, is a daisy with pink rays surrounding orange centers.

Chapter 21

Ten Killer Combinations

*F*lower grouping is currently one of the hottest topics in perennial gardening. You can find whole books about coordinating perennials so that every flower enhances and brings out the best in its companions. The idea behind coordinating flowers is the same as consuming red wine with strong cheese to improve the flavor of each.

The easiest way to make perennial groupings work is to concentrate on placing complementary pairs or trios together within the larger framework of the flower bed. Sometimes, an effective partnership is based on contrast and the drama it creates. Other associations rely on repetition or similarity to catch the eye in a more calming fashion. Some combinations take the stage separately but are useful for hiding one another's entrances and exits. Some just knock your socks off. Of the infinite number of relationships you can come up with, this chapter contains ten possibilities, just to get you started.

All the combinations in this chapter are based on color, but none would survive for long if the plants' needs weren't also met. Water, light, and climate preferences must be as compatible as the colors. Within the following groupings, the flowers share cultural requirements.

Red Daylilies, Goldenrod, and Yellow Yarrow

For a combination that sizzles in late summer, plant these strong colors near each other. The silky red trumpets of the daylilies contrast markedly with the dull texture and golden yellow flowers of goldenrod and yellow yarrow. Additionally, the daylilies' yellow throats carry the yellow across all three.

Tulips, Forget-Me-Nots, and Lamb's Ears

In this grouping, the tulips and forget-me-nots bloom simultaneously. The tiny blue forget-me-nots complement any tulip color. The soft, furry foliage of the lamb's ears can hide the ripening and browning tulip leaves. The lamb's ears bloom in midsummer, filling the gap left by the dormant tulips.

Daffodils and Daylilies

Daffodils and daylilies are recommended for planting together so often that they've practically become a flower-garden cliché. They're perfect partners because their leaves are nearly identical. After the daffodils finish their splendid spring show, their dying leaves aren't such an appealing sight. The daylilies grow up and over the daffodils, completely disguising the daffodils' fall from grace. In midsummer, the daylilies put on their own magnificent show.

Shade Lilies and Virginia Bluebells

Virginia bluebells are one of the earliest flowers to bloom in spring; shade lilies like to sleep in late. When planted together, they camouflage one another's faults. Virginia bluebells go dormant — their leaves turn brown and die back to the ground — about the same time that the shade lily leaves start to wake up and emerge from the ground. Think of these two perennials as roommates who share the same apartment but work different shifts.

Feather Reed Grass, Burgundy Blanket Flower, and Jupiter's Beard

These are three of the hardest working perennials you can grow — they bloom tirelessly for up to six months. Placed together, they also make great team players. The spikes of the feather reed grass provide an interesting counterpoint to the blanket flower's daisies. The open spikes of Jupiter's beard complement both forms. This trio also has colors that coordinate nicely. The flower spikes of feather reed grass open much the same shade of burgundy as the blanket flower. The peachy pink blossoms of Jupiter's beard keep the group from getting monotonous.

Baby's Breath, Lilies, and Shasta Daisies

Sometimes, the simplest combination is the prettiest. This grouping is a variation on the florist's tradition of setting off roses with a sprig of baby's breath, but here the lily gets to be the centerpiece in a cloud of tiny white baby's breath flowers. White is carried over into the petals of the Shasta daisies, while their yellow centers echo the gold of the lilies. The overall effect is as perky as a sunny-side-up fried egg on a lace doily.

Frikart's Aster, Russian Sage, and Butterfly Flower

For a late summer morale booster, you can't miss with the cheerful blue daisies of Frikart's aster teamed up with the steely blue spikes of Russian sage and the soft orange of butterfly flower. Think of these blooms as your reward for surviving another miserably hot summer.

Purple Coneflower, Lamb's Ears, and Sedum 'Vera Jameson'

These three pink flowers prove that a grouping of a single color doesn't have to be monotonous. The flower forms are all dissimilar, which does help prevent the group from becoming boring. But in this case, the foliage does most of the work. The silvery gray, furry leaves of lamb's ears contrast elegantly against the waxy, pink- and purple-tinged foliage of *Sedum* 'Vera

Jameson' — much like an opal pendant on an angora sweater. Add the dark green leaves and bright pink daisies of purple coneflower, the even brighter flower clusters of the sedum, and the near-lavender blossom spikes of lamb's ears, and the effect is anything but dull.

Pink Yarrow, Pink Daylilies, and Golden Marguerite

Here is another simple but striking combination of only two colors — this time clear yellows and pinks. Choose a pink daylily with a yellow throat to coordinate with the yellow daisies of golden marguerite. The flat-topped cluster of pink yarrow can be exactly the same shade of pink as the daylilies. These two flowers are shaped so differently that they don't cancel one another out.

Lady's Mantle, Jacob's Ladder, and Golden Feverfew

In the shady flower bed, these three plants bring out the best in one another. The flowers of lady's mantle are sort of a yellowish chartreuse froth. This color may sound truly dreadful, but actually it goes with everything. The blossoms of Jacob's ladder are silvery blue, and the little white daisies of feverfew lend a casual touch.

Chapter 22

Ten Ways to Accessorize Your Garden

. . . .

In This Chapter

▶ Museum pieces and pink flamingoes

▶ Recycled treasures

▶ A touch of nature

▶ A place to sit and admire your hard work

▶ Sundials — sculpture with a practical purpose

▶ Garden railroads

▶ Bird paraphernalia

▶ Arches for ambiance

▶ Wind chimes — music in the garden

▶ Gazing globes

. . . .

*G*arden designers and other tasteful types get nervous about the topic of accessorizing your garden. They envision a huge collection of painted gnomes or a flock of plastic pink flamingos and shudder at the thought. You need to resist the protestations of these folks and remind yourself that this is your own personal garden and you can do whatever you like in it (within the laws of the land and of your neighborhood covenants). You can dress up your garden in an endless number of ways, so let your imagination run wild.

Besides, decorating the garden has a long and honorable tradition. The 18th and 19th century aristocrats ornamented their gardens with live swans, sheep, peacocks, and the occasional hired hermit (no, I am not making this up). They built faux Greek and Roman temples, bridges where there was no water, and dank and amazingly awful grottoes. One guy moved an entire picturesque village, complete with villagers, into his garden (it was a rather large garden). Who can object to a few windsock geese compared to that?

Scoping Out Sculpture

Sculptures run the gamut from museum treasures (bolt them down and install a security system) to the previously mentioned gnomes and flamingos. Currently popular in Colorado is chain saw art — dead trees carved into local wildlife images such as squirrels, raccoons, and bears. Within hours, an old stump is transformed into a work of art. Sculpture of any sort just naturally looks good in a garden setting because of the old leather and lace contrast — positioning radically different materials next to one another highlights their dissimilarities.

Finding Objects

Your only limit is your imagination with found objects. Cow skulls and wagon wheels are the stereotypical western U.S. artifacts. In England, mushroom-shaped straddle stones are all the rage. A friend of mine has a large boulder with golf balls stuffed into every suitably shaped hole. Another friend uses discarded furniture for trellises.

Warming Up with Rocks and Boulders

Rocks and boulders lend a natural touch to the garden. Large boulders also create mini-microclimates — borderline-hardy perennials may survive in a colder climate if they can tuck up next to a boulder for protection. One caution: Use care when mixing rock types. Having granite next to sandstone next to quartz can easily get more cluttered than the look you had in mind. Large fossils and polished stones are also fun in the garden, and strategically placed boulders can double as seating.

Bringing in Benches

A bench is the one item that makes garden designers agree with the cluttering-up-the-garden mentality. Every garden needs a bench or some other sort of seating. Guests can sit and visit with you while you work. Or you may actually find a spare moment to sit on the bench with a cup of coffee or tea and enjoy the fruits of your labor. Benches also make handy tool holders, where you can stack small pruning shears and scissors out of the way until you need them.

Setting Out a Sundial

You can find free-standing sundials with their own bases, or you can perch a sundial on a marble post, stove pipe or chimney, or even on a birdbath base (after the bowl has cracked). I have mine on a 3-foot-tall, white-barked birch log. You can also put sundials directly onto the ground, but small ones tend to get lost in the flowers.

Railroading through the Garden

You can use electric trains (just like the kind you had as a kid, but larger) to create garden railroads that wind through your daylilies and tunnel beneath your bellflower. People have been known to create tunnels, bridges, and even miniature villages for their garden railroads. Garden railroads are so popular that they have their own clubs of fanciers.

Decorating for the Birds

Bird baths and flowers just go together. If you live in a really cold climate, remember that you need to move concrete bird baths indoors in winter to keep them from cracking. Buy one you can actually lift unless you're prepared to hire someone to move it twice a year. Bird feeders are fun, too, but don't put them in the flower bed where dropped seeds can grow into a private weed patch (most bird seed is not made up of desirable flower seeds). Many types of bird feeders are available, from conservative to quirky.

Adding an Arch

No, not the famous golden arches, although you certainly can paint your arches yellow. Every garden center sells wooden arches that you can bring home and plop into the garden for instant ambiance. If you're handy with tools, you can construct your own. Some types have a bench built in; others go over a path so that you can walk under and through it. Use several in a row to create a tunnel effect, or put one arch at the entrance to the flower garden to let visitors know that they are about to enter a separate and special place. Arches are also handy for screening bad views, giving the garden a sense of height, and providing extra trellising for flowering vines.

Chiming in the Wind

People either really love or really despise wind chimes. Checking with your neighbors to find out where they stand is a good idea, *before* they call the police and report you for disturbing their peace.

Going Global

Globes are another item that you either love or hate, but at least they don't make noise. These look like shiny, giant Christmas tree balls, and are available in many colors. Whether displayed on a post or dropped into the flower bed, their mirrored surface reflects light and images of the garden. Globes were popular in Victorian times and are currently enjoying a resurgence of fame. Really.

Chapter 23
Ten Sets of Ten Perennials

● ●

In This Chapter
▶ Ten everlastings for dried arrangements

▶ Ten perennials for fresh flower bouquets

▶ Ten perennials for instant gratification in the garden

▶ Ten practically unkillable perennials

▶ Ten tasty perennials

▶ Ten hummingbird magnets

▶ Ten perennials to beckon butterflies

▶ Ten herbs to liven up your cooking

▶ Ten perennials for growing in containers

▶ Ten sweet-smelling perennials

● ●

*P*erennials are multipurpose flowers. Some types make glorious arrangements, cut or dried. Others aren't just another pretty face; they attract wildlife to your garden. Some perennials are as instant as annuals — blooming the first year when grown from seed. A few are surprisingly good to eat. In this chapter are ten categories of practical perennials with ten selections listed in each category. Many more are available; these lists are just a taste.

Ten Everlasting Perennials

Every flowerhead, seedpod, stem, and leaf has potential for dried flower arrangements. The best dried flowers are the *everlastings* — flowers that open fairly stiff and papery to the touch without much moisture content to their blossoms. They hold their color well for several months, especially when dried out of direct sunlight. The best everlastings endure for a very long time — up to several years — with only an occasional dusting.

Cut the flowers with long stems and dry them in a vase or upside down with the bunch held together by a rubber band. Most everlastings keep their shape and color better when harvested just as their flowers open.

All the perennials in this list are everlasting except *Artemisia,* which is dried for its felted silver foliage, and Siberian iris, which has satiny brown, woody seedpods that form after the flowers fade and die.

- ❀ Yarrow *(Achillea)*
- ❀ Pearly everlasting *(Anaphalis)*
- ❀ Wormwood *(Artemisia)*
- ❀ Globe thistle *(Echinops exaltatus)*
- ❀ Sea holly *(Eryngium)*
- ❀ Baby's breath *(Gypsophila paniculata)*
- ❀ Siberian iris *(Iris sibirica)*
- ❀ Lavender *(Lavandula)*
- ❀ Sea lavender *(Limonium)*
- ❀ Showy oregano *(Origanum laevigatum* 'Herrenhausen')

Ten Perennials for Long-Lasting Cut Flowers

The price of cut flowers is incentive enough to grow a few flowers in your garden. Follow these guidelines to help your cut flowers last longer in a vase:

- ✔ Always cut flowers early in the day before the dew has burned off.
- ✔ Take a bucket of water into the garden with you and plunge the stems into the water immediately.
- ✔ Place your finished arrangement in a cool room out of strong sunlight and change the water daily.

By careful selection, you can have fresh flowers in the house the whole growing season. The following perennials last at least one to two weeks as cut flowers when treated properly.

❦ Yarrow *(Achillea)*

❦ Golden marguerite *(Argyranthemum frutescens)*

❦ Pinks *(Dianthus)*

❦ Coral bells *(Heuchera)*

❦ Peonies *(Paeonia)*

❦ Orange coneflower *(Rudbeckia fulgida* 'Goldstrum'*)*

❦ Pincushion flower *(Scabiosa)*

❦ Goldenrod *(Solidago)*

❦ Stokes' aster *(Stokesia laevis)*

❦ Speedwell *(Veronica)*

Ten Perennials for Instant Gardens

Instant gratification is the one thing that you can't rely on perennials to provide. Most perennial flowers take several years to settle in and start to reach their full potential. But sometimes you don't have several years to wait.

If you have only a few weeks to put together an instant garden, buy the largest-sized container-grown flowers you can find of the flowers from the following list. Choose plants with buds rather than those in full bloom so that they won't be entirely past their prime by the time the event takes place.

If you have several months to plan, you can save some money by choosing smaller plants from this list. All these plants mature and start to bloom the same season you transplant them into the garden. In fact, if you have six months, grow these flowers from seed by using the techniques outlined in Chapter 19. Then you can stuff the garden full of color for very little cost.

❦ Yarrow *(Achillea* Summer Pastels Series*)*

❦ Aster *(Aster)*

❦ Blue cupid's dart *(Catananche caerulea)*

❦ Tickseed *(Coreopsis grandiflora)*

❦ Perennial larkspur *(Delphinium belladonna)*

❦ Purple coneflower *(Echinacea purpurea)*

❦ Blue flax *(Linum perenne)*

❦ Lupine *(Lupinus* hybrids*)*

❦ Rose campion *(Lychnis coronaria)*

❦ Hollyhock mallow *(Malva alcea* 'Fastigiata'*)*

Ten Tough Perennials for Difficult Sites

Sometimes, you need a perennial with a really rugged constitution. The following flowers are tough enough for commercial parking lots and street medians. All thrive on occasional neglect without too much complaint. They are *almost* unkillable. If nothing else grows for you, give some of these a try.

- ❀ Yarrow *(Achillea)*
- ❀ Wormwood *(Artemisia)*
- ❀ Clustered bellflower *(Campanula glomerata)*
- ❀ Tickseed *(Coreopsis grandiflora)*
- ❀ Cushion spurge *(Euphorbia polychroma)*
- ❀ Blanket flower *(Gaillardia aristata)*
- ❀ Sunflower heliopsis *(Heliopsis helianthoides)*
- ❀ Catmint *(Nepeta faassenii)*
- ❀ Oriental poppy *(Papaver orientale)*
- ❀ Balloon flower *(Platycodon grandiflorus)*
- ❀ 'Autumn Joy' sedum *(Sedum telephium* 'Autumn Joy')
- ❀ Checkerbloom *(Sidalcea malviflora)*
- ❀ Lamb's ears *(Stachys byzantina)*
- ❀ Feverfew *(Tanacetum parthenium)*

Ten Edible Perennials

You don't generally associate perennials with the vegetable garden, but a few double-duty plants easily make the transition from ornamental to edible. Some, such as asparagus and rhubarb, are traditionally grown for the table. But these plants are also pretty enough to grace the flower bed. For example, the blossoms of 'Pink Panda' strawberry are every bit as pretty as the berries are tasty. This selection of edible perennials are all too attractive to hide away in the vegetable garden. Put them in the flower bed where you can enjoy their beauty *and* eat them. The part of the plant that is edible is listed after the botanical name.

Remember, some perennials are toxic. Don't eat any plant unless you're quite certain that you've identified it correctly!

❀ Horseradish (*Armoracia rusticana* — root)

❀ Asparagus (*Asparagus officinalis* — shoots)

❀ Sea kale (*Crambe maritima* — leaves)

❀ Sweet fennel (*Foeniculum vulgare* — leaves and seeds)

❀ 'Pink Panda' strawberry (*Fragaria* 'Pink Panda' — berries)

❀ Jerusalem artichoke (*Helianthus tuberosus* — tubers)

❀ Daylilies (*Hemerocallis* hybrids — flowers)

❀ Mint (*Mentha* — flowers and leaves)

❀ Rhubarb (*Rheum rhubarbarum* — stems)

❀ Violets, pansies, and johnny–jump-ups (*Viola odorata, Viola wittrockiana, Viola tricolor* — flowers)

Ten Perennials That Attract Hummingbirds

Hummingbirds are besotted with red and orange flowers and will come from miles away to check them out. After you've lured them into your garden, these feathered blurs of activity are just as happy to sip nectar from flowers of many colors. The following are ten perennials guaranteed to attract every hummingbird in the vicinity.

❀ Double-bubble mint (*Agastache cana*)

❀ Coral bells (*Heuchera sanguinea*)

❀ Lion's tail (*Leonotis leonurus*)

❀ Cardinal flower (*Lobelia cardinalis*)

❀ Maltese cross (*Lychnis chalcedonica*)

❀ Bee balm (*Monarda* 'Cambridge Scarlet')

❀ Common beardtongue (*Penstemon barbatus*)

❀ Sage (*Salvia*)

❀ Scarlet hedgenettle (*Stachys coccinea*)

❀ California fuchsia (*Zauschneria californica*)

Ten Perennials That Attract Butterflies

Any patch of color attracts butterflies. Plant a diverse mixture of flowers, and you'll probably include one or two of the food sources for the local populations. Don't kill the caterpillars if you want more butterflies. The damage caterpillars do usually isn't severe or noticeable enough to be bothersome. Though butterflies often are very specific about which flowers they prefer in the garden, the following perennials are universal favorites of a large variety of butterflies.

- ❀ Butterfly flower *(Asclepias tuberosa)*
- ❀ Aster *(Aster)*
- ❀ Blue wild indigo *(Baptisia australis)*
- ❀ Butterfly bush *(Buddleia davidii)*
- ❀ Knapweed *(Centaurea montana)*
- ❀ Purple coneflower *(Echinacea purpurea)*
- ❀ Joe-pye weed *(Eupatorium maculatum)*
- ❀ Beardtongue *(Penstemon grandiflorus)*
- ❀ Orange coneflower *(Rudbeckia fulgida* 'Goldstrum')
- ❀ Goldenrod *(Solidago)*
- ❀ Verbena *(Verbena)*

Ten Herbs Used as Perennials

The majority of herbs are perennial and live for several years in the garden. Most herbs also have beautiful flowers and foliage, so they shouldn't be confined to separate gardens. Plant your favorite herbs from the following list amongst the flowers and enjoy their aroma whenever you work in the garden. You can also pinch off a few leaves or twigs of culinary herbs to liven up dinner.

- ❀ Anise hyssop *(Agastache foeniculum)*
- ❀ Garlic chives *(Allium tuberosum)*
- ❀ Archangel *(Angelica gigas)*
- ❀ Tarragon *(Artemisia dracunculus* 'Sativa')
- ❀ Hyssop *(Hyssopus officinalis)*
- ❀ Mallow *(Malva sylvestris)*

❀ Peppermint *(Mentha piperita)*

❀ Bee balm *(Monarda didyma)*

❀ Rosemary *(Rosemarinus officinalis)*

❀ Pineapple sage *(Salvia elegans)*

Ten Perennials for Containers

Whenever you can't create conditions exactly to the liking of a particular perennial in the garden, you can put the plant in a container instead. Controlling the soil, water, and drainage conditions in a small, confined space is easy. If your soil is wet, heavy, and poorly drained, for example, and you want to grow perennials that demand perfect drainage, a pot is the answer.

You can also grow perennials that aren't hardy to your climate in containers and then keep them indoors over the winter. I grow rosemary and African lilies in pots and bring them inside to live in a sunny kitchen window during the winter months.

For a pleasing arrangement, plant several perennials together in one container, varying the color, shape, and size of the flowerheads and foliage of each — just like in the flower bed. Ivy and other small vines are pretty when tumbling over the edge of the pot. You can create effective still lifes by placing several pots of flowers together wherever you need a spot of color.

Buy the largest containers you can afford, especially if you live in a hot or dry climate. Pots dry out very quickly and may need watering as often as twice a day in hot weather. (Plastic pots dry out more slowly than clay pots.) Then fill the containers with a selection of flowers from the following list:

❀ African lily *(Agapanthus)*

❀ Asparagus fern *(Asparagus setaceus)*

❀ Bulbs (see Chapter 10)

❀ Tickseed *(Coreopsis grandiflora)*

❀ Ferns

❀ Coral bells *(Heuchera)*

❀ Plantain lilies *(Hosta)*

❀ Lavender *(Lavandula)*

❀ Purple fountain grass *(Pennisetum setaceum* 'Rubrum')

❀ Pansies *(Viola wittrockiana)*

Bulbs in pots

To plant bulbs in a container, follow these steps:

1. **Choose a container with drainage holes.**

2. **Fill the container to within a few inches of the top with good quality potting soil.**

3. **Place the bulbs on the soil and barely cover them with more mix.**

4. **Water the pots and place them in an unheated garage where temperatures stay around 40° F (4.5° C).**

6. **Water again whenever the mix dries out.**

   After several weeks, white roots start to come out of the holes in the bottom of the pot.

5. **Bring the pot inside to a cool room in front of a sunny window.**

   Within a few weeks, you have flowers.

Ten Fragrant Perennials

Unless you enjoy the perfume section in department stores with its medley of competing scents, you probably don't want to plant all the aromatic flowers from the following list in the same bed. Place one or two by a walk or a patio where you can enjoy their fragrance every time you walk by.

- ❀ Calamint *(Calamintha grandiflora)*
- ❀ Daphnes *(Daphne)*
- ❀ Pinks *(Dianthus)*
- ❀ Gas plant *(Dictamnus albus)*
- ❀ Daylilies *(Hemerocallis* hybrids)
- ❀ Lavender *(Lavandula)*
- ❀ Lilies *(Lilium)*
- ❀ Bee balm *(Monarda didyma)*
- ❀ Peonies *(Paeonia* hybrids)
- ❀ Summer phlox *(Phlox paniculata)*

Appendix
Sources for Perennials

* *

*M*ost countries are justifiably reluctant to admit new diseases and insect plagues across their borders. Live plants can carry both, which is why commerce laws make shipping live plant material across international borders almost impossible. Seeds and bulbs usually don't have such strict restrictions because they can be cleaned of hitchhiking pests, but you'll find the whole mail-order process less frustrating if you stick to sources within your own country when buying live plants.

Check out garden magazine ads for more mail-order nurseries. In fact, one of the surest methods to receive dozens of unsolicited (and free) catalogs is to subscribe to a garden magazine. Having your name sold to eager companies is a real convenience, in this case.

Most mail-order nurseries charge for their first catalog but generally refund the catalog cost with your first order. Many catalogs are well worth the money because they're filled with gorgeous color photos, descriptions, and detailed information on how to grow each plant.

USA

Bulbs

B&D Lilies, P.O. Box 2007-H, Port Townsend, WA 98368. Full-color catalog $3.

Caladium World, P.O. Box 629, Sebring, FL 33871; phone 941-385-7661, fax 941-385-5836. More than 20 fancy strap- and dwarf-leaf varieties.

Connell's Dahlias, 10616 Waller Rd. East, Tacoma, WA 98446; phone 206-531-0292, fax 206-536-7725. Catalog $2. More than 350 varieties.

The Daffodil Mart, 85 Broad St., Torrington, CT 06790; phone 800-255-2852, fax 800-420-2852. More than 1,000 different flower bulbs.

Dutch Gardens, P.O. Box 200, Adelphia, NJ 07710; phone 800-818-3861, fax 908-780-7720. Spring and summer bulbs, perennials.

McClure & Zimmerman, 108 W. Winnebago, P.O. Box 368, Friesland, WI 53935; phone 414-326-4220, fax 414-326-5769. Wide selection of spring- and autumn-blooming bulbs.

Van Bourgondien Brothers, 245 Rte. 109, P.O. Box 1000, Babylon, NY 11702; phone 800-622-9959, fax 516-669-1228. Importers and distributors of bulbs and perennials.

Seeds

W. Atlee Burpee & Co., 300 Park Ave., Warminster, PA 18974; phone 800-333-5808, fax 800-487-5530. Home page: http://garden@burpee.com. Wide selection of flower seeds and supplies.

Fragrant Path, P.O. Box 328, Fort Calhoun, NE 68023. Catalog $2. Seeds of fragrant, rare, and old-fashioned plants.

Park Seed Co., Cokesbury Rd., Greenwood, SC 29647-0001; phone 800-845-3369, fax 800-275-9941. More than 1,800 kinds of bulbs and seeds.

Select Seeds — Antique Flowers, 180 Stickney Hill Rd., Union, CT 06076-4617; phone 860-684-9310, fax 860-684-9224. Catalog $1. Vintage flowers for color or cutting; vines for arbors.

Shepherd's Garden Seeds, 30 Irene St., Torrington, CT 06790; phone 860-482-3638, fax 860-482-0532. Catalog features herbs and old-fashioned flower varieties.

Thompson & Morgan Seed Co., P.O. Box 1308, Jackson, NJ 08527; phone 800-274-7333 or 908-363-2225, fax 888-466-4769. Wide selection of English flowers.

Plants

Andre Viette Farm & Nursery, P.O. Box 1109, Fishersville, VA 22939; phone 540-943-2315, fax 540-943-0782. Catalog/resource guide/landscaping kit $5. Top perennials from around the world.

Bluestone Perennials, 7211 Middle Ridge Rd., Madison, OH 44057; phone 800-852-5243, fax 216-428-7198. More than 400 perennials.

Busse Gardens, 5873 Oliver Ave. SW, Cokato, MN 55321-4229; phone 320-286-2654, fax 320-286-6601. Catalog $2. Cold-hardy and unusual perennials and native plants.

Heronswood Nursery, Ltd., 7530 NE 288th St., Kingston, WA 98346; phone 360-297-4172, fax 360-297-8321. Catalog $4. Rare and hard-to-find trees, shrubs, vines, and perennials.

High Country Garden, 2902 Rufina St., Santa Fe, NM 87505-2929; phone 800-925-9387. Drought tolerant perennials and natives.

Kurt Bluemel, 2740 Greene Ln., Baldwin, MD 21013-9523; phone 410-557-7229, fax 410-557-9785. Catalog $3. Bamboo, ferns, ornamental grasses, perennials, and water plants.

Milaeger's Gardens, 4838 Douglas Ave., Racine, WI 53402-2498; phone 800-669-9956 or 414-639-2371, fax 414-639-1855. Catalog $1. Many varieties of hostas, daylilies, and other perennials.

Niche Gardens, 1111 Dawson Rd., Chapel Hill, NC 27516; phone 919-967-0078. Perennials for southeastern gardens.

Roslyn Nursery, 211 Burrs Ln., Dix Hills, NY 11746; phone 516-643-9347, fax 516-484-1555. Catalog $3. A large selection of perennials and shrubs for shady and woodland gardens.

Wayside Gardens, 1 Garden Lane, Hodges, SC 29695-0001; phone 800-845-1124, fax 800-457-9712. Bulbs, perennials, roses, trees, and shrubs.

Weiss Brothers Nursery, 11690 Colfax Hwy., Grass Valley, CA 95945; phone 916-272-7657, fax 916-272- 3578. More than 400 varieties of perennials and herbs.

White Flower Farm, 30 Irene St., Torrington, CT 06790; phone 800-503-9624 or 860-496-9600, fax 860-482-0532. Lavishly illustrated catalog includes more than 700 varieties of annuals, perennials, bulbs, and shrubs.

Canada

Bulbs

Lindel Lilies, 5510 239th St., Langley, BC, V34 7N6; phone 604-534-4729, fax 604-534-4742.

Seeds

The Butchart Gardens, P.O. Box 4010, Victoria, BC, V8X 3X4; phone 604-652-4422, fax 604-652-3883.

William Dom Seeds, P.O. Box 8400, 279 Hwy. 8 (Flamborough), Dundas, ON, L9H 6M1.

Dominion Seed House, P.O. Box 2500, Georgetown, ON, L7G 5L6; phone 905-873-3037.

Gardens North, 34 Helena St., Ottawa, ON, K1Y 3M8.

Ontario Seed Co., Ltd., 330 Phillip St., Waterloo, ON, N2J 3Z9; phone 519-886-0557, fax 519-886-0605.

T&T Seeds, Ltd., P.O. Box 1710, Winnepeg, MB, R3C 3P6; phone 204-895-9962.

WH Perron & Co., Ltd., 2914 Labelle Blvd., Chomeday Laval, PQ, H7P 5R9; phone 514-332-3619, fax 514-682-4959.

Plants

Alberta Nurseries & Seed Co., P.O. Box 20, Bowden, AB, T0M 0K0; phone 403-224-3544, fax 403-224-2455.

Ferncliff Gardens, 8394 McTaggart St., Mission, BC, V2V 6S6; phone 604-826-2447, fax 604-826-4316.

Hortico, Inc., 723 Robson Rd., Rt. 1, Waterdown, ON, L0R 2H0; phone 905-689-6984.

Iris & Plus, P.O. Box 903, 1269 Rt. 139, Sutton, PQ, J0E 2K0; phone 514-538-2048, fax 514-538-0448.

McFayden, P.O. Box 1800, Brandon, MB, R7A 6N4; phone 204-725-7300, fax 204-725-1888.

Morden Nurseries, Ltd., P.O. Box 1270, Morden, MB, R0G 1J0; phone 204-822-3311.

Sherry's Perennials, P.O. Box 39, Cedar Springs, ON, N0P 1E0; phone 519-676-4541.

Windy Ridge Nursery, Box 12, Site 3, Hythe, AB, T0H 2C0; phone 403-356-2167, fax 403-356-3694.

England

Bulbs

Broadleigh Gardens, Dept. AGS2, Bishops Hull, Taunton, Somerset, TA4 1AE; phone 01823 286231.

De Jagers (TG), of Marden, Kent, TN12 9BP; phone 01622 831235.

VanTubergen UK, Dept. 727, Bressingham, Diss., Norfolk, 1P22 2AB; phone 01379 688282.

Seeds

Chiltern Seeds, Dept. R, Bortree Stile, Ulverston, Cumbria, LA12 7PB; phone 01229 581137.

Thompson & Morgan, Ltd., Poplar Lane, Ipswich, 1P8 3BU; phone 01473 601090, fax 01473 680199.

Plants

Croftway Nursery, Yapton Road, Barnham, Bogner Regis, West Sussex, P022 0BH; phone 01243 552121.

Hartside Nursery Garden, nr. Alston, Cumbria, CA9 3BL; phone 01434 381372.

Holden Clough Nursery, Holden, Bolton-by-Bowland, Clitheroe, Lancashire, BB7 4PF; phone 01200 447615.

Kettlesing Nurseries, The Old Post Office, Kettlesing, Harrogate, North York, AG3 2LB; phone 01423 770831.

Lingen Nursery & Garden, Lingen, nr. Bucknell, Shropshire, SY7 0DY; phone 01544 267720.

Merriments Gardens, Hawkshurst Rd., Hurst Green, East Sussex, TN19 7RA; phone 01580 860666.

Perhill Nurseries, Worcester Rd., Great Witley, Worcester, WR6 6JT; phone 01299 896329.

South View Nurseries, Dept. G, Eversley Cross, Hants, R27 0NT; phone 01734 732206.

West Acres Gardens, West Acre, Kings Lynn, Norfolk, PE32 1UJ; phone 01760 755562.

Australia

Bulbs

JN Hancock & Co., Jacksons Hill Rd., Menzies Creek, Victoria 3159; phone (61) 3.754.3328.

Van Dieman Quality Bulbs, Rd. 20, Table Cape, Wynyard TAS 7325; phone (004)422012.

Seeds

Eden Seeds, M.S. 316 Gympie 4570; phone and fax (074)86.5236.

LSA Goodwin & Sons, Goodwins Rd., Bagdad So., Tasmania 7030; phone (002)68.6233.

Plants

Alberts Garden, 9 Beltana Road, Pialligo, ACT 2609; phone (06)248.0300.

The Braidwood Nursery, 62 Wilson St., Braidwood, NSW 2622; phone (048)42.2057.

Cloudehill, 89 Olinda-Monbulk Rd., Olinda, Victoria 3788; phone (03)751.1009.

Good Nature Nursery, 482 Dignams Creek Road, via Narooma, NSW 2546; phone (064)93.6739.

Lambley Nursery, "Burnside," Lesters Rd., Ascot, Victoria 3364; phone (053)43. 4303.

Leura Country Gardens Nursery, Rear/156 Megalong St., Leura, NSW 2780; phone (047)84.3146.

Mountain View Daylily Gardens, Box 458GJ, Maleny, Queensland 4552; phone (074)94.2346.

Otway Herbs Cottage Garden, Biddles Rd., Apollo Bay, Victoria 3233; phone (052)37.6318.

Woodbank Nursery, RMB 303, Kingston, Tasmania 7150; phone and fax (002) 39.6452.

Index

• D •

• *N* •

• *O* •

• *P* •

FREE six month subscription to **National Gardening** magazine

No other magazine gets to the root of planting and growing like *National Gardening*. That's because here at *National Gardening*, we haven't forgotten what down-to-earth, practical gardening is all about. And we're talking about all kinds of gardening—fruits, vegetables, roses, perennials— you name it and *National Gardening* knows it.

We bring you hands-on growing information you can use to become a more successful gardener. Make smarter variety selections. Time your plantings more efficiently for better results. Extend your growing season. Fertilize your garden more effectively, and protect it from pests using safe, sensible, and effective methods. Harvest healthier, tastier, more beautiful crops of all kinds.

Plus: Swap tips and seeds with other avid gardeners from around the country and around the world. Choose the best, most practical gardening products for your needs. Get expert gardening advice. Let the gardening experts at NGA help you grow everything more successfully!

Special offer to ...*For Dummies*® readers:
For a limited time, you're entitled to receive a six month (3 issue) subscription to *National Gardening* magazine—absolutely FREE. Just fill out the coupon and mail it to the address listed or call **1-800-727-9097**, today! Offer limited to new subscribers only.

❑ **YES** — Please sign me up for a free six month (3 issue) subscription to *National Gardening* magazine. Send the subscription to the name and address listed below.

_____
MY NAME

_____
ADDRESS

_____
CITY/STATE/ZIP   **R7DB**

*Offer limited to new subscribers only. Clip (or copy) and mail coupon today to: National Gardening Magazine, Dept. R7DB, P.O. Box 52874, Boulder, CO 80322-2874

Visit our Web site at *http://www.garden.org*

Van Bourgondien

Van Bourgondien Dutch Bulbs & Perennials

QUALITY DUTCH BULBS & PERENNIALS - FOR YEARS & YEARS OF CONTINUOUS BLOOMS!

From Daylilies and dahlias to poppies and primrose, you'll find over 1,500 varieties of the finest quality Holland & domestic-grown bulbs and perennials at great prices - all guaranteed! FREE CATALOG!

Order your FREE color catalog today, and include the $5 discount coupon when you place your Van Bourgondien order. If ordering by phone, please mention code #4715 to receive your special one-time $5 discount.

1-800-622-9959 x4715

VAN BOURGONDIEN BROS.

P.O.Box 1000-4715, Babylon, NY 11702-9004   Email: blooms@dutchbulbs.com

Van Bourgondien
Dutch Bulbs & Perennials

$5 off

YOUR FIRST ORDER
OF $25 OR MORE

1-800-622-9959 x4715

VAN BOURGONDIEN BROS.

P.O.Box 1000-4715, Babylon, NY 11702-9004
Email: blooms@dutchbulbs.com

FISKARS®

PowerGear Lopper

The Fiskars PowerGear Lopper, endorsed by the American Rose Society, is the perfect tool to take along in your garden bag when you're ready to tackle a day's worth of pruning. Its compact design and light weight make it easy to cut all day!

Find the Fiskars PowerGear Lopper on the Fiskars Home Page at http://www.fiskars.com

Call or write to find out who carries the PowerGear Lopper in your area. Return the coupon with proof of purchase for a **FREE Pruning Tips Guide** from Fiskars!

WA7214

FISKARS®
FREE Pruning Tips Guide!
With Proof Of Purchase
1-800-500-4849
*Fiskars Wallace Division, Dept. CSCR
780 Carolina St.
Sauk City, WI 53583*

Daylily Discounters

Award Winning Daylilies at Fantastic Prices!

Beautify your home and garden with the world's finest daylilies & enjoy blooms year after year! America's most carefree perennial in a rainbow of great colors and sizes comes direct from the grower. 200 beautiful photographs make this acclaimed color catalog indispensable. Informative planting guide included.

Daylily Discounters Catalog $2.00. Take $5 off first order.

ONE DAYLILY PLAZA
ALACHUA, FL 32615
1-904-462-1539

1997 Catalog & Planting Guide

$5 OFF
FIRST ORDER!

1997 Catalog & Planting Guide

1-904-462-1539

---

http://www.garden.org — VALUABLE ONLINE GARDENING COUPONS AND RESOURCES

ComposTumbler®

How to Make Compost in Just 14 Days!

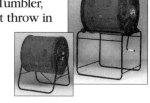

Making compost is easy with the ComposTumbler, the world's best-selling drum composter. Just throw in your leaves, grass clippings, kitchen scraps, and any organic wastes. Fasten the door and give the drum a few easy turns. Turning mixes and aerates the materials for proper oxygen content and decomposition so temperatures reach 160° — hot enough to kill weed seeds. After 14 days you'll have rich compost — nature's fertilizer.

Call **1-800-880-2345** for FREE Information about this marvelous machine used by more than 150,000 gardeners.

Use the coupon to save up to $97!
ComposTumbler, Dept. 84037C, 160 Koser Rd., Lititz, PA 17543

ComposTumbler®

$97 off 18-Bushel Size
$75 off 9.5-Bushel Size

Plus! A Free Compost Thermometer

1-800-880-2345

ComposTumbler®, Dept. 84037C
160 Koser Rd., Lititz, PA 17543

Burpee Seed Company

Shop America's favorite home gardening catalog . . .

for the highest quality gardening supplies. A huge selection of flowers, vegetables, bulbs and garden accessories all backed by our 100% guarantee. From beginner to expert, from gardening to outdoor entertaining, the Burpee catalog has it all!

Call or write for your FREE Burpee catalog and include the $5 coupon with your order to receive this special discount.*

*Cannot be combined with any other offers.

Burpee Seed Company

$5 off a $30 Order

1-800-888-1447

Burpee Seed Co., Dept. 012369
300 Park Ave., Warminster, PA 18974

Spring Hill Nurseries

Beautify your home with perennial flowering plants, roses, trees and shrubs.
Choose from over 27 professionally designed gardens!
Every plant in our 40-page catalog is guaranteed to grow.

Call for your FREE catalog

1-800-662-2589

and mention code NA9489A9

AMERICA'S #1 MAIL ORDER GARDEN CENTER

Reservation Center, 6523 North Galena Rd., Peoria, IL 61632

FREE
Mystery Gift

(Value at least $7.99)
With your order of $30 or more.

Call **1-800-662-2589** anytime!
and mention code NA9489A9

AMERICA'S #1
MAIL ORDER GARDEN CENTER

Reservation Center
6523 North Galena Rd., Peoria, IL 61632

---

http://www.garden.org — VALUABLE ONLINE GARDENING COUPONS AND RESOURCES

Johnny's Selected Seeds

Buy from the catalog that gardeners rate "Best"!

Johnny's catalog is packed with information. Truly a gardeners' source book for successful gardening. All Johnny's seed is trial grown by us to insure that our gardeners have the best tasting, most productive vegetables and herbs. We also conduct extensive flower trials so we can provide you with the newest, most beautiful flowers.

Johnny's, in association with Eliot Coleman, offers an extensive selection of gardening tools, accessories and books.

For award-winning service, a 100% satisfaction guarantee and one-stop shopping for all your gardening needs. **Send for Your Free Catalog Today!**

Foss Hill Road, Albion, ME 04910
(207) 437-4301
http://www.johnnyseed.com

Take $5.00 off
any $30.00 order*

Foss Hill Road, Albion, ME 04910
(207) 437-4301
http://www.johnnyseed.com

*Offer cannot be combined with other offers.

Bluestone Perennials

BEAUTIFUL PERENNIALS at a pleasing price.

At Bluestone, we've grown and shipped our specialty perennials for over 25 years. Our plants return to bloom season after season for years of easy pleasure. Let us help beautify your home with our economical plants, bulbs and shrubs. Over 600 varieties are available in the spring and fall - easy to plant and every plant guaranteed. Write today for our FREE color catalog that's packed with information. Send in the coupon with your order and we'll pay the shipping!

7211 Middle Ridge Road
Madison, Ohio 44057
1-800-852-5243

BLUESTONE
PERENNIALS

7211 Middle Ridge Road
Madison, Ohio 44057
1-800-852-5243

$ FREE SHIPPING $
ON YOUR ORDER

http://www.garden.com

At www.garden.com, you will find over 6,000 plants, books, tools and gifts from high quality, brand name suppliers that you can purchase directly over the Internet for delivery to your doorstep!

http://www.garden.com

Visit the ultimate garden bookmark on the World Wide Web

We search the world for the finest products and bring them together exclusively on the World Wide Web!

$10.00 gift certificate
valid toward any purchase

Mail this coupon to:
Garden Escape
Customer Coupon Program
515 Congress Ave., Suite 1350
Austin, TX 78701

For your $10 gift, you must include:
your name:_____
your address: _____
your state: _____
zip: _____
your e-mail: _____

Mantis SprayMate

Mantis Spraymate

Professional gardeners and landscapers already know the importance a good spraying program has on a beautiful rose garden. It's one of their most important secrets of success. **Spraymate** by **Mantis** is the first portable sprayer designed and built exclusively for the busy suburban homeowner who wants a safer way to have a more beautiful bug-free lawn and garden.

Call **Mantis** now for FREE information on **SprayMate** and our one-year home trial **1-800-366-6268 ext. P9058**, or write: **Mantis, 1028 Street Road, Southampton, PA 18966, Dept. P9058**

Division of Schiller-Pfeiffer, Inc.

FREE
16 oz. bottle of
Safer® Insecticidal Soap
with the purchase of a
Mantis SprayMate

$10 VALUE

Division of Schiller-Pfeiffer, Inc.

1-800-366-6268

1028 Street Road, Dept. P9058
Southampton, PA 18966

Shady Oaks Nursery

Enjoy shade gardening at its best! Our catalog offers you hundreds of perennial plants including Hosta, Ferns, Ground Covers and Grasses that are suitable for shade gardening.

Contact us for your free copy of our catalog today. Return the coupon with your order for 10% off the catalog prices.

1-800-504-8006   FAX: 1-507-835-8772
112 10th Ave. S.E., Waseca, MN 56093

Plants for shady places

Shady Oaks Nursery LLP
112 10th Ave. S.E.
Waseca, MN 56093

10% OFF CATALOG PRICE ON FIRST ORDER

Coupon must accompany order.
Not valid with any other offer.

A.M. Leonard

Save on the best and most reliable gardening tools available. Buy direct from a firm that has been serving nurserymen, landscapers, foresters, arborists and serious gardeners since 1885!

Request a **FREE** 100+ page catalog for a huge selection of top-quality tools and supplies to help you grow and care for the living things around you.

Call 1-800-543-8955

PD597

Sensible Tools for the Serious Gardener

FREE Catalog...
Fantastic Savings!
PD597

FOR A NEW CATALOG, CALL

1-800-543-8955

or mail your request to:
A.M. Leonard • P.O. Box 816
Piqua, OH 45356

---

http://www.garden.org — VALUABLE ONLINE GARDENING COUPONS AND RESOURCES

The Fun & Easy Way™ to learn about computers and more!

7/29/96

Windows® 3.11 For Dummies,® 3rd Edition
by Andy Rathbone
ISBN: 1-56884-370-4
$16.95 USA/
$22.95 Canada

Mutual Funds For Dummies™
by Eric Tyson
ISBN: 1-56884-226-0
$16.99 USA/
$22.99 Canada

DOS For Dummies,® 2nd Edition
by Dan Gookin
ISBN: 1-878058-75-4
$16.95 USA/
$22.95 Canada

The Internet For Dummies,® 2nd Edition
by John Levine & Carol Baroudi
ISBN: 1-56884-222-8
$19.99 USA/
$26.99 Canada

Personal Finance For Dummies™
by Eric Tyson
ISBN: 1-56884-150-7
$16.95 USA/
$22.95 Canada

PCs For Dummies,® 3rd Edition
by Dan Gookin & Andy Rathbone
ISBN: 1-56884-904-4
$16.99 USA/
$22.99 Canada

Macs® For Dummies,® 3rd Edition
by David Pogue
ISBN: 1-56884-239-2
$19.99 USA/
$26.99 Canada

The SAT® I For Dummies™
by Suzee Vlk
ISBN: 1-56884-213-9
$14.99 USA/
$20.99 Canada

Here's a complete listing of IDG Books' ...For Dummies® titles

Title	Author	ISBN	Price
DATABASE			
Access 2 For Dummies®	by Scott Palmer	ISBN: 1-56884-090-X	$19.95 USA/$26.95 Canada
Access Programming For Dummies®	by Rob Krumm	ISBN: 1-56884-091-8	$19.95 USA/$26.95 Canada
Approach 3 For Windows® For Dummies®	by Doug Lowe	ISBN: 1-56884-233-3	$19.99 USA/$26.99 Canada
dBASE For DOS For Dummies®	by Scott Palmer & Michael Stabler	ISBN: 1-56884-188-4	$19.95 USA/$26.95 Canada
dBASE For Windows® For Dummies®	by Scott Palmer	ISBN: 1-56884-179-5	$19.95 USA/$26.95 Canada
dBASE 5 For Windows® Programming For Dummies®	by Ted Coombs & Jason Coombs	ISBN: 1-56884-215-5	$19.99 USA/$26.99 Canada
FoxPro 2.6 For Windows® For Dummies®	by John Kaufeld	ISBN: 1-56884-187-6	$19.95 USA/$26.95 Canada
Paradox 5 For Windows® For Dummies®	by John Kaufeld	ISBN: 1-56884-185-X	$19.95 USA/$26.95 Canada
DESKTOP PUBLISHING/ILLUSTRATION/GRAPHICS			
CorelDRAW! 5 For Dummies®	by Deke McClelland	ISBN: 1-56884-157-4	$19.95 USA/$26.95 Canada
CorelDRAW! For Dummies®	by Deke McClelland	ISBN: 1-56884-042-X	$19.95 USA/$26.95 Canada
Desktop Publishing & Design For Dummies®	by Roger C. Parker	ISBN: 1-56884-234-1	$19.99 USA/$26.99 Canada
Harvard Graphics 2 For Windows® For Dummies®	by Roger C. Parker	ISBN: 1-56884-092-6	$19.95 USA/$26.95 Canada
PageMaker 5 For Macs® For Dummies®	by Galen Gruman & Deke McClelland	ISBN: 1-56884-178-7	$19.95 USA/$26.95 Canada
PageMaker 5 For Windows® For Dummies®	by Deke McClelland & Galen Gruman	ISBN: 1-56884-160-4	$19.95 USA/$26.95 Canada
Photoshop 3 For Macs® For Dummies®	by Deke McClelland	ISBN: 1-56884-208-2	$19.99 USA/$26.99 Canada
QuarkXPress 3.3 For Dummies®	by Galen Gruman & Barbara Assadi	ISBN: 1-56884-217-1	$19.99 USA/$26.99 Canada
FINANCE/PERSONAL FINANCE/TEST TAKING REFERENCE			
Everyday Math For Dummies™	by Charles Seiter	ISBN: 1-56884-248-1	$14.99 USA/$22.99 Canada
Personal Finance For Dummies™ For Canadians	by Eric Tyson & Tony Martin	ISBN: 1-56884-378-X	$18.99 USA/$24.99 Canada
QuickBooks 3 For Dummies®	by Stephen L. Nelson	ISBN: 1-56884-227-9	$19.99 USA/$26.99 Canada
Quicken 8 For DOS For Dummies,® 2nd Edition	by Stephen L. Nelson	ISBN: 1-56884-210-4	$19.95 USA/$26.95 Canada
Quicken 5 For Macs® For Dummies®	by Stephen L. Nelson	ISBN: 1-56884-211-2	$19.95 USA/$26.95 Canada
Quicken 4 For Windows® For Dummies,® 2nd Edition	by Stephen L. Nelson	ISBN: 1-56884-209-0	$19.95 USA/$26.95 Canada
Taxes For Dummies,™ 1995 Edition	by Eric Tyson & David J. Silverman	ISBN: 1-56884-220-1	$14.99 USA/$20.99 Canada
The GMAT® For Dummies™	by Suzee Vlk, Series Editor	ISBN: 1-56884-376-3	$14.99 USA/$20.99 Canada
The GRE® For Dummies™	by Suzee Vlk, Series Editor	ISBN: 1-56884-375-5	$14.99 USA/$20.99 Canada
Time Management For Dummies™	by Jeffrey J. Mayer	ISBN: 1-56884-360-7	$16.99 USA/$22.99 Canada
TurboTax For Windows® For Dummies®	by Gail A. Helsel, CPA	ISBN: 1-56884-228-7	$19.99 USA/$26.99 Canada
GROUPWARE/INTEGRATED			
ClarisWorks For Macs® For Dummies®	by Frank Higgins	ISBN: 1-56884-363-1	$19.99 USA/$26.99 Canada
Lotus Notes For Dummies®	by Pat Freeland & Stephen Londergan	ISBN: 1-56884-212-0	$19.95 USA/$26.95 Canada
Microsoft® Office 4 For Windows® For Dummies®	by Roger C. Parker	ISBN: 1-56884-183-3	$19.95 USA/$26.95 Canada
Microsoft® Works 3 For Windows® For Dummies®	by David C. Kay	ISBN: 1-56884-214-7	$19.99 USA/$26.99 Canada
SmartSuite 3 For Dummies®	by Jan Weingarten & John Weingarten	ISBN: 1-56884-367-4	$19.99 USA/$26.99 Canada
INTERNET/COMMUNICATIONS/NETWORKING			
America Online® For Dummies,® 2nd Edition	by John Kaufeld	ISBN: 1-56884-933-8	$19.99 USA/$26.99 Canada
CompuServe For Dummies,® 2nd Edition	by Wallace Wang	ISBN: 1-56884-937-0	$19.99 USA/$26.99 Canada
Modems For Dummies,® 2nd Edition	by Tina Rathbone	ISBN: 1-56884-223-6	$19.99 USA/$26.99 Canada
MORE Internet For Dummies®	by John R. Levine & Margaret Levine Young	ISBN: 1-56884-164-7	$19.95 USA/$26.95 Canada
MORE Modems & On-line Services For Dummies®	by Tina Rathbone	ISBN: 1-56884-365-8	$19.99 USA/$26.99 Canada
Mosaic For Dummies,® Windows Edition	by David Angell & Brent Heslop	ISBN: 1-56884-242-2	$19.99 USA/$26.99 Canada
NetWare For Dummies,® 2nd Edition	by Ed Tittel, Deni Connor & Earl Follis	ISBN: 1-56884-369-0	$19.99 USA/$26.99 Canada
Networking For Dummies®	by Doug Lowe	ISBN: 1-56884-079-9	$19.95 USA/$26.95 Canada
PROCOMM PLUS 2 For Windows® For Dummies®	by Wallace Wang	ISBN: 1-56884-219-8	$19.99 USA/$26.99 Canada
TCP/IP For Dummies®	by Marshall Wilensky & Candace Leiden	ISBN: 1-56884-241-4	$19.99 USA/$26.99 Canada

Microsoft and Windows are registered trademarks of Microsoft Corporation. Mac is a registered trademark of Apple Computer. SAT is a registered trademark of the College Entrance Examination Board. GMAT is a registered trademark of the Graduate Management Admission Council. GRE is a registered trademark of the Educational Testing Service. America Online is a registered trademark of America Online, Inc. The "...For Dummies Book Series" logo, the IDG Books Worldwide logos, Dummies Press, and The Fun & Easy Way are trademarks, and ---- For Dummies are, and ... For Dummies are registered trademarks under exclusive license to IDG Books Worldwide, Inc., from International Data Group, Inc.

For scholastic requests & educational orders please call Educational Sales at 1. 800. 434. 2086

FOR MORE INFO OR TO ORDER, PLEASE CALL ▶ 800 762 2974

For volume discounts & special orders please call Corporate Sales, at 415. 655. 3000

Title	Author	ISBN	Price
The Internet For Macs® For Dummies® 2nd Edition	by Charles Seiter	ISBN: 1-56884-371-2	$19.99 USA/$26.99 Canada
The Internet For Macs® For Dummies® Starter Kit	by Charles Seiter	ISBN: 1-56884-244-9	$29.99 USA/$39.99 Canada
The Internet For Macs® For Dummies® Starter Kit Bestseller Edition	by Charles Seiter	ISBN: 1-56884-245-7	$39.99 USA/$54.99 Canada
The Internet For Windows® For Dummies® Starter Kit	by John R. Levine & Margaret Levine Young	ISBN: 1-56884-237-6	$34.99 USA/$44.99 Canada
The Internet For Windows® For Dummies® Starter Kit, Bestseller Edition	by John R. Levine & Margaret Levine Young	ISBN: 1-56884-246-5	$39.99 USA/$54.99 Canada

MACINTOSH

Title	Author	ISBN	Price
Mac® Programming For Dummies®	by Dan Parks Sydow	ISBN: 1-56884-173-6	$19.95 USA/$26.95 Canada
Macintosh® System 7.5 For Dummies®	by Bob LeVitus	ISBN: 1-56884-197-3	$19.95 USA/$26.95 Canada
MORE Macs® For Dummies®	by David Pogue	ISBN: 1-56884-087-X	$19.95 USA/$26.95 Canada
PageMaker 5 For Macs® For Dummies®	by Galen Gruman & Deke McClelland	ISBN: 1-56884-178-7	$19.95 USA/$26.95 Canada
QuarkXPress 3.3 For Dummies®	by Galen Gruman & Barbara Assadi	ISBN: 1-56884-217-1	$19.95 USA/$26.99 Canada
Upgrading and Fixing Macs® For Dummies®	by Kearney Rietmann & Frank Higgins	ISBN: 1-56884-189-2	$19.95 USA/$26.95 Canada

MULTIMEDIA

Title	Author	ISBN	Price
Multimedia & CD-ROMs For Dummies® 2nd Edition	by Andy Rathbone	ISBN: 1-56884-907-9	$19.99 USA/$26.99 Canada
Multimedia & CD-ROMs For Dummies® Interactive Multimedia Value Pack, 2nd Edition	by Andy Rathbone	ISBN: 1-56884-909-5	$29.99 USA/$39.99 Canada

OPERATING SYSTEMS:

DOS

Title	Author	ISBN	Price
MORE DOS For Dummies®	by Dan Gookin	ISBN: 1-56884-046-2	$19.95 USA/$26.95 Canada
OS/2® Warp For Dummies® 2nd Edition	by Andy Rathbone	ISBN: 1-56884-205-8	$19.99 USA/$26.99 Canada

UNIX

Title	Author	ISBN	Price
MORE UNIX® For Dummies®	by John R. Levine & Margaret Levine Young	ISBN: 1-56884-361-5	$19.99 USA/$26.99 Canada
UNIX® For Dummies®	by John R. Levine & Margaret Levine Young	ISBN: 1-878058-58-4	$19.95 USA/$26.95 Canada

WINDOWS

Title	Author	ISBN	Price
MORE Windows® For Dummies® 2nd Edition	by Andy Rathbone	ISBN: 1-56884-048-9	$19.95 USA/$26.95 Canada
Windows® 95 For Dummies®	by Andy Rathbone	ISBN: 1-56884-240-6	$19.99 USA/$26.99 Canada

PCS/HARDWARE

Title	Author	ISBN	Price
Illustrated Computer Dictionary For Dummies® 2nd Edition	by Dan Gookin & Wallace Wang	ISBN: 1-56884-218-X	$12.95 USA/$16.95 Canada
Upgrading and Fixing PCs For Dummies® 2nd Edition	by Andy Rathbone	ISBN: 1-56884-903-6	$19.99 USA/$26.99 Canada

PRESENTATION/AUTOCAD

Title	Author	ISBN	Price
AutoCAD For Dummies®	by Bud Smith	ISBN: 1-56884-191-4	$19.95 USA/$26.95 Canada
PowerPoint 4 For Windows® For Dummies®	by Doug Lowe	ISBN: 1-56884-161-2	$16.99 USA/$22.99 Canada

PROGRAMMING

Title	Author	ISBN	Price
Borland C++ For Dummies®	by Michael Hyman	ISBN: 1-56884-162-0	$19.95 USA/$26.95 Canada
C For Dummies® Volume 1	by Dan Gookin	ISBN: 1-878058-78-9	$19.95 USA/$26.95 Canada
C++ For Dummies®	by Stephen R. Davis	ISBN: 1-56884-163-9	$19.95 USA/$26.95 Canada
Delphi Programming For Dummies®	by Neil Rubenking	ISBN: 1-56884-200-7	$19.99 USA/$26.99 Canada
Mac® Programming For Dummies®	by Dan Parks Sydow	ISBN: 1-56884-173-6	$19.95 USA/$26.95 Canada
PowerBuilder 4 Programming For Dummies®	by Ted Coombs & Jason Coombs	ISBN: 1-56884-325-9	$19.99 USA/$26.99 Canada
QBasic Programming For Dummies®	by Douglas Hergert	ISBN: 1-56884-093-4	$19.95 USA/$26.95 Canada
Visual Basic 3 For Dummies®	by Wallace Wang	ISBN: 1-56884-076-4	$19.95 USA/$26.95 Canada
Visual Basic "X" For Dummies®	by Wallace Wang	ISBN: 1-56884-230-9	$19.99 USA/$26.99 Canada
Visual C++ 2 For Dummies®	by Michael Hyman & Bob Arnson	ISBN: 1-56884-328-3	$19.99 USA/$26.99 Canada
Windows® 95 Programming For Dummies®	by S. Randy Davis	ISBN: 1-56884-327-5	$19.99 USA/$26.99 Canada

SPREADSHEET

Title	Author	ISBN	Price
1-2-3 For Dummies®	by Greg Harvey	ISBN: 1-878058-60-6	$16.95 USA/$22.95 Canada
1-2-3 For Windows® 5 For Dummies® 2nd Edition	by John Walkenbach	ISBN: 1-56884-216-3	$16.95 USA/$22.95 Canada
Excel 5 For Macs® For Dummies®	by Greg Harvey	ISBN: 1-56884-186-8	$19.95 USA/$26.95 Canada
Excel For Dummies® 2nd Edition	by Greg Harvey	ISBN: 1-56884-050-0	$16.95 USA/$22.95 Canada
MORE 1-2-3 For DOS For Dummies®	by John Weingarten	ISBN: 1-56884-224-4	$19.99 USA/$26.99 Canada
MORE Excel 5 For Windows® For Dummies®	by Greg Harvey	ISBN: 1-56884-207-4	$19.95 USA/$26.95 Canada
Quattro Pro 6 For Windows® For Dummies®	by John Walkenbach	ISBN: 1-56884-174-4	$19.95 USA/$26.95 Canada
Quattro Pro For DOS For Dummies®	by John Walkenbach	ISBN: 1-56884-023-3	$16.95 USA/$22.95 Canada

UTILITIES

Title	Author	ISBN	Price
Norton Utilities 8 For Dummies®	by Beth Slick	ISBN: 1-56884-166-3	$19.95 USA/$26.95 Canada

VCRS/CAMCORDERS

Title	Author	ISBN	Price
VCRs & Camcorders For Dummies™	by Gordon McComb & Andy Rathbone	ISBN: 1-56884-229-5	$14.99 USA/$20.99 Canada

WORD PROCESSING

Title	Author	ISBN	Price
Ami Pro For Dummies®	by Jim Meade	ISBN: 1-56884-049-7	$19.95 USA/$26.95 Canada
MORE Word For Windows® 6 For Dummies®	by Doug Lowe	ISBN: 1-56884-165-5	$19.95 USA/$26.95 Canada
MORE WordPerfect® 6 For Windows® For Dummies®	by Margaret Levine Young & David C. Kay	ISBN: 1-56884-206-6	$19.95 USA/$26.95 Canada
MORE WordPerfect® 6 For DOS For Dummies®	by Wallace Wang, edited by Dan Gookin	ISBN: 1-56884-047-1	$19.95 USA/$26.95 Canada
Word 6 For Macs® For Dummies®	by Dan Gookin	ISBN: 1-56884-190-6	$19.95 USA/$26.95 Canada
Word For Windows® 6 For Dummies®	by Dan Gookin	ISBN: 1-56884-075-6	$16.95 USA/$22.95 Canada
Word For Windows® For Dummies®	by Dan Gookin & Ray Werner	ISBN: 1-878058-86-X	$16.95 USA/$22.95 Canada
WordPerfect® 6 For DOS For Dummies®	by Dan Gookin	ISBN: 1-878058-77-0	$16.95 USA/$22.95 Canada
WordPerfect® 6.1 For Windows® For Dummies® 2nd Edition	by Margaret Levine Young & David Kay	ISBN: 1-56884-243-0	$16.95 USA/$22.95 Canada
WordPerfect® For Dummies®	by Dan Gookin	ISBN: 1-878058-52-5	$16.95 USA/$22.95 Canada

Windows is a registered trademark of Microsoft Corporation. Mac is a registered trademark of Apple Computer. OS/2 is a registered trademark of IBM. UNIX is a registered trademark of AT&T. WordPerfect is a registered trademark of Novell. The "...For Dummies Book Series" logo, the IDG Books Worldwide logos, Dummies Press, and The Fun & Easy Way are trademarks, and ---- For Dummies and ... For Dummies are registered trademarks under exclusive license to IDG Books Worldwide, Inc., from International Data Group, Inc.

Fun, Fast, & Cheap!™

NEW!

The Internet For Macs® For Dummies® Quick Reference
by Charles Seiter

ISBN:1-56884-967-2
$9.99 USA/$12.99 Canada

NEW!

Windows® 95 For Dummies® Quick Reference
by Greg Harvey

ISBN: 1-56884-964-8
$9.99 USA/$12.99 Canada

SUPER STAR

Photoshop 3 For Macs® For Dummies® Quick Reference
by Deke McClelland

ISBN: 1-56884-968-0
$9.99 USA/$12.99 Canada

SUPER STAR

WordPerfect® For DOS For Dummies® Quick Reference
by Greg Harvey

ISBN: 1-56884-009-8
$8.95 USA/$12.95 Canada

Title	Author	ISBN	Price
DATABASE			
Access 2 For Dummies® Quick Reference	by Stuart J. Stuple	ISBN: 1-56884-167-1	$8.95 USA/$11.95 Canada
dBASE 5 For DOS For Dummies® Quick Reference	by Barrie Sosinsky	ISBN: 1-56884-954-0	$9.99 USA/$12.99 Canada
dBASE 5 For Windows® For Dummies® Quick Reference	by Stuart J. Stuple	ISBN: 1-56884-953-2	$9.99 USA/$12.99 Canada
Paradox 5 For Windows® For Dummies® Quick Reference	by Scott Palmer	ISBN: 1-56884-960-5	$9.99 USA/$12.99 Canada
DESKTOP PUBLISHING/ILLUSTRATION/GRAPHICS			
CorelDRAW! 5 For Dummies® Quick Reference	by Raymond E. Werner	ISBN: 1-56884-952-4	$9.99 USA/$12.99 Canada
Harvard Graphics For Windows For Dummies® Quick Reference	by Raymond E. Werner	ISBN: 1-56884-962-1	$9.99 USA/$12.99 Canada
Photoshop 3 For Macs® For Dummies® Quick Reference	by Deke McClelland	ISBN: 1-56884-968-0	$9.99 USA/$12.99 Canada
FINANCE/PERSONAL FINANCE			
Quicken 4 For Windows® For Dummies® Quick Reference	by Stephen L. Nelson	ISBN: 1-56884-950-8	$9.95 USA/$12.95 Canada
GROUPWARE/INTEGRATED			
Microsoft® Office 4 For Windows® For Dummies® Quick Reference	by Doug Lowe	ISBN: 1-56884-958-3	$9.99 USA/$12.99 Canada
Microsoft® Works 3 For Windows® For Dummies® Quick Reference	by Michael Partington	ISBN: 1-56884-959-1	$9.99 USA/$12.99 Canada
INTERNET/COMMUNICATIONS/NETWORKING			
The Internet For Dummies® Quick Reference	by John R. Levine & Margaret Levine Young	ISBN: 1-56884-168-X	$8.95 USA/$11.95 Canada
MACINTOSH			
Macintosh® System 7.5 For Dummies® Quick Reference	by Stuart J. Stuple	ISBN: 1-56884-956-7	$9.99 USA/$12.99 Canada
OPERATING SYSTEMS:			
DOS			
DOS For Dummies® Quick Reference	by Greg Harvey	ISBN: 1-56884-007-1	$8.95 USA/$11.95 Canada
UNIX			
UNIX® For Dummies® Quick Reference	by John R. Levine & Margaret Levine Young	ISBN: 1-56884-094-2	$8.95 USA/$11.95 Canada
WINDOWS			
Windows® 3.1 For Dummies® Quick Reference, 2nd Edition	by Greg Harvey	ISBN: 1-56884-951-6	$8.95 USA/$11.95 Canada
PCs/HARDWARE			
Memory Management For Dummies® Quick Reference	by Doug Lowe	ISBN: 1-56884-362-3	$9.99 USA/$12.99 Canada
PRESENTATION/AUTOCAD			
AutoCAD For Dummies® Quick Reference	by Ellen Finkelstein	ISBN: 1-56884-198-1	$9.95 USA/$12.99 Canada
SPREADSHEET			
1-2-3 For Dummies® Quick Reference	by John Walkenbach	ISBN: 1-56884-027-6	$8.95 USA/$11.95 Canada
1-2-3 For Windows® 5 For Dummies® Quick Reference	by John Walkenbach	ISBN: 1-56884-957-5	$9.95 USA/$12.95 Canada
Excel For Windows® For Dummies® Quick Reference, 2nd Edition	by John Walkenbach	ISBN: 1-56884-096-9	$8.95 USA/$11.95 Canada
Quattro Pro 6 For Windows® For Dummies® Quick Reference	by Stuart J. Stuple	ISBN: 1-56884-172-8	$9.95 USA/$12.95 Canada
WORD PROCESSING			
Word For Windows® 6 For Dummies® Quick Reference	by George Lynch	ISBN: 1-56884-095-0	$8.95 USA/$11.95 Canada
Word For Windows® For Dummies® Quick Reference	by George Lynch	ISBN: 1-56884-029-2	$8.95 USA/$11.95 Canada
WordPerfect® 6.1 For Windows® For Dummies® Quick Reference, 2nd Edition	by Greg Harvey	ISBN: 1-56884-966-4	$9.99 USA/$12.99/Canada

Microsoft and Windows are registered trademarks of Microsoft Corporation. Mac and Macintosh are registered trademarks of Apple Computer. UNIX is a registered trademark of AT&T. WordPerfect is a registered trademark of Novell. The "...For Dummies Book Series" logo, the IDG Books Worldwide logos, Dummies Press, The Fun & Easy Way, and Fun, Fast, & Cheap! are trademarks, and ---- For Dummies and ... For Dummies are registered trademarks under exclusive license to IDG Books Worldwide, Inc., from International Data Group, Inc.

For scholastic requests & educational orders please call Educational Sales at 1. 800. 434. 2086

FOR MORE INFO OR TO ORDER, PLEASE CALL ▶ 800 762 2974

For volume discounts & special orders please call Corporate Sales, at 415. 655. 3000

Order Center: **(800) 762-2974** *(8 a.m.–6 p.m., EST, weekdays)*

Quantity	ISBN	Title	Price	Total

Shipping & Handling Charges

	Description	First book	Each additional book	Total
Domestic	Normal	$4.50	$1.50	$
	Two Day Air	$8.50	$2.50	$
	Overnight	$18.00	$3.00	$
International	Surface	$8.00	$8.00	$
	Airmail	$16.00	$16.00	$
	DHL Air	$17.00	$17.00	$

*For large quantities call for shipping & handling charges.
**Prices are subject to change without notice.

Ship to:

Name _____

Company _____

Address _____

City/State/Zip _____

Daytime Phone _____

Payment: ☐ Check to IDG Books Worldwide (US Funds Only)

☐ VISA   ☐ MasterCard   ☐ American Express

Card # _____ Expires _____

Signature _____

Subtotal _____

CA residents add
applicable sales tax _____

IN, MA, and MD
residents add
5% sales tax _____

IL residents add
6.25% sales tax _____

RI residents add
7% sales tax _____

TX residents add
8.25% sales tax _____

Shipping _____

Total _____

Please send this order form to:

IDG Books Worldwide, Inc.
Attn: Order Entry Dept.
7260 Shadeland Station, Suite 100
Indianapolis, IN 46256

*Allow up to 3 weeks for delivery.
Thank you!*

IDG BOOKS WORLDWIDE REGISTRATION CARD

RETURN THIS REGISTRATION CARD FOR FREE CATALOG

Title of this book: **Perennials For Dummies™**

My overall rating of this book: ❑ Very good [1] ❑ Good [2] ❑ Satisfactory [3] ❑ Fair [4] ❑ Poor [5]

How I first heard about this book:

❑ Found in bookstore; name: [6]   ❑ Book review: [7]

❑ Advertisement: [8]   ❑ Catalog: [9]

❑ Word of mouth; heard about book from friend, co-worker, etc.: [10]   ❑ Other: [11]

What I liked most about this book:

What I would change, add, delete, etc., in future editions of this book:

Other comments:

Number of computer books I purchase in a year: ❑ 1 [12] ❑ 2-5 [13] ❑ 6-10 [14] ❑ More than 10 [15]

I would characterize my computer skills as: ❑ Beginner [16] ❑ Intermediate [17] ❑ Advanced [18] ❑ Professional [19]

I use ❑ DOS [20] ❑ Windows [21] ❑ OS/2 [22] ❑ Unix [23] ❑ Macintosh [24] ❑ Other: [25]_____
(please specify)

I would be interested in new books on the following subjects:
(please check all that apply, and use the spaces provided to identify specific software)

❑ Word processing: [26]   ❑ Spreadsheets: [27]

❑ Data bases: [28]   ❑ Desktop publishing: [29]

❑ File Utilities: [30]   ❑ Money management: [31]

❑ Networking: [32]   ❑ Programming languages: [33]

❑ Other: [34]

I use a PC at (please check all that apply): ❑ home [35] ❑ work [36] ❑ school [37] ❑ other: [38] _____

The disks I prefer to use are ❑ 5.25 [39] ❑ 3.5 [40] ❑ other: [41]_____

I have a CD ROM: ❑ yes [42]   ❑ no [43]

I plan to buy or upgrade computer hardware this year: ❑ yes [44]   ❑ no [45]

I plan to buy or upgrade computer software this year: ❑ yes [46]   ❑ no [47]

Name: Business title: [48]   Type of Business: [49]

Address (❑ home [50] ❑ work [51]/Company name:)

Street/Suite#

City [52]/State [53]/Zipcode [54]:   Country [55]

❑ **I liked this book!** You may quote me by name in future
   IDG Books Worldwide promotional materials.

   My daytime phone number is _____

IDG BOOKS

THE WORLD OF
COMPUTER
KNOWLEDGE

☐ YES!

Please keep me informed about IDG's World of Computer Knowledge.
Send me the latest IDG Books catalog.

BUSINESS REPLY MAIL

FIRST CLASS MAIL   PERMIT NO. 2605   FOSTER CITY, CALIFORNIA

IDG Books Worldwide
919 E Hillsdale Blvd, STE 400
Foster City, CA 94404-9691

NO POSTAGE
NECESSARY
IF MAILED
IN THE
UNITED STATES